THE GATEWAY TO THE MIDDLE AGES
ITALY

The Gateway
to the Middle Ages
ITALY

by Eleanor Shipley Duckett

ANN ARBOR PAPERBACKS

THE UNIVERSITY OF MICHIGAN PRESS

TO

MARY ELLEN CHASE

AND

OUR CAMBRIDGE FAMILY

CAMBRIDGE, ENGLAND

1934–1936

ABBREVIATIONS

PL	*Patrologia Latina*
PG	*Patrologia Graeca*
M.G.H.	*Monumenta Germaniae Historica*
M.H.B.	*Monumenta Historica Britannica*
R.I.S.	*Rerum Italicarum Scriptores* (Muratori)
Script. rer. Merov.	*Scriptores Rerum Merovingicarum*
Script. rer. Lang. .	*Scriptores Rerum Langobardicarum*
C.S.H.B. . . .	*Corpus Scriptorum Historiae Byzantinae*
C.S.E.L.	*Corpus Scriptorum Ecclesiasticorum Latinorum*
P.L.M.	*Poetae Latini Minores*
P.W.	*Real-Encyclopädie,* ed. Pauly-Wissowa
C.M.H.	*Cambridge Medieval History*
H.S.C.P.	*Harvard Studies in Classical Philology*
C.P.	*Classical Philology*
Schanz	Schanz-Hosius-Krüger: *Geschichte der römischen Literatur,* IV, 2, 1920
Manitius . . .	M. Manitius: *Geschichte der lateinischen Literatur des Mittelalters,* I, 1911
Bardenhewer . .	O. Bardenhewer: *Geschichte der altkirchlichen Literatur,* V, 1932

PREFACE

THE GATEWAY TO THE MIDDLE AGES is made up of three parts. This one deals with Italy in the sixth century.

This "gateway" opened with the passing of Italy, seat of government of the Western part of the Roman Empire, into rude barbarian hands, when Ravenna and Rome, chief cities of this Roman Empire in the West, fell in 476 to the invader Odovacar and his Germanic hordes; when, in his turn, Odovacar was forced, some seventeen years later, to yield to another barbarian conqueror, who seized his throne at Ravenna, overran his kingdom, killed him by his own hand, and thus became lord of Italy and its people.

Here, then, stretching before us, we see the Middle Ages. This Gothic barbarian was to be known as Theodoric the Great. Ignorant himself both of diplomacy and of culture, face to face with the skill and experience of the Romans whom he was to rule, his mind conceived the ideal of an Italy under himself as king, supported in counsel and in learning by the finest of his Roman subjects. His should be a twofold state, uniting the young barbarian energy of muscle and daring with the Roman genius and knowledge in matters of law and administration.

And so he worked until he died in 526, and Italy once more fell upon strife. The Roman Empire of the East, ruled from Constantinople, sent out its armies to regain from barbarian control this Western portion of its imperial dominion. For more than sixty years battle and siege,

hatred and fear, famine and massacre, pass before us in
these pages, while commanders of Constantinople's counter-
invasion, Belisarius and Narses, fight the Gothic kings who
succeed one another on Italy's throne. Victory and defeat
fall to either side. At length Roman power driving from
the East prevails, and Italy is once more wholly united
under Rome's imperial law, ruling from Constantinople.

Yet not for long. Toward the end of the sixth century,
the Lombards, a new barbarian host, pour down upon the
land, seize its northern cities, and in 599 compel Constantinople to strike treaty of partition. Italy in days to come is
to be divided: its north under Lombard chieftains, its cen-
ter and south under the Roman Empire of the East.

From out this land ruled by barbarian kings have come
writings of deep interest and worth to readers of history:
the letters and other documents which Cassiodorus the
Roman wrote as official secretary for his Gothic sovereigns;
the story by Jordanes, himself a Goth, of his Gothic people;
the picture of Theodoric drawn by Ennodius, bishop of
Pavia in northern Italy.

Above all, the reign of Theodoric the Great has left for
us the thought of Boethius, who, noble Roman though he
was, and devoted to his Catholic Church, served loyally
under Theodoric, heretic and barbarian; who was accused
of treachery, thrown into prison, and in 525, under Theodoric, was put to death. From his prison has come to us
that dialogue with the Lady Philosophy, the famous *Consolation of Philosophy,* which lived for the scholars and
poets of the Middle Ages and the Renaissance, which still
lives for all who would look into the mystery of man's soul
and its hope. As John Bunyan long after him, so here the
captive Boethius strives in meditation to discover the meaning of his fate. Here at last philosophy draws him up from

PREFACE

his misery to understand the riddle of human life; to look away from his sorrow to the Perfect Goodness, the Oneness, the God for Whom all creatures yearn, do they know it or not; to reach an insight into the problems that have beset all thinkers in all time: of Providence and Predestination; of Fortune and Freewill; of God's foreknowledge and of man's final destiny.

In these records of her history, in this wrestling with philosophy, Italy of the sixth century opens out a way to the struggles and the victories of medieval ages to come.

As in the original book, I again acknowledge here with gratitude permission to quote from the Loeb edition of the *Theological Tractates* of Boethius.

E.S.D.

Northampton, Massachusetts, 1960

INTRODUCTION

The fifth century of our era in Europe makes sad and dreary reading. Its records are filled with death and decay, destruction of lands and wasting of resources, the misery of the poor, the careless ease of the rich. Its preachers pointed the thoughts of men away from this world's false dream of evil to a City not built with hands, eternal in the heavens. Monastic enclosure, retirement from secular affairs, was the refuge of its devout layfolk, choosing rather to save their own souls than to hand down to children the burden they themselves had borne. Its thinkers, Augustine, Orosius, Salvian, each gave a different answer to the many who asked why God dealt thus with a Christian State of Rome? Its poets turned back to the story of man's fall from innocence, the drop of evil which long ago had tainted at its source the stream of human history. Its rulers ended the line of the Roman Empire in the West.

The thread of the sixth century's narrative is no less caught in an unending tangle of siege and battle, of famine and murder, distress of nations gripped in duel throughout its time. During its years the Roman Empire, still surviving in the East, struggled from Constantinople to defend Italian lands from the Eastern Goths, who first with triumph and afterward with despair clung to the Italian crown and territory they had seized by force of arms. At its ending both Romans and Goths yielded place to another wave of barbarians from the north. In Gaul the sons and grandsons of Clovis wrote a century's full chapter of restless fighting for land and wealth. Along the Rhine German tribes exulted within the ruined towns from which the last Roman defenders had now been banished by death or exile. In Spain the successors of Alaric the second gave rein to an ambition which stopped at nothing in its desire. In Britain the Celts had fled to their mountains and caves before their conquerors from overseas.

Yet once again the old as it passed from life into history gave birth to the new.[1] First, in things political. The dream which Theodoric the Great now longed to realize in a marriage of young barbarian vigour with ancient Roman civilization found its fulfilment later under Charlemagne. Even now a fresh national spirit was emerging through the settling of different peoples in Europe on their own chosen soil. The sixth century saw the Lombards in occupation of northern Italy, saw the broad fields of France taken and retaken by the Merovingian Kings: in preparation for the time when Franks and Lombards united under the same Charles the Great should make his brief dream of one barbarian empire splendid throughout mediaeval times. Spain became for a period the battle-ground of the Visigothic monarchs. Britain in these days of harrying learned to know herself as motherland of the children of her Saxon conquerors.

But the rising tide of new life came to its fullness in the things of religion. In the Far East this century saw the birth of Mahomet and the dawning of Islam, soon to lay violent hands upon a Catholic West. In the nearer East the buzzings of theologians were busy for attack or for defence over the fruit gained by the Church in the fifth century at the Council of Chalcedon. Catholic and Monophysite were still contending stubbornly around the Mystery of the Christ; schism still for many years divided Patriarchs in Constantinople from Popes in Rome. In the West, always the world of practical energy rather than speculative, it was secular conflict that vexed the Church. Neverthe-

[1] For a general discussion of this see Ferdinand Lot, *The End of the Ancient World and the Beginnings of the Middle Ages,* 1931.

less, as the wordy debates of the East gradually disclosed positive truth among the dross of repartee and discord, so amid strife in Western lands new visions were born.

By the baptism of Clovis just before the century dawned the Franks of Gaul had led the way for barbarians in conversion from the Arian creed. The Bishops of Gaul contended for their hope throughout its length. Its closing years saw formal confession of the Faith by Recared, Visigothic King of Spain: the starting-point of the broken yet persistent Catholic history of that land. As it reached its end the Church laid her mark on the last of the Arian kingdoms, when she received the little son of the Lombard ruler in Italy.

So in the work of missionaries and monks. In Burgundy fresh vigour, pumped into the channels of religion from Irish sources by Columban, gave to the Church countless schools for her priests and saints for her roll of honour. In Britain, Christian already in the fourth century, though crippled by invasion of Saxons in the south, of Picts and Scots in the north this sixth century saw a great quickening of faith and fervour through the work of two men. From Ireland Columba sailed to make a Celtic beacon-fire of Christianity in his monastic house on the island of Iona, home of Aidan and a host of other crusaders who were to labour in the north. Toward the end of this age Augustine with his brethren landed on the Kentish shore, in a mission born of Pope Gregory's longing to win also the English to fellowship in his Christ.

Within the cloister, also, these years found light for troubled souls. Of the different monastic Rules formed and practised in this same period, that of Columban was too severe, those of Caesarius and of Cassiodorus too limited in their appeal. It remained for Benedict, "Father of Monks," to create of his spiritual genius in this century a discipline that should endure for all time for all sorts and conditions of men.

INTRODUCTION

Nor was the age wanting in new growth that was to bear varied fruit thereafter for mind and intellect. Flooded as it was with extravagance of form and magnifying of matter, it yet contained within its writings the hint of mediaeval lyric in Venantius Fortunatus, in either Gregory the progress of anecdotes and legends and tales, both secular and spiritual, concerning saint and sinner, bird and beast. It was after this sort that mediaeval chronicle developed its spicy narratives.

Far more important, as sprung from this century's brain, was the joining hand in hand of science and faith : in lesser degree by the statesman Cassiodorus, in greater, by the philosopher Boethius. To the intellectual discipline imposed by Cassiodorus upon his monastic copyists in southern Italy mediaeval manuscripts owed an incalculable debt. In Boethius, striving to use his Aristotle in the service of the highest truth, mediaeval scholasticism found its forerunner : in substance, by the due relating of logic and spiritual wisdom ; in form, by the creation for the Schoolmen of words and definitions in which to express their thought.

Finally, with Gregory the Great the Papacy of the Middle Ages rose on the horizon of the world. And when in 600 A.D. his days were drawing to a close, his world had already passed through the gateway to the mediaeval spirit and the mediaeval mind. As W. P. Ker observes in his *Dark Ages:* "Almost everything that is common to the Middle Ages, and much that lasts beyond the Renaissance, is to be found in the authors of the sixth century." [2]

[2] pp. 101ff.

CONTENTS

THE GATEWAY TO THE MIDDLE AGES
ITALY

CHAPTER I

THE HISTORICAL SCENE IN ITALY

In our viewing of the writers of this sixth century after Christ we shall naturally begin with those of Italy. But first it will be necessary to sketch into the picture some background of her history during these years.

Since the time of the Emperors Valentinian and Valens, in the fourth century of the Christian era, the Roman Empire had been divided under two rulers. The Emperor in the East governed from Constantinople, the Emperor in the West made his capital at Rome, as might be expected. Early in the fifth century, however, the Emperor Honorius, terrified by the advancing menace of Alaric the Goth, moved his court from Rome to Ravenna, a city geographically convenient, happily secure in the midst of great marshes. By this time his throne had lost the power and glory it had enjoyed during the fourth century, and its decline, due to various reasons, social, bureaucratic and military, prepared the way for its end in 480. In this year Julius Nepos, last of a line of empty figureheads propped up by external forces, last lawful Emperor of Rome in the West, by his death extinguished this branch of the double Imperial line. Already in 475 his actual reign had ended when he had been driven from rule by one of his officers called Orestes, who placed on the seat of Empire at Ravenna his own son Romulus, a boy about fourteen years old, dubbed "Augustulus" in derision by those who sadly recalled the golden Augustan age.

Here we meet the first figure of note in our sixth century

records. Among men of prominence in the pay of the "Emperor" Romulus was a young barbarian, Odovacar by name, of Germanic race, who had crossed the Alps in search of fortune and had risen into popular notice under the patronage of Ricimer, maker and destroyer of one after another of the puppet emperors of Rome in these last days. Shortly afterward the barbarian mercenaries of "Augustulus" rose in rebellious outcry for a rewarding of their services, and even demanded a third of the soil of Italy as their portion.

Orestes refused to rob his son's subjects for the payment of his hired legions. Here, then, our young alien, Odovacar, saw his chance and seized it. With a bold offer to procure for these rebels the land they coveted he won their favour, and in 476 by their overwhelming force "Augustulus" was driven into exile, his father Orestes was slain, and Odovacar promptly established himself on the throne at Ravenna. The Roman Empire of the West had passed into barbarian hands.

From Ravenna Odovacar controlled Italy for seventeen years; not indeed independently, but with the consent and under the overlordship of Zeno, who governed from Constantinople the Roman Empire of the East during the years 474 to 491. The Fall of the West had brought Italy under the suzerainty of Constantinople as head of the surviving portion of Rome's power. But the harmony between Odovacar in the western part and his superior in the eastern part of the Empire lessened as time went on. From docile acquiescence in directions from Constantinople the young barbarian ruler passed to the gratifying of his own ambition by military conquests, which penetrated almost to the very border of Zeno's realms.

This rift between secular governors, moreover, was deepened by religious controversy between the Sees of Rome and of Constantinople, set in motion by the Emperor Zeno's attempt to conciliate all parties of the Church in 482 through the articles

of his famous *Henoticon*. For this *Henoticon* was not of sufficiently orthodox Catholicity to meet with approval from Rome.
It did not uphold with sufficient loyalty the pronouncements
by which the Council of Chalcedon in 451 had defined the
Catholic doctrine of the Two Natures in One Person of the
Lord Christ. It tried too patently to conciliate the Patriarchs
of the East, ever suspected of leanings toward the Monophysite
doctrine of which the East was full. And so the long schism
of thirty-five years began, and Rome and Constantinople issued
decree and counter-decree of excommunication, and Patriarch
after Patriarch in Constantinople struggled in vain against the
unbending determination of Pope after Pope in Rome. It was
well on in the sixth century when Chalcedon emerged triumphant, and the name of Acacius, the Patriarch who had dared
to issue judgment of excommunication against the Papal
throne, was expunged from the company of faithful children
of the Church.

Such discord was not likely to cause friendly feeling toward
the ruler of Italy on the part of his Lord, author of the *Henoticon*. For a long time Zeno endured his vassal with growing
discontent, till finally in 487 a happy occasion of deliverance
offered itself to his mind. It came through another barbarian,
Theodoric, afterwards known as "Theodoric the Great." Ostrogothic in race and Amal in kindred, he had led a life of roving
adventure from the age of seven, when he had been sent as
hostage for the good behaviour of his people to the court of
Leo I, predecessor of Zeno as Emperor at Constantinople. That
was in 461, and at the Eastern Court Theodoric had lived ten
years, drinking in as he grew up the fair conception of ordered
rule, the ideal of culture and harmony which never left him
through all his chequered life.

Pannonia had once been the home of this Ostrogothic race,
ruled there by three brothers, of which one was Theodemir,

father of this Theodoric. About the time that the son was restored from Constantinople to his own people the father had
been chosen as their leader. Theodoric himself at once gave
proof of a spirit brave and daring enough to satisfy all, and on
his father's death in 471, he, too, became in his turn Chief of
the Ostrogoths: all bound to him and to one another, more or
less, in one vast family of blood relationship. For nearly twenty
years he wandered hither and yon in Central Europe, seeking a
country where his warriors might find food and shelter for themselves and for the women and children who trekked with them
in their endless roamings: from the Aegean to the Roman
Scythia, from Scythia to Macedonia, from Macedonia to
Northern Greece, from Greece to Thrace. For himself he
dreamed of a secure Lordship under the Roman Empire,
wherein without insult to his royal blood of the Amal kings he
might rule his subjects in freedom and in peace. At times during these years he held military office under his former host, the
Emperor Zeno, and aided him in war; in 484 he was actually
consul of the Roman State in the East. At other times, in despair
of attaining his hopes for himself and his multitude, he threw
off all allegiance and gave his energies to open rebellion, ravaging and invading wherever he could. Once, in 487, he even
dared to lay waste the land of the Eastern Empire just outside
the precincts of Constantinople itself.

It was a problem for Zeno—how to content and quiet the
restless ambition of this leader of threatening hordes—till a
pleasant solution for both his problems at home and in Italy
offered itself, whether from his own inventive skill or from the
petition of Theodoric, we do not know. Our authorities are
divided in the matter. Procopius of Caesarea, who lived in the
sixth century and has left us in Greek his *History* of its various
wars, declares that it was Zeno who urged Theodoric to the
conquest of Italy; "for Zeno could always arrange things com-

fortably for himself." [1] Why not, then—whether Zeno so exhorted Theodoric, or Theodoric so begged Zeno—subdue the
obnoxious Odovacar and feed the appetites of these hungry
Ostrogoths by allowing Theodoric to march into Italy? That
would give the eager warrior something to ravage far away
from the fields around Constantinople, and, doubtless, if Theodoric survived the struggle for control of Italy, he would be
content in gratitude to rule it with deference to his benefactor,
the Emperor of New Rome in the East.

So Theodoric went forth to conquer. It was the year 488,
and soon in three great battles the invaders were victorious: at
the River Sontius (Isonzo) near Aquileia; at Verona; and at
the River Addua, ten miles from Milan. No time was lost before they laid siege to Ravenna, Odovacar's Imperial city,
which held its stand amid the protection of its marshes for
three years of terrible sufferings. Little, however, is known
concerning them in actual detail. From one chronicler we learn
that the citizens were driven to eat "hides and other foul and
horrid things," and that "many, saved from the sword, died of
famine"; from another source we gain a grim remark, that "a
bushel of wheat was priced at six *solidi*," three hundred and
sixty times the price asked after Theodoric had established his
rule over Italy in peace.[2] In 493 Ravenna could no longer
resist, and its surrender was quickly completed by the submission of Odovacar himself.

At first the two chieftains agreed to share the rule of Italy
in Ravenna with equal partnership. But the suspicion of
treachery was soon whispered against Odovacar, and probably
Theodoric chafed against a division of power. At all events,
we are told on good tradition that he invited his conquered

---

[1] *History of the Wars,* Loeb edition, V, i, 10ff.; cf. *Anon. Vales.* II, 11
(49).
[2] Agnellus, *Lib. Pont. Rav.* 39, p. 108; *Anon. Vales.* II, 12 (53);
Hodgkin, *Italy and her Invaders,*[2] III, pp. 227, 233.

rival to a banquet in the Palace of the Laurel Grove at Ravenna, and that the banquet ended in the slaying of Odovacar, either by order of Theodoric or, as it would seem, by Theodoric himself.[3] For the story goes that while Odovacar was sitting at the feast of goodwill two men drew near him and grasped his hands under pretence of offering a petition. Immediately a group of soldiers who had treacherously lain in wait, hidden on either side of the hall, came forward with drawn swords. One look at their intended victim was enough, however; they hesitated and dared no more. Then Theodoric ran forward and with his own sword struck Odovacar down. As he fell he cried aloud, "Where is God?" and was answered by the taunt, "This didst thou, too, to my kindred!" The mighty blow rent his body to the loin, and it is said that Theodoric remarked, "Methinks the villain had no bones at all!" The family, friends and military companions of Odovacar, all who could be found by diligent search, shared in his fate.

It was a sorry beginning. None the less, in his reign of some thirty-three years Theodoric worked a splendid chapter for the records of Italy. Procopius wrote of him: "Theodoric was in name a usurper, but in reality he was a true King, no less than any of those who at any time have held this rank with honour. Love of him grew strong both among the Goths and the Italians, even beyond the common fashion of mankind. . . . At his death he was feared by all his enemies, but sorely missed by all those whom he had ruled."[4]

His fame rests on a determined and noble attempt to combine into one glorious State of Rome the best in both elements of his rule: the experienced wisdom and sagacity of the Roman, the barbarian's young energy and muscular strength. Human-

---

[3] Cf. Agnellus, *ibid.* 39, p. 110, and John of Antioch, frag. 214a, *F.H.G.* V, p. 29; Procopius, *Hist. Wars,* V, i, 25; Gibbon, *Decline and Fall,* ed. Bury, IV, p. 180, note 30.

[4] *Hist. Wars,* V, 1, 29ff.

ity as opposed to savage cruelty, order as against lawlessness, justice in place of rape, brotherly feeling in exchange for each man's hand against his fellow: this was the King's dream. It was never forgotten by him, in spite of lapses due to fear and passion, during all the years he ruled Italy from his court within the stronghold of Ravenna. The character given him in Latin chronicle, though exaggerated in its praise, is founded on truth: "Theodoric was distinguished in renown, and of goodwill toward all. In his day such prosperity visited Italy for thirty years that there was peace also for those who followed him. For he did nothing wrong. He united in one the Romans and the Goths. His own creed was Arian, but he did no harm to the Catholic faith. By the splendour of his public games he merited from the Romans the renown of Trajan, by the Goths he was held most mighty for his maintaining of the law he established . . . He was generous in his gifts. He found the public treasury full of straw and by his toil refilled it with gold." [5]

Above all, his merit stands out against the dark record of the years that closed down on Italy when he was no longer King. The noise of arms was then to resound through the land, as his barbarians fought long and bitterly to maintain their hold. Famine and disease were to stalk rampant from north to south; taxation was to sap the hope and energy of its miserable people; towns with their citizens were to fall before the battering-rams, now of one side, now of another, in conflict between Roman and Goth. Service in the field then took its toll of death and imprisonment; suicide and murder were the last resort of men and women, desperate between the future which could promise nothing, and present military or civil exactions which demanded all. In such surroundings the culture which had encouraged the Romans to keep alive the art

[5] *Anon. Vales.* II, 14 (59f.). The same fragment notes the order given by Theodoric to attack the Catholic Church and counts his death shortly afterward as punishment: 32(94f.).

of writing at Theodoric's behest speedily disappeared; only in remote places solitary individuals, unprofitable for active struggle, still laboured with the pen. The barbarian settler in Italy soon forgot the great aims of Theodoric as he quickly reverted to his normal self: a man of primitive passion for the satisfying of his soul and body, in fighting and its victory, in lust and its attainment, in the immediate need of driving hunger from his door.

The King died in 526, and left as heir a grandson ten years old, Athalaric, son of his daughter Amalasuntha and her husband Eutharic, kinsman of Theodoric in Amal descent and Ostrogothic race. Because of the tender years of the young heir the regency of Italy devolved upon Amalasuntha. We are told to picture her as a woman of strong will and quick mental force, "most penetrating in her intelligence and sense of justice, but tending too far to the masculine in her nature." [6] She inherited from her father his passion for Roman civilization and his interest in matters of the intellect. The governing of Rome promised to her joy in practical matters as well. But there was one grave defect; she lacked natural sympathy for her own Gothic people. It would have been hard enough for a woman to hold her own as temporary ruler of a host of Gothic warriors, even had she done all in her power to rear her son in the approved tradition of the Gothic race: in its stern discipline of arms, in recreation of hunting and carousal, duel and tournament. Her ideal was the wisdom and grace of Roman learning from East to West, and she delighted in trying to foster in her wayward and weak-willed son a love of pen and book which filled the Gothic leaders with discontent. He ran to them whenever she punished him for some childish fault, and they hurled at her many bitter words; saying that she wanted to

---

[6] Procopius, *ibid.* V, ii, 3. References cited without title hereafter in this chapter indicate this work (Loeb edition).

make an end of the boy with all speed that she might take another husband and be ruler with him over Goths and Italians alike. "Learning," they stormed at her, "has nothing to do with manliness, and the teachings of old men generally bring forth a cowardly and supine spirit in their charges. If you want your son to be daring in act and great in fame, away with this cringing before teachers! Give him to training of armour; let him have companions of his own age, who will encourage in him that brave heart which is the tradition of the Gothic race!" [7]

At length his mother gave way; for she feared for her own rule if she defied these fierce patriots. Athalaric was sent from the schoolroom to run wild among the sturdy young Goths, who soon made havoc of his carefully guarded temperance by their boisterous enjoyment of pleasures of wine and women. His physical strength was as feeble as his moral force, and a brief career of unchecked indulgence soon ended in his death at the age of seventeen.

By this time Amalasuntha herself had lost all hope of controlling her subjects or of holding her own in Italy. *Dux femina facti* found no echo for her among either Romans or Goths. Two courses were open to her as a last refuge. She might of her own accord surrender her rule to Justinian, since 527 Emperor in Constantinople, who was already turning over in his own mind all possible roads to this end. Or she might ally herself with Theodahad, her kinsman by race and the nephew of Theodoric, a man most worthy of the contempt and dislike he earned wherever he went. He had, however, the training in culture so dear to Amalasuntha's heart: "well read in Latin works and in Platonic philosophy, knowing nothing of a soldier's work or of practical matters of any kind, but marvellously keen on making money." [8] Justinian saw in his weakness one source of hope for the regaining of Italy by the Roman Empire.

[7] V, ii, 11ff.   [8] V, iii, 1.

Negotiations had taken place between the two even before
Athalaric died, and Theodahad had seriously contemplated
treachery to the Gothic King and his Regent mother in return
for substantial favours from the East. But now Amalasuntha
decided for him in preference to Justinian, and in 534 the two
were proclaimed King and Queen of Italy in a strange partnership born of her despair.

It led to no good end. The natural lethargy of this King was
spurred into action by his covetous wife Gudeliva and by the
eagerness of the Goths in Italy to find for themselves once more
a man to lead them to arms. Amalasuntha was soon compelled
to retire to Martana, a tiny island in the Lake of Bolsena, near
Orvieto. There for a little while she was held captive by Theodahad, who felt it politic to send letters to Justinian at Constantinople, excusing his act on the ground that the Queen was
receiving only just and, to boot, merciful treatment in return
for grievous wrongs she had inflicted on himself, her partner
in government. The poor lady was also forced to declare the
same in her own writing to the Eastern Court.

The fall of Italy's Queen was promptly seized by Justinian
for his own devices. When he heard of Amalasuntha's imprisonment, he sent off word to her that he was anxious to do
everything in his power for her aid ; in this way he hoped to stir
up trouble for Theodahad and his Gothic army. But before
the messenger could reach Italy, certain Goths had petitioned
Theodahad to punish in their name this woman, who had put
to death three of their kinsfolk on the ground of rebellion against
her rule. Theodahad had not dared to refuse, and these Goths
themselves had gone at once to the island and murdered Amalasuntha—to their own personal satisfaction, but to the dismay
of both their race and the Italians in general. After all, she
was their Queen.

The news was not altogether bitter, we may well believe, in

the ears of Constantinople. Now the Empire in the East could seriously plan to spread out its hands once again over its Western counterpart; the avenging of the death of Theodoric's daughter would prove a most righteous call to arms. In 535 Justinian proclaimed war against the Goths in Italy, and with the onset of this struggle we are brought face to face with its hero, Belisarius.

Belisarius, born in the East of a Macedonian people, had entered the service of Justinian as a young man. His dramatic career shines brilliantly in the pages of the historian Procopius, whom he took with him on his campaigns as one expert in legal problems. But Procopius was more than a counsellor in delicate situations. He was for many years the devoted admirer and friend of his Chief, and the last tragic years of Belisarius are made the darker by the change from keen enthusiasm in the writings of Procopius as he describes the exploits of Belisarius in Asia and Africa and Italy, to the scorn and hatred which he pours upon him in the malicious *Anecdota,* published after the writer's death.

At the time when Justinian decided to prosecute his own ends by punishing Theodahad and his Ostrogoths, Belisarius was already well known in Constantinople.[9] He had won merit as a soldier in the East, fighting the Persians. He had quelled by force of arms in Constantinople the memorable riot of the "Nika," when in 532 a vast and furious mob had raised the cry of "Vanquish!" throughout the city, in rebellion against the taxes bound upon them by greedy officials and the ever-hungry Imperial purse. He had won glory in Africa by his conquest of Gelimer, which had brought the Vandal kingdom under the power of Justinian in 534. Now he was to magnify the Eastern

[9] For the East in this sixth century see Holmes, *The Age of Justinian and Theodora,* I-II, 1905-1907; Moss, *The Birth of the Middle Ages,* 1935, pp. 79ff., and, on the side of religion, Duchesne, *L'Église au sixième siècle,* 1925.

Empire by asserting its claim over the Gothic usurpers of Italy. He proceeded, therefore, to take possession of Sicily; Theodahad shivered with terror and the way was open for invasion. Then suddenly he was diverted to Africa by a rising of the barbarian soldiers who were holding it for Justinian. The Emperor had neither rewarded their services by grants of Vandal lands, which were kept to feed the Imperial revenues, nor in his Catholic zeal suffered them to profess the Arian faith so dear to their souls. The mutiny, however, was finally quelled by Germanus, nephew of Justinian, and Belisarius, recalled for action, in 536 was already in Italy pounding at the gates of Naples.

Procopius pictures the citizens of Naples remonstrating with this enemy, so famous for conquest, when first his ships anchored in their harbour and his soldiers settled down in camp near their walls.[10] In vain they suggested that Rome, chief city of Theodahad as King of Italy, would be better worth the toil of a siege than their lesser town! Belisarius answered by bidding them think hard before they dared resist Justinian, Lord of the Roman Empire equally in Italy of the West as in Constantinople of the East. The debate was long and the defenders were anxious. But at length confidence in their store of provisions and in the promise of loyal co-operation on the part of the Goths who lived within the city determined them to fight with all their power. The Goths undertook to guard the outer wall, which Belisarius repeatedly attacked in vain, as it was also protected in part by the sea and in part by rough and precipitous land. He then proceeded to destroy the aqueduct which furnished the city's water. Yet even here the inhabitants triumphed through an abundant supply of springs inside the walls.

So matters went on for long weary months till the besiegers

[10] V, viii, 6ff.

began to think of abandoning the blockade altogether in their discouragement at the stout resistance offered and the slipping away of precious time as the year advanced. Rome still lay ahead, and an attack on Rome in the winter was no joyful prospect. Just as they were preparing to depart, their luck turned. The brilliant idea occurred to one of the Isaurian mercenaries in the invading army—a man given to exploring on his own account—that it might be possible to enlarge the channel of the aqueduct, which Belisarius had cut, and to penetrate into the city by this secret way. There follows a thrilling tale of men creeping stealthily by night along the narrow pipe, while by instructions of Belisarius one of his officers parleyed with shouts of ringing Gothic gutturals in the ears of its barbarian defenders, lest any sound should be heard from the soldiers crawling on hands and knees below. Finally they reached a place where the aqueduct stood bare to the sky, and found themselves faced by a mass of sheer rock. The courage of one saved all. He promptly scaled the height, and drew his fellows after him by throwing down to them the end of a stout leather rope which he fastened round an olive tree growing on the top. They reached the city wall in safety, killed the guards they encountered, and opened a way of conquest for the rest of their host. Thus in 536 Naples was taken, and Justinian's victorious soldiers fell to slaughter and pillage. But Belisarius, always represented to us as great in generosity as he was in generalship, quickly bade them refrain, gave back to the people of Naples their possessions, and saved from harm women, children and slaves. The Italian men were granted their liberty, and the Goths who had been taken prisoners were treated by him as his own men and invited to enroll in his army if they would.

During all this time of distress Theodahad had refused to heed the city's repeated appeals for aid. It was only what was to be expected from him. Before Belisarius had even entered Italy this miserable King had held secret audience for an Imperial legate from Constantinople. "Your joy is to pursue paths of philosophy," argued this subtle officer. "It belongs to Justinian to be a noble Emperor of the Romans. Surely you know from your study of Plato that killing men is no business for a philosopher; and, moreover, Justinian is not to be blamed for laying claim to land which by right belongs to him."[11]

Theodahad found it convenient to see the point; manliness, we are told, was not one of his virtues. There is a story, believe it or not as you will, says our chronicler, Procopius, that he was addicted to consultations with fortune-tellers. So now he asked one of these how this invasion of Belisarius would fare, and was bidden to shut up swine in three huts, ten in each; the three herds were to represent, one the Goths, one the soldiers of Justinian, and one his own Italian troops. After a few days he was told to go and look at the swine. Nearly all the "Goths" were dead, of the "Romans of Italy" half had perished and all were mangy and bald, but close by all the "soldiers of Justinian" were alive and flourishing. The interpretation was evident, and Theodahad left the citizens of Naples to their fate.[12]

Revenge was quick in coming. The Gothic warriors, stung by this treachery and cowardice, assembled near Terracina at a place then called Regata, about forty miles south-east of Rome, and elected one of their own number, Witigis, as King of Italy. Witigis was only a simple soldier, and elderly at that. But he had courage and distinction in battle to his credit, and the Goths knew no better man. He at once ordered the capture of Theodahad, who had fled toward Ravenna. Unfortunately for the fugitive, the Gothic soldier dispatched on this mission had a private grievance against his quarry. The Gothic King some time before had taken from him his heart's joy, a very beautiful young woman well endowed with this world's goods, and had given her to another man. Loyalty to Witigis was thus sweetened for the pursuer by his own thoughts of vengeance. With all speed he hastened day and night toward Ravenna, caught up with Theodahad, and, as we are told, "cast him to the ground on his back and sacrificed him like some victim at the altar." [13]

Then Witigis proceeded to Rome, where he held a great assembly of the Goths and besought the Pope, Silverius, and the Roman Senate and people to support his race and help to bring back the days of Theodoric the Great. With this vision in mind he marched on to Ravenna, seized the daughter of Amalasuntha and sister of Athalaric, a young girl named Matasuntha, and forced her to wed most unwillingly with him, a man old enough to be her father, in order to secure some real claim of legal kinship with the family of her grandfather, that same Theodoric.

It was a mistake on the part of Witigis to forego a seat of rule in Rome for the more retired and inaccessible Ravenna: a lack of imagination which cost him a great chance of rallying and enheartening his soldier adherents.

And there was cause enough for discouragement. Emboldened by a message from Pope Silverius and the people of Rome, who in spite of oaths of allegiance exacted from them by Witigis preferred to think of themselves under the power of Justinian's general rather than starving and slain in the fate of their compatriots of Naples, Belisarius marched upon Rome by the Latin Way. The Goths who were guarding the walls abandoned them as the invading army approached, and retreated to Ravenna, with the exception of their captain, Leuderis. At the same moment the soldiers of Belisarius entered the city by another gate. Its keys and the brave Gothic chieftain were

[13] V, xi, 6ff.

sent in triumph to the Eastern Court, and thus in December, 536, "Rome, lost for sixty years, once again passed into Roman hands."[14] Measures were immediately taken for defence against attempts of the Goths at recapture, though many of the Roman soldiers thought it folly to try to guard a place that needed so many defenders for its vast circuit of walls, and lay, moreover, too far from the sea to be adequately supplied with food.

Then the shame of Witigis, watching from his retreat at Ravenna the capture of his chief city and a considerable part of its neighbouring land, drove him forth in an attempt to regain his loss. News had come through refugees from Rome that Belisarius carried only a small force of soldiers with him. But it was learned, too, that lieutenants in the invading army had already seized important cities in Tuscany: Narnia (Narni), Spoletium (Spoleto), and Perusia (Perugia). So the Gothic King turned Romewards with all his army, and in March, 537, arrived at the Salarian Bridge over the Anio.[15] We are told that by this time he was as eager to find Belisarius in Rome as he had been ready to avoid him before. On the way, as he was urging on his men, he met a priest journeying from Rome, and asked him anxiously whether Belisarius was still there. "Do not worry about that," was the answer. "Belisarius is still in Rome and will surely stay." This was excellent hearing, and Witigis made more haste than ever, in the hope of catching his enemy before he might retreat.[16]

The Salarian Bridge had been fortified as a precaution by Belisarius in anticipation of this movement of his enemy. But when the Roman guards saw the great horde of Goths coming down upon them, they fled and left the crossing open. On the farther side, however, the Goths were met by Belisarius himself,

[14] V, xiv, 14.
[15] See Bury, *Later Roman Empire*, 1923, II, p. 182.
[16] V, xvi, 19ff.

coming out from the city to attack with a thousand horsemen. In the battle that followed he fought so furiously that he took no thought for his office and the welfare of his army depending on him, but contended in the very front of the battle, like a private of the ranks. He was also brought into even greater peril through his horse, "White-face," a splendid creature, all grey except for this distinguishing feature. Deserters who had fled from Belisarius to the Goths pointed out the mark to the men of Witigis, calling out to them to "aim at the white-faced horse." Fortunately the animal was very sagacious and well accustomed to battle, and we are glad to read that it saved again and again its rider's life.[17] So, though he was constantly in the thick of the fight, Belisarius escaped unscathed, and after many adventures entered safely within the walls of Rome once more.

Witigis now set to work at the siege of Rome, expecting to capture the city without delay on account of the smallness of the force defending it. Yet it resisted from this date, March, 537, for a whole year, held stubbornly by Belisarius in the face of terrific assault. The Goths repaid him in his own coin by destroying the aqueducts, cutting off the water supply, and stopping the mills. He met this emergency to some extent by placing the mills on boats and working them through the strong current of the Tiber near the Pons Aurelius. Thus enough wheat was ground to feed the city, and water could be drawn in sufficient measure from wells, though the people grumbled because there was no means of bathing and because their plentiful provision of food was dealt out by a firm and sparing hand. Their nights, too, were broken by enforced military vigils, and it was truly vexatious to see the invaders plundering their lands outside the city wall. Belisarius was the target of all these complaints. "Why," protested the citizens, "did you

[17] V, xviii, 6ff.

venture to attack the Goths before you had been provided with
a respectably-sized army by Justinian?" [18]   Rumours of this
discontent reached Witigis and encouraged him to send pro-
posals for surrender, to which Belisarius made brief retort that
he would hold Rome as long as he himself held life.

He merely laughed at the advancing towers and battering
rams with which the besiegers terrified his imprisoned citizens.
Yet he did send an appeal to Justinian, asking for reinforcements in order that he might meet the Gothic attack on an equal
footing. If his men should now be conquered, he reminded
the Emperor, both Italy and the Imperial army would be lost,
to say nothing of the shame to Constantinople. "I know for
myself," he ended, "that I owe death as my duty to your Empire, and no man shall drive me from this city as long as I am
alive. But think what kind of reputation such an end of Belisarius will bring to you!" [19]

This gloomy letter had its effect, and Justinian quickly sent
off a message announcing the despatch of troops to the rescue.
In the meantime Belisarius sent away to Naples all the women
and children, and all servants who were not needed for the
defence of Rome. Through a strange lack of ability and of
military experience shown by Witigis they were allowed to
escape safely, and for the same reasons provisions were constantly brought in from outside to the besieged.

At this point rumours spread through Rome that the Pope
Silverius was negotiating secretly with the Goths for the surrender of the city, a happening which brings us to a little describing of intrigue done in the name of religion during this
sixth century.[20]

Theodora, wife of Justinian, and therefore Augusta or Empress of Rome in the East, was as devoted an adherent of the

[18] V, xx, 5ff.   [19] V, xxiv, 17.
[20] *Vita Silverii* in *Gesta Pont. Rom.* I, ed. Mommsen, *M.G.H.* pp.
144ff.; *Lib. Pont.* I, ed. Duchesne, pp. 290ff.; Liberatus, *Brev.* cc. 21f.

Monophysite belief, which held that our Lord was of One Nature only, as her husband was firm in adherence to the Catholic Christology set forth at Chalcedon. Her story begins badly. She was daughter of an attendant in the amphitheatre of Constantinople, and in her early youth was famed as an actress on its public stage. The staid and ambitious Justinian, for all his eagerness to hold both the glories of this world and the mysteries of heaven in his grasp, fell a helpless victim to her fascination, overcame all obstacles and made her his lawful wife. She exercised in his Court all the power and influence which had brought her to it and was a most formidable enemy of anyone who opposed her, especially in the vital matter of her creed.

Great, therefore, had been her wrath when Agapetus, Pope of Rome from 535 till 536, arriving at Constantinople to plead for the miseries of Italy, had refused to hold friendship or communion of the Church with Anthimus, Patriarch of Constantinople, on account of the Patriarch's Monophysite sympathies. And more than this. The Pope had even caused the deposition of Anthimus from his office for this same reason, and had himself consecrated and appointed one Menas as Patriarch in his place. Shortly afterward Agapetus died at Constantinople, just as he was preparing his return to Italy.

Then, as our ancient chroniclers tell, the Lady Theodora set her busy brain to work. She summoned to the Palace the Archdeacon Vigilius, Papal legate at Constantinople of the Church in Rome. He was well liked by her, and she hoped to play upon the secret ambition which she thought to read in his heart. Before him she held out openly the hope of succeeding now to the See of Rome. She would write to Belisarius and to his wife, Antonina, who held Belisarius as closely under her spell as Theodora did Justinian. Only Vigilius must promise to do all in his power as Pope to promote the Monophysite faith.

Vigilius, from what our sources tell us, appeared not indifferent to this dazzling prospect, and set out for Italy and Belisarius at once. But when he arrived, the clergy of Rome had already approved for the Papal Chair Silverius, a subdeacon, son of Hormisdas, Pope of Rome from 514 till 523, by a marriage ended, of course, before he held the Holy See.

The indignation of the Empress at Constantinople waxed doubly hot when this news arrived. She wrote to Pope Silverius a note: "Come here to see me, or, at any rate, reinstate Anthimus in his office." When Silverius received this message, he groaned, crying, "I know now that she has made an end of my life!" But, blessed man (so we read), with faith in God and Saint Peter, he wrote back: "Lady Empress, never will I do this—that I should recall a heretic damned in his iniquity."

In spite of this temporary disappointment, Vigilius steadily pursued his mission and declared Theodora's will both to Belisarius and to the Lady Antonina at Rome. It placed the unhappy General in a terrible dilemma, torn between his conscience and his fear of the Empress, with whom his beloved Antonina was on intimate terms. Long he meditated, and finally he said: "I do what is ordered of me. But as for him who shall be concerned in the death of Silverius the Pope, let him give account of his deeds to our Lord Jesus Christ."

Thereupon witnesses declared that they had found Pope Silverius sending word to Witigis, King of the Goths: "Come to the Gate called Asinarian near the Lateran, and I will hand over to you both Belisarius and the city of Rome." The report was undoubtedly false, and indeed one of our ancient records gives us the names of two men said to have forged the letter bearing the signature of Silverius.[21] Belisarius, who had taken up his quarters during the siege in the Pincian Palace, sent for Silverius, and showed him this letter, begging

[21] Liberatus, c. 22.

him, as also did Antonina, to try to propitiate the Empress
Theodora by turning from the Catholic creed to promote
Monophysite belief. The Pope took refuge for a while in the
Church of Saint Sabina in Rome, but came forward against
the advice of his friends when another message arrived summoning him again to the Pincian, under oath of safe return.
He did return, but after yet another summons, as this story
reads, "he was no more seen," and "was sent into exile at
Patara, a city of Lycia." [22] Another chronicler tells us that on
coming into the Palace Silverius was led to an inner private
room, where he found Antonina lying on a couch and her
husband Belisarius sitting at her feet.[23] "Tell me, my Lord
Silverius the Pope," said Antonina, "what have we done to
you and the Romans that you should want to hand us over to
the Goths?" At that same moment a subdeacon, John by
name, came into the room and stripped the pallium, the sacred
vestment of the Popes, from the shoulders of Silverius. Next,
taking him aside to a bedroom, John despoiled him of all his
robes of office and clothed him in the dress of a simple monk.
Then announcement was made by another subdeacon to the
clergy of Rome that the Pope had been deposed, and all fled at
the news.

Belisarius now called an assembly of the clergy and bade
them elect Vigilius as Pope. Amid general hesitation and with
the refusal of some who were present, Vigilius was elected, and
consecrated on March 29, 537.

The sequel of the story is of interest to the historians of the
Church. The Bishop of Patara, indignant at the suffering of
the illustrious exile in his diocese, went to Justinian in protest.
"The Kings of this world are many," he said gravely. "There
is but one Pope, Head of the Church throughout the world, and

[22] ibid.
[23] Gest. Pont. Rom. I, p. 147; Lib. Pont. I, p. 292.

he has been banished from his See." [24] Justinian, much perturbed, at once gave order that Silverius should be recalled to
Rome to stand trial. "If the letter on which his accusation
rests be proved true," he ordained, "let Silverius exercise his
office as Bishop in some other city; if false, let him be restored
to his own See of Rome."

So Silverius returned to Rome. But Vigilius, in terror of los-
ing the Papal dignity, sent word to Belisarius: "Hand over
Silverius to me; otherwise I cannot perform what you seek."
The request was granted, and the captive was borne back into
exile, this time on the island of Palmaria,[25] where, "sustained
by the bread and water of affliction," he died on June 20, 538,
and is celebrated as Saint, Pope, and Martyr in the Roman
Missal by a Mass each year on this same day.[26] Hereupon
Vigilius became Pope in lawful right, as he had been by unlaw-
ful tenure since March, 537.

Meanwhile the siege of Rome went on steadily. Witigis now
determined to try to stop the entry of provisions into the city
by seizing the harbour called "Portus," at the northern mouth
of the Tiber. This was successfully carried out, and as the
entry into the other harbour, Ostia, was too dangerous an
undertaking, Belisarius was obliged to bring in food carried
by way of Antium and thence a day's journey by land to Rome.
Food, then, of some sort was still forthcoming, and operations
went on with sallies on the part of the besieged, even a pitched
battle outside the walls in the Plain of Nero near the Cornelian
Gate. But in this the soldiers of Belisarius were defeated by the
Goths, and for the future only ventured out from the city in
short dashes of attack.

Thus the winter passed, and in the warmer spring season

[24] Liberatus, c. 22.   [25] In the Tyrrhenian Sea.
[26] *Lib. Pont.* I, p. 293. Liberatus says he died of starvation; Procopius,
Anecdota (Historia Arcana) i, 14; i, 27, that he was murdered by Eugenius,
a servant of Antonina, in her desire to propitiate Theodora.

of 538 the imprisoned people began to suffer terribly from hunger and disease. The Goths had by this time raised a fortified position on the meeting of two aqueducts between the Latin and the Appian Roads, which effectively prevented the entrance of provisions. As long as the harvest lasted, some of the more adventurous of the Roman soldiers had crept out of the city by night to bring in corn from the fields and sell it for huge sums to the highest bidders. When even this supply failed, the whole populace of Rome lived miserably, as her poorer inhabitants long had done, on grasses and plants growing in the streets and on the walls, and even on sausage meat made from the carcasses of mules dead through lack of food.

At last human nature could bear no more, and a deputation of leading citizens begged Belisarius to hazard a general battle with the Goths. Any form of death, they said, was preferable to that of starvation; to which the General retorted that "great as was their eagerness, their folly was equal to it. Watchful waiting was the only proper course, in view of the fact that an army which no man could number had already been assembled by Justinian for their support from all over the earth. Even now it was on its way, with a fleet such as the Romans had never seen before." [27] Then Procopius, and Antonina as well, were sent off secretly to Naples to await the arrivals from the East, and to superintend loading of ships with corn in preparation for this happy escort shortly expected. And, in truth, aid did appear soon after from various directions, especially in an army led by a general known as John "the Bloodthirsty," nephew of one Vitalian, who in 513 had stirred up rebellion against Anastasius I, Roman Emperor in the East from 491 till 518.

On their side the Goths had also been suffering greatly from famine and sickness and the raids of the besieged. When, therefore, they heard of the arrival of this new force, with all the

[27] Procopius, VI, iii, 8ff.

natural exaggerations of its size and power, they decided in great discouragement to send ambassadors to Belisarius. Their argument ran that Odovacar had driven Romulus "Augustulus" from the throne of Italy, that Theodoric had been suffered by Zeno to punish Odovacar for this wrong-doing and to rule afterward as lawful King. From that time, they maintained, the Goths had governed justly in accordance with the traditions laid down by the Emperors of Roman race in older days. Belisarius retorted that the Emperor Zeno had, no doubt, commissioned Theodoric to conquer Odovacar, but in order that Italy might be under the sovereign supremacy of Zeno himself, not of Theodoric the Goth.

In the debate which followed various offers of reconciliation were made. The Goths proposed to hand over Sicily to Justinian for the sake of retaining Italy, and Belisarius responded with equal magnificence that Justinian would undoubtedly yield to them the whole of Britain, a far greater territory than Sicily, if they would renounce their claims to the Roman throne of Italy. The envoys were not tempted. They went further, even promising to pay annual tribute to Constantinople. But Belisarius remained unmoved, and only a truce was the point of this conference.[28]

By the aid of their reinforcements the Romans were now enabled to receive necessary supplies within their city. For the besiegers, although they were stationed at the Northern Harbour, took no measures to prevent the passage of ships along the Tiber and finally abandoned this station altogether. The last blow to their persistence was given by John "the Bloodthirsty." When he had captured Ariminum (Rimini), his fame became so great that the Goths, still half dead with hunger, decided that they must at length abandon the attack upon Rome. In fact, Matasuntha, the young and romantic

[28] *ibid.* VI, vi, 1ff.

wife of Witigis, already tired to death of her elderly husband
and her dreary days in his court at Ravenna, sent a secret
message to the hero that if he would carry her off as his bride,
she would secretly betray to him the keys of that city also!

So the Goths withdrew from the territory of Rome in March,
538, after a siege of twelve months and nine days. The months
that followed were notable especially for the capture of Milan
by the soldiers of Belisarius, and for the siege of Ariminum,
held by his lieutenant, the John of sanguinary reputation. This
was almost successful, engineered as it was by Witigis himself
and his whole army. Belisarius, hoping that the Goths would
pass by Ariminum without notice if it were not guarded by a
great force, had sent a small detachment to hold it under two
officers, Martin and Ildiger, with word to John that he should
relinquish its command to these. When John refused to comply
with this order, the siege began in earnest, as the General-in-
Chief had feared. Soon matters became desperate for the defenders. At the very last moment in deeply wounded pride
John was compelled to send a message to the General he had
disobeyed: the city must surrender within seven days, since its
garrison was starving and the enemy could no longer be resisted: "a situation," he wrote, "which, I suppose, might excuse
us if we should act contrary to our code." [29] It was saved by the
arrival of relief from the East commanded by one Narses, of
all men the most unlikely to prevail in such a case, yet strangely
destined to prove himself most famous of all the Roman generals engaged in this war.

He belonged by birth to Persarmenia, and had been trained
as a eunuch to serve in the Court of Constantinople. By his
subtle and quick mind he had risen stage by stage to become,
first one of the Keepers of the archives of the Imperial household, and afterward, in middle age, the *Praepositus sacri cubi-*

[29] VI, xvi, 16.

culi, Grand Chamberlain of the Court. This position naturally gave him constant access to conference with Justinian; and Theodora, also, had used his confidential services to good effect in her intrigues. Of his courage and his loyalty to the Eastern throne we have good evidence. For when Justinian was in peril through the "Victory" riot of 532 and the rival adherents of different colours in the circus races were pouring fuel on the flames of strife, Narses, going out secretly from the Palace, distributed bribes to certain of the "Blues," the party ever noted for its support of the Emperor. Thus encouraged, the "Blues" had risen in force for the throne, and the soldiers of Belisarius had finished the work begun by the cunning of Narses the Court official.[30] Narses was, moreover, an eager Catholic. He was devoted to the Madonna, our Lady, from whom he was said to receive immediate direction for his acts, and "so keen on fasting and prayer that he prevailed rather by his fervent supplications to heaven than by his use of the weapons of war." [31]

It might, indeed, seem strange that Justinian should send this man, already about sixty years old and trained in domestic matters of the Court far from the fields of battle, on so desperate a mission as the rescue of Italy from Witigis and his Gothic warriors. Yet the reason has easily been traced by shrewd students of the times. The Emperor was beginning to be alarmed at the fame of the exploits of Belisarius in Asia, Africa and Italy. It would be well, he must have decided, to dim this lustre somewhat by sending to Belisarius a colleague who could be counted on to place his master's interests above his own. A eunuch advanced in age, deeply involved in the Imperial service, would not be dangerous to Justinian, however successful he might be in subduing Witigis.

[30] See Procopius, *Persian War,* I, 24; John Malalas, *Chron. C.S.H.B.* pp. 473ff.; *Chron. Pasch.* I, *C.S.H.B.* pp. 620ff.; Theophanes, ed. de Boor, pp. 181ff.

[31] Evagrius, *Eccles. Hist.* IV, 24; Paul. Diac. *Hist. Lang.* II, 3.

His coming did bring trouble for Belisarius. But it also brought for the time a retarding of Justinian's own cause. Ariminum, certainly, was rescued, for Narses was a great friend of John "the Bloodthirsty," and strongly advised the sending of a relief force to save him there. Ildiger, the lieutenant of Belisarius, was despatched, and so terrified the Goths by the sight of his incoming fleet that they fled in panic and disorder. Belisarius, arriving himself shortly afterward, could not help feeling sorry for John, because "he and his soldiers were white of face and terribly unkempt to look upon." But neither could he refrain from remarking that John had better be thankful to Ildiger. To which John retorted that if it had not been for Narses, he would have perished. From that moment history traces the beginning of jealousy between the two commanders of Justinian's army. "Was not Narses," argued his friends, "a confidential adviser of the Emperor? Was he to be ordered about by a man who was but a military officer? Should not Narses himself gain renown by conquering Italy rather than simply aid Belisarius to carry everything off as his own right?"[32]

Narses listened to this talk and consistently opposed the counsels of Belisarius, still by title his superior. A Staff Assembly was called; but the General to no purpose warned all present that the crisis admitted of no waste of time in petty quarrels. At last he tried to bring about harmony by producing a letter which Justinian had sent to his officers on this Western front: "We did not send our steward Narses to Italy to be Commander-in-Chief of the army. For we desire that Belisarius alone should direct matters as he shall judge best, and it belongs to you all to follow him for the advantage of our state." The answer of Narses was, of course, that Belisarius was *not* acting for the advantage of the state, and need not, therefore, be obeyed.[33]

From this time disloyalty steadily increased, till matters came

[32] Procopius, VI, xviii, 1ff.   [33] *ibid*. VI, xviii, 28.

to a head when through lack of co-operation Milan was re-taken by the enemy and destroyed. Its male citizens were put to death and its women sold as slaves by the rage of the Goths under Uraias, nephew of Witigis. Then at last Justinian re-called Narses to Constantinople and left Belisarius to work his will alone.

The massacre of the citizens of Milan is one of the deepest stains upon Ostrogothic records; doubtless it was due to anger at its former yielding to Belisarius. We read, however, that the lives of its soldier defenders were spared.

Progress now blessed the efforts of the Imperial General, and the Goths, in terror that Ravenna itself would shortly be at-tacked by him, sent envoys praying for aid from the Lombards and the Persians. From the Lombards they obtained no re-sponse. The Persian King, Chosroes, did make plans for hostili-ties, which bore fruit in the Second Persian War (540-545), but remained for the present barren of good.

Then suddenly hope arose from an unexpected quarter. The Franks of Gaul, scenting the occasion of capture of land and other booty for themselves in the exhausted state of both Goths and Romans, marched into Italy under Theodebert, their King, apparently on the Gothic side. The joy of the Goths knew no bounds. Often before now they had made splendid offers to the Franks, offers which had been accepted in word. But noth-ing had come of it. In fact the Franks, "in affairs of honour the most slippery of mankind," [34] had even concluded an alliance with the Romans on their own account.

And so with great enthusiasm they saw these new allies arrive at Ticinum (Pavia), and helped them to cross the river Po. Their happiness, alas! was short-lived. Once the Franks had gained possession of the bridge, they promptly abandoned pretence of friendship, seized all the women and children of the

[34] VI, xxv, 2.

Goths whom they could find, and threw them into the river. They then engaged in battle for themselves against some of the soldiers of Belisarius and defeated them. Belisarius addressed to Theodebert a tactful letter, advising him not to break his treaty with Justinian. Sickness, caused through bad food and water, was a more potent factor of discouragement, ravaging men and beasts in the troops of the invaders, and the Frankish King at last yielded to the complaints of his suffering host and retreated homewards to Gaul.

The distress of Italy was now extreme. Siege after siege brought famine and death in its train, and while Belisarius thundered at the gates of Italian towns, people in city and country perished indiscriminately. Procopius had ghastly stories to tell of these days, of things he had seen and heard himself as one of the train of Belisarius: of strange diseases brought on by horrible substitutes for decent food, of the dying who fell as they struggled to pluck even a tuft of grass, of the dead who lay unburied, of frightful deeds done by starving men. And by women, too. There is one story of two women who were left alone in their village when all the other inhabitants had perished through sickness and famine, so that travellers passing that way often rested for the night in their cottage. As time went on, hunger drove them to murder their guests as they slept and to feed on human flesh. Seventeen men died in this way; the eighteenth awoke just in time to learn what was in store for him and to destroy these victims of a craving beyond all control.[35]

The misery of the soldiers in Justinian's army was no less, especially as the Goths refused to surrender, even in these straits. After Narses had departed, Belisarius captured Auximum (Osimo), the chief town of Picenum, and then at last laid siege to the city where Witigis held his royal state. It was a

[35] VI, xx, 22ff.

hard situation for the Gothic leader. If Ravenna fell, he and
his warriors would surely be sent to magnify their victor's
triumphant procession before the eyes of Justinian and to live
the wretched remainder of their lives as prisoners of the Byzantine Court. At one time Witigis thought of yielding to envoys
from the Franks, once again anxious to possess themselves of
this land in her weakness. "We propose, if you are willing,"
said they, "to share with you the rule of Italy." [36] But at last
a different counsel prevailed, fruit of a great despair of his
situation, and a tiny hope in the urgings of his men. He decided
to throw himself upon the pride of his attackers and to offer
the throne of Italy to Belisarius himself.

Belisarius had no intention of betraying Justinian's trust.
But his loyalty to the Emperor is cast here into the shadow of
treachery toward the Goths who took him simply at his word.
Promising to protect them, he declared he would give oath
concerning the crown before Witigis himself. This they interpreted as consent, and in May, 540,[37] he entered Ravenna as
ruler of the West, surrounded by the cheers of his own army,
the rejoicings of the Goths, and the thanksgivings of the citizens
whom he was rescuing from starvation. Procopius, who was
present, pondered on the divinity that shapes men's paths as
he watched the Roman soldiers on their way. He tells that
when the women of Ravenna saw the inferiority of the Romans
both in numbers and in muscular strength to their own male
populace, they pointed with scorn at the conquerors marching
past, and turned to spit upon the faces of their husbands, as
cowards and no true men.[38]

The treasures of the city, with King Witigis himself, were
promptly secured by the victor and kept closely under guard,
while the news of this double capture opened to Belisarius almost all the cities in North-Eastern Italy. Only in Verona and

[36] VI, xxviii, 15.   [37] Agnellus, 62, p. 176.   [38] VI, xxix, 32ff.

in Ticinum do we still read of Gothic garrisons unsubdued. The defenders of Verona were ruled by Ildibad, nephew of Theudis, the Visigothic King in Spain, and in Ticinum the nephew of Witigis, Uraias, was in command. Ildibad did, indeed, send conciliatory messages to Ravenna, because Belisarius had found and seized his children there.

As time went on and Belisarius took no steps toward confirming this new Kingship, when whispers even began to creep about that he was planning an early departure for Constantinople, the fresh hope of the Goths slowly turned sour with dismay. Their fears were only too well founded. Partly because of rumours of these doings in Ravenna, speedily carried to Constantinople by the vigilant enemies of the Commander-in-Chief in Italy, partly because of threatenings of the Second Persian War, Justinian now decided to recall Belisarius to the East.

Thrown back upon their own fate, the chief warriors of the Goths first begged Uraias to become their King, and when he refused through fear of seeming disloyalty to his uncle Witigis, they next asked Ildibad to lead them. He, said Uraias, would surely be aided by his uncle in Spain. And so Ildibad was invested with the marks of sovereignty.

One more appeal, however, was made to Belisarius. At the advice of Ildibad himself, nervous lest he be unable to bring the Gothic rule out of danger, envoys were sent after him, promising that if only he would keep his plighted word like a true and honourable soldier (so they put it), Ildibad the King would come and lay down his royal robes in homage at his feet, proclaiming him conqueror of Ravenna and its future Lord. As Theodoric once before, so Belisarius should now reign in harmony over both Romans and Goths.

But to no avail. In this year, 540, Belisarius set out for Constantinople, carrying with him Witigis his prisoner and the young Matasuntha, whose appeal to the hero, John "the Bloodthirsty," had not availed to release her from the long boredom of Ravenna. Justinian was thrilled by the sight of all this brave array of barbarian captives, enhanced by the presence of their King and Queen. The treasure of the Goths must also have been a welcome sight, though we are told that jealousy of the notable success of Belisarius and of the rapturous welcome given him by the people of Constantinople was not so pleasant. The fame of this General was to increase by leaps and bounds as dismal news filtered in from Italy through the months yet to come. At the same time it is fair to remember with Bury that Belisarius had left behind him an unconquered country, unsettled and embittered.[39]

The hesitating mind of Justinian was always an obstacle in the road of success. The same spirit of economy regarding expenditure abroad which had governed him throughout would not now permit of one single General in command on the Italian front; and the divided administration which he established was fruitful of nothing but dispute. His eternal need of revenue led, moreover, to increased tyranny of taxation throughout Italy. This was superintended by an officer sent specially from Constantinople, who had attained there such notorious fame for gaining funds for the Imperial treasury by unfair means that he was generally known as Alexander "the Clipper." He promptly set to work to gain fresh laurels in this western land by all sorts of fines inflicted on civilians, and by dealing out the barest pittance to the soldiers on his own side.

Thus the seeds of grievances, sown by Romans and Goths alike, bore sweet fruit to Ildibad. Constantinople was becoming seriously disturbed by relays of bad news when suddenly a blaze flared up in the Gothic Court, kindled from a woman's wrath. The Queen of Italy, Ildibad's wife, held herself insulted by the wife of Uraias, who, on entering one day into the Baths

[39] *Later Roman Empire,* II, p. 214.

of Ravenna with great magnificence of dress and retinue, had utterly disdained to notice the First Lady of the Land. Ildibad had not received any royal allowance with his royal crown, and his Queen was dressed but shabbily. However, her spirit was proud enough, and in tears she rushed to her Lord and husband to beg him to punish such an outrage. Therefore Ildibad spread evil tales about Uraias and ended by secretly causing his death.

This nephew of Witigis was popular among the Goths, and his murder caused bitter offence. But no one dared take any open action till another tiny spark was fired. For some unexplained reason King Ildibad gave away the betrothed of Velas, one of his barbarian guards, to another man in marriage. It was the story of Theodahad over again. Velas was passionately attached to his intended wife, and the deed, whether in malice or ignorance, had been done during his absence from the Court on military service. On his return he at once struck in revenge. It was the spring of 541, and he murdered Ildibad during the festivity of a banquet given by the King to propitiate his angry followers.

For a few months the rule of Italy was held by a Goth of Rugian birth, called Eraric. His own people, among whom he held great influence, had proclaimed him King, and the Goths in general were at first too discouraged to refuse a passive assent, though they were by no means enthusiastic over their new Chief. Would it not be far better to take their chance under Totila, Ildibad's nephew, who was at this time in charge of the Gothic garrison at Tarvisium (Treviso) in Northern Italy?

The career of this Totila (also known as Baduila) had not begun with great glory, it would seem, even if Procopius describes him as "of very great shrewdness, energy and high repute among the Goths." [40] After tidings had reached him of

[40] VII, ii, 7.

the violent death of Ildibad, his uncle, he had offered to yield himself and his whole garrison of Goths to the Romans if his own safety might be assured. The Roman commander at Ravenna, with whom he discussed this proposal, was delighted. The bargain was on the point of being carried out, when the Goths finally decided that Eraric was not their man, and sent messengers to Tarvisium, calling Totila to rule as King over them. Totila made no secret of his private treaty with Ravenna, but at the same time had no objection to making another with the Goths. If, said he, they would see that Eraric was murdered before the date of the surrender he had promised to the Romans, he would readily do all they wanted. Nothing remained, therefore, for this happy consummation but to slay Eraric by cunning. This was promptly carried out, and Totila became King of the Goths in 541. The deed was made easier by the facts that the times were desperate, that Eraric was no general, and that many people were loudly asserting that he had conveniently removed Ildibad from his path.

The King who now entered upon his eventful reign of eleven years has always been given a prominent place in the pages of historians, ancient and modern, though the quality of their description varies from the "very perfite gentil knight" of Thomas Hodgkin to the "ordinary perfidious barbarian" of Bury's detailed criticism.[1] Bury's colder judgment saw with reason in the downfall of Totila after so brilliant a career an irresistible appeal to the sympathy of enemies as well as of friends. Totila was certainly barbarian, and sometimes perfidious. But he was not ordinary, and now and again he was illumined by some nobler impulse for good.

In the next year, after some minor successes in Northern Italy, he worked his way southwards, meeting with no great

[1] *Italy and her Invaders,* IV, pp. 439, 724f.; *Lat. Rom. Emp.* II, pp. 268f.

fortune till he reached Samnite territory and captured Bene-
ventum. He then proceeded to invest Naples. When the rigour
of blockade had brought its inhabitants to all loss of hope,
Totila spoke to them from the ramparts, promising safety to
themselves and to their commander Conon with his soldiers if
all would surrender. For, said he, he remembered well their
loyalty to the Gothic cause in the bitter siege of 536. Only
after the most stubborn resistance had they then been compelled to yield to Belisarius. In answer the besieged stipulated
that they should wait yet a little while in the hope of receiving
aid from the Roman general. When none came, they yielded
in the spring of 543.

Already in connection with this siege various incidents reflect the varied character of the new King. Procopius tells
that, after the city had fallen, Totila showed such humanity to
his prisoners as was "characteristic neither of an enemy nor of
a barbarian." [42] He kept his promise, and both military and
civil population departed in safety where they would. He even
supplied horses, money, and guards for Conon and his men.
During the actual work of destroying part of the walls of
Naples he found time to consider the case of one of his own
spearmen, who had assaulted a girl belonging to the captured
city. The soldier was of special value to the Gothic army, and
the leading Goths interceded for him. But Totila put the man
to death and handed over to his victim all the offender's savings.

Such magnanimity is sharply contrasted with another story
of Totila, concerning Demetrius, governor of Naples during
the beginning of the siege. Demetrius was famous as a daring
sailor. But his boldness knew no bounds of discretion, and he
constantly walked about the city hurling evil words at the
Gothic King. At length he gained permission from Conon to
steal out from Naples in a little boat to ask relief from the

[42] VII, viii, 1.

Roman fleet in Sicily. Success favoured him, and ships set
sail bringing aid. They had even reached the coast near Naples
when Gothic guards attacked them; a few of the sailors escaped, many were killed, many were captured. Among the last
was Demetrius, on whom Totila wreaked a terrible vengeance.
He cut off his prisoner's hands, deprived him of power of
speech, and then set him free, the victim, so the judgment ran,
of an "undisciplined tongue." [43]

Despatches to Constantinople became so gloomy that Justinian was driven to bethink him of Belisarius again. The first
glory of return had long been dimmed for this hero by the
Imperial censure and coldness, which had denied him the
honour of an official triumph. Far worse trouble, however,
had wrecked his life in private through the unfaithfulness of
his wife Antonina. She had once been his comrade in Italy,
and, as we have noted, he adored her with a passion like that
of Justinian for Theodora.

The lives of these two women have many other points in
common. Both had risen from the plebeian life which strove
tumultuously in the rival factions of the Circus; both were
given to political intrigue which kept the Court in a ferment;
both were devoted to luxury in matters personal and public;
both before their marriages to their distinguished husbands had
played fast and loose with morality. But Theodora, in spite
of the malice of hostile gossip, seriously reformed her ways in
her career as Empress. On the other hand, the sordid love of
Antonina for the young man whom Belisarius had adopted as
son had embittered her husband's life, since the time he discovered it when fighting to secure Sicily for Justinian in 535. [44]
This affair had been at its height when Belisarius, shortly after
his recall from Italy, had set out for the East in 541 to fight for

[43] VII, viii, 12ff., vi, 26.
[44] See the *Anecdota* of Procopius for details.

Justinian in the Second Persian War. The Empress had aided and abetted her friend Antonina, and even, as Procopius tells, compelled Belisarius after his return to beg humbly from his erring wife for a renewal of affection and peace in his home.[45]

Early in 544 came the report that Totila was marching toward Rome. Belisarius had already been recalled from his campaign against Chosroes in Persia. Procopius declares that he spoke indiscreet words and was brought back at the request of the angry Theodora. For a while, this story goes on, he lived in Constantinople a perfectly miserable life, idle and neglected, begging to be sent back to the East. But however disinclined Theodora and her Imperial spouse might be to honour Belisarius, the fact remained that Justinian had no one else on whom he could depend in this struggle in Italy. The fact was, perhaps, the more tolerable because, "as men say," Procopius cautiously adds, Belisarius promised to pay all the expenses of a campaign in Italy if led by him.[46]

Of course he could not keep his word. The next year, 545, when Totila was besieging Firmum (Fermo) and Asculum (Ascoli), when Belisarius was actually on the Italian front of battle and knew not where to turn for its defence, he sent home a letter to Justinian which tells better than any formal description the plight of the Roman army. Men, horses, arms and money are lacking, the General writes. All his efforts in enlisting volunteers have gained him but a tiny band, ignorant and unequipped. The few survivors of his original force are terrified by their frequent disasters; there are no funds for their payment; the greater part have already deserted to the Goths. "If, then," he ends, "your only aim, my Lord, was to send me to Italy, this has been done, and here I am. But if you desire to conquer, you must provide the other things needful. No one can be a commander without men to carry out his commands.

[45] *Anec.* IV, 27ff.   [46] *ibid.* IV, 39.

It is meet, therefore, that men should be sent me, both my own soldiers and many barbarians, with money for their hire." [47]

But the messenger to whom this letter was entrusted, no less a person than John "the Bloodthirsty," carried out none of the promises he had made concerning it, and nothing resulted. Belisarius shut himself up in Ravenna, while Totila gained control of the Great Flaminian Way between Ravenna and Rome by the yielding of the towns which lay in or near it, Fermo and Ascoli, Spoleto and Assisi. Finally, probably toward the end of 545, having effectually blocked the sending of supplies from Ravenna, Totila began his siege of Rome.

The story of this siege surpasses in its horrors any of the previous ones in Rome or Naples. Naples was, of course, in the hands of the Goths, and a fleet stationed there barred any provision which might be despatched by sea. Nearer Rome Gothic ambush did the same, when not long after the beginning of the blockade Pope Vigilius, who was staying in Sicily, sent off from there toward Rome a number of ships laden with corn. All were seized and their crews put to death. More ruthless was the capture of a certain bishop who had taken passage in one of these ships. He was conducted into the presence of the Gothic King for questioning, but did not talk long. Totila cried out that his answers were all lies and in a rage cut off his hands.

Another blow now befell the troubled Belisarius. By the surrender of Placentia, an important city on the Aemilian Way and the River Po, the whole of Aemilia passed under the control of the Goths, who already held most of Picenum and Tuscany. The citizens of Placentia had held out most gallantly for a whole year, till they were brought to the extremity of eating human flesh. Misery almost as terrible soon prevailed in Rome. Its inhabitants even sent the deacon Pelagius, who afterward succeeded Vigilius as Pope from 555 to 561, to beg Totila for

[47] *Hist. Wars,* VII, xii, 9f.

a truce of a few days, promising that if no help came to them within that time they would surrender to him. Before Pelagius even began to speak, the Gothic King informed him with all courtesy that his desires would be granted, save in three matters: The Romans must not ask any clemency for Sicily, which they had used as a base of operations against the Goths; they must not expect immunity for the walls of Rome when captured; they must not request the return of those of their own slaves who had fled from Rome to the Gothic camp.

Pelagius resented so keenly the determination shown in this speech that he returned without even presenting his petition. Only three things now seemed possible to the citizens of Rome in their utter wretchedness. They begged the commanders of the army in charge of the defence either to find sufficient food to sustain life decently for them; or to let them go forth from the city to their fate outside; or to put them to death then and there. When the answer was given that the first proposal was impossible, the second unsafe, and the third impious, that the only hope for all was to wait for Belisarius, the city settled down to eke out its days as best it could. It lunched and supped on dogs and mice, with an occasional banquet if a horse chanced to die, and when all animals failed, on husks of corn and boiled nettles. After this diet, too, began to fail, and suicide proved the only refuge, the officers then allowed all who would to leave. Most of the fugitives perished of weakness on their way or were captured and killed by the Goths. "To such things as this," wrote Procopius, "had sunk the fortune of Rome—her Senate and her People!"[48]

In the meantime Belisarius, bitterly regretting the folly which had led him to concentrate his strength in Ravenna, had left that city for Dyrrhachium (Durazzo) in Greek Illyricum, where he had received reinforcement from Constantinople under the

[48] VII, xvii, 25.

leadership of John "the Bloodthirsty." He directed John to march by land toward Rome, while he himself planned to approach by sea. John set out, but was turned aside by a force of Goths sent by Totila, and Belisarius was left to act alone when he duly arrived at the northern harbour. This still remained in the hands of the Imperialists, and the problem before him was how to carry food into the starving city. It was extremely difficult, as Totila's energy had barricaded the River Tiber by a fortified bridge.

The tale of the attempt of Belisarius to overcome the hindrance is one of the many tragedies of this war. First, he built a contrivance of boats locked together, bearing in a high tower upon their decks a mass of inflammable matter. He then launched this structure on the river, guarding it with other boats manned by his men, who were ordered to shoot at the enemy from behind barriers of wood. On one of these boats he himself set sail. The Lady Antonina and the harbour town of Portus were left in charge of an Armenian officer called Isaac, with strict orders to guard the town through all perils as a place of refuge in case of defeat.

Unfortunately, thirst for fame was dearer to Isaac than caution. When news arrived that his Chief had actually destroyed the intervening bridge and was about to attack Rome, he rushed forward to capture his own victory from the Goths and was taken prisoner. Belisarius, on receiving the message, jumped to the conclusion that the town at the harbour was lost and that his wife was in the hands of the enemy. At once he ordered his men to retreat. After the mistake was discovered and he learned that both were safe, his disappointment preyed on his mind till he lay prostrate in high fever. The miserable Isaac paid the penalty of his disobedience by death at the hands of Totila.

At last in 546 the city of Rome fell through treachery, when its walls were betrayed by four barbarian mercenaries posted as sentinels at the Asinarian Gate. The few citizens who were still within the walls fled for refuge to the Church of Saint Peter and other sacred shrines, and at the petition of Pelagius Totila stopped bloodshed after a number had been killed, though plundering was freely permitted. A letter announcing his capture of Rome was despatched by him to Justinian, proposing that he should be left in peace as ruler of Italy. "For," he wrote, "if these words should perhaps find favour with thee, thou mightest rightly be called my father and thou wilt have us as allies against any thou mayest desire to attack in time to come." [49] The suggestion fell on deaf ears, and Justinian merely referred Totila to Belisarius as his accredited representative.

The Gothic King burst into renewed wrath, and further provocation in the shape of the attacking and slaughter of his men in Lucania silenced all thought of peace. It even drove him to destroy a third of the fortifications of Rome, and he was only stopped from working its utter ruin and "making Rome into a meadow for oxen" by the prayer of his enemy. In the pages of Procopius Belisarius pleads with the King, in the name of beauty and of reason, that he refrain from such a senseless act. [50] Totila was persuaded, and the city stood, deprived only of part of its defence.

Presumably he thought that it was now safe from attack by the Romans, especially as their General was reported as grievously sick. At all events the Gothic army was ordered to retire to Algedon, some twenty miles from Rome. And then the unexpected happened. Belisarius boldly came, looked, and devised an extraordinary feat. Bringing up nearly all his army to the places where the ramparts lay in ruins, he constructed in haphazard fashion rough masonry for patching up their yawning gaps, and actually within a month saw the city in his own

[49] VII, xxi, 24.   [50] VII, xxii, 7ff.

hands, entrenched again behind completed walls. This was in the year 547. Rome once more belonged to the Empire, and in dramatic fashion its keys were again forwarded to Justinian in Constantinople. The Gothic nobles were bitterly grieved at the folly of their King, in that, as they said, he had neither defended Rome himself nor destroyed it utterly.

Shortly afterward Antonina set out for Constantinople in the hope of convincing the Empress that ampler provision for war must be sent to Italy. On her arrival she learned that Theodora had just died (on June 28, 548), and she turned her energies to persuading Justinian to recall Belisarius. It was, indeed, impossible for him to win any lasting result in Italy without generous support from the Imperial purse; but the lady gained her desire the more easily because Justinian was worried by the war with Persia. This time it was a final farewell that Belisarius said to Italy as he returned to Constantinople in 549, a bitterly disappointed man.

His arrival was greeted with mixed feelings. The rank and file welcomed him with loud enthusiasm as the deliverer of Italy. The Emperor and his nobles, as before, were jealous of his popularity and quick to remark, as Belisarius himself knew only too well, that his second campaign in Italy had failed of any great and lasting result.

His remaining years make a sad story. He was sent, it is true, to command an expedition against Zabergan, King of the Kotrigur Huns, and rejoiced in some renewal of his former success.[51] But he was recalled before he could accomplish his full end, and lived henceforth practically in retirement, though in name he still held high office under the Eastern Court. About two years before his death in 565 he was accused of treason, brought to trial and deposed from his honourable estate in the Imperial city. After a while Justinian relented and restored

[51] Agathias, *Histories, C.S.H.B.* V, 15.

him to his old position. Yet he remained but a shadow of his former self and died scarcely noticed, forgotten in the rushing tide of the life within the Court where once he had been held all-powerful.[52]

We return to Italy. Its wretchedness was now still further intensified by a third siege of Rome, carried on by Totila in a mood of bitter resentment at the refusal of the Franks to listen to his offer of alliance and of marriage with a princess of their race. The Franks had turned by this time their goodwill toward the cause of Justinian, with whom they had a source of common sympathy in the Catholic faith they professed, so far apart from the Arian creed of the Goths. In spite of their aid, however, Totila entered the city again triumphantly in 549, and when Justinian again would not heed any proposal of diplomatic correspondence, the Goths plundered and captured far and wide. The Emperor's contempt for these barbarians on Roman soil was only exceeded by his need of keeping all the money he could get for his own purposes, for the renown and splendour of his reign in Constantinople. It infuriated him that Italy, his rightful source of supply, as he considered, should in fact be a never-ceasing drain of expense. Moreover, he still had a war with Persia to divert his attention and empty his purse.

But there was a still stronger distraction standing between Justinian and storm-tossed Italy. At the moment neither Italy nor Persia nor any secular question could hold the thoughts of this devoted wrestler of the Church; nothing less than the theological battling which was his passion now held him in its grip. We may perhaps be glad that the intricacies of the struggle of "The Three Chapters" are not forced upon our study here. It will be enough to say that Justinian, eager to propitiate his

---

[52] The story that Belisarius spent his last days as a blind beggar by the roadside is apocryphal.

Empress and her beloved Monophysites without breaking away from his own position as upholder of the creed defined at the Council of Chalcedon, had pounced joyfully upon a chance, as it seemed to him, of repairing an error that had somehow been perpetrated by the good Bishops of that Assembly. They had allowed to pass as orthodox the works of three Syrian prelates—all three, when Justinian's alert eye fell on their writings, departed to peace from this troubled life. They were Theodore, Bishop of Mopsuestia, Theodoret, Bishop of Cyrrhus in Syria, and Ibas, Bishop of Edessa in the same country. We can imagine the enthusiasm with which our royal student greeted word from an episcopal friend that these writings were full of Nestorian heresy. Would he not look into the matter? But certainly! He was only too happy to shut himself up among his Patristic tomes.

Hence ensued a long drawn duel between the lay theologian of Constantinople and Vigilius, Pope of Rome, lasting ten years and ended only shortly before the death of Vigilius in 555. Italy might suffer, might be lost to the Empire; but Justinian remained thrilled with the joy of battle in this subtle Greek dispute. It is sad to read of the vacillatings in the mind of the unhappy Vigilius, forced meanwhile to submit to violence, terror, and all indignity. At last the contention brought forth the Fifth Oecumenical Council of the Church, at which the condemnation of these writings was sealed in 553.

Some years before that time, however, the din of secular arms and the cry of the suffering had penetrated even behind the closed doors of the Imperial study. As we saw, Rome was now once more in the hands of the Goths. The capture had been won by treachery of the Isaurian guards, discontented through neglect of their pay. Totila actually worked it by aid of a simple ruse, bidding trumpets sound at one part of the walls to direct attention of the besieged to that spot, while the Isaurians opened the gates in another quarter. And since the King of the Franks in rejecting the proffered alliance with Totila had rudely said "that Totila was not, and never would be King of Italy," the Gothic Chief, immediately after his possession of Rome, rebuilt all the damaged parts of the city and proposed to settle within it both Goths and Romans, nobles and ordinary citizens, under himself as its supreme Lord.

On the other side, after a time of fluctuating decisions, Germanus, nephew of Justinian, was well provided with funds and ordered to the front. The Roman army was delighted, for Germanus was universally popular among soldiers and civilians alike. The Goths for the same reason fell into gloomy forebodings, vastly increased when it became known that Germanus was planning to advance his cause through marriage with Matasuntha, grandchild of the great Theodoric and widow by this time of the Gothic leader Witigis. It would be hard for them, as Germanus foresaw, to fight against one whose wife was of their own race.

All seemed ready for a revival of Roman hopes in Italy. But just as Germanus was recruiting his soldiers for the campaign, preparing everything with immense enthusiasm, Justinian was horrified by news of a mighty invasion of Sclaveni into Roman territory in Thessalonica. In his panic he thought that nothing would suffice to meet this except the power of Germanus, and orders were quickly sent that the new army divert its march and proceed against the barbarian hordes. The terror was quelled, the invaders vanquished, and the conqueror emerged from this menace a hero to enemy and patriots both; only to fall seriously ill and die at the height of his promise. Procopius paints his character in glowing terms of praise. As General, we read, he was of the highest talent, self-reliant and shrewd; in peace he guarded well the laws and constitution of the government, a most honest judge, a lender of great sums of money to those in need, without thought of interest; in public life he was grave and commanding, among his own family and intimate friends delightfully informal and gracious.[53] No wonder that Justinian was much perturbed when he received the news of his death.

Something, however, had to be done, and promptly. By this time hardly any part of Italy remained to the Empire; its funds were exhausted, its defenders unpaid, its people destitute, its fields ravaged and robbed. It was impossible for the Catholic Emperor of Rome, Old as well as New, to leave the problem in further neglect, and John "the Bloodthirsty" was commanded to lead the expedition forward into Italy. He reached Dalmatia and spent the winter there, unable to cross the water as he had no fleet, yet judging it impracticable at that season to journey the long way round by land. Meanwhile Totila worked havoc freely in Sicily. When at length spring had come and John was busy preparing the transport by sea, suddenly a despatch arrived, replacing him as Imperial Commander in Italy by Narses the eunuch.

Procopius tries to theorise on the reason for this abrupt change, and decides that Justinian was afraid lest the subordinate officers in his army would not obey John, as one of insufficient standing in Constantinople. He also recalls a remark made during the reign of Athalaric by a man of that Etruscan race so famous for skill in prophecy: "Some day a eunuch shall bring to nought the ruler of Rome." Who knows whether Justinian was not unconsciously swayed by fate? Or was necessity only wrought by chance? So muses our historian.[54] Certainly Narses did take over the command, and certainly Justinian did once more try to make up for past neglect, pressed hard this time by the determination of his new General either to march forth well equipped or not to march at

[53] VII, xl, 9.   [54] VIII, xxi, 7ff.

all. A vast army was collected; veterans and recruits were gathered in from Constantinople, from Thrace and from Illyricum; Herculians, Persians, Gepids, Huns, all swelled the assembling multitude. There came also John "the Bloodthirsty," with his own soldiers, as well as those once led by Germanus.

There came also—an interesting detail—twenty-five hundred warriors sent by the King of the Lombards. Audoin was his name, and he was induced, we read, by a great sum of money and by memory of alliance with Justinian. Justinian had not only made treaty with the Lombards, but had given to Audoin as wife a sister of the Thuringian Amalafrid, who had been brought to Constantinople as captive with Witigis and had been given office in the army there. The Lombards came of a German race that once had dwelt near the Baltic and had then occupied lands about the Danube; like the Ostrogoths under Theodoric they were seeking a permanent home by the axe and the sword. But their naked joy in plunder and their barbarian savagery made the Gothic spirit a thing of decency in comparison.

These preparations for war on Justinian's side were greatly furthered by the character of the new commander. Not only did Narses spare no pains to aid his cause by lavish use of money, but also men were induced to enlist under him because of kindly usage at his hands in days past and high hopes of like generosity in the future. With an anxious heart Totila sent to Verona one of his most distinguished officers, Teias, to delay the enemy's march southward in every possible way.

In 552 the armies met in the Apennine mountains for the decisive battle. Procopius describes the camping place of the Goths under Totila as a village named Taginae, and that of the Romans under Narses as Busta Gallorum, "the Tombs of the Gauls." Modern historians place the encounter in the neighbourhood of Tadinum (Gualdo Tadino), near the present Fabriano.[55]

Details of the struggle are also given by Procopius in a vigorous narrative.[56] It opens with a despatch from Narses to Totila, bidding him sue for peace, as in no wise able to ward off the whole power of Rome. If, however, Totila should prove obstinate, the envoys were instructed to request him to set a day for the battle. So it happened, and Totila readily answered, "In eight days let us meet." But Narses was too wary to believe and prepared to fight on the morrow, when, in truth, Totila did march forward for war right in face of his enemy.

Exhortations were given on either side. Narses, as a devout Catholic, bade his men to be ever mindful of God fighting for them against those "who, placing over themselves as their ruler one from the common herd of men, have prevailed for the time in rascally fashion to confuse the Roman empire." Totila frankly declared that all hope for the Goths lay in the issue of this one day. Both generals also had recourse to stranger measures. Narses, we are told, held up armlets and necklaces and gold bridles before his army as rewards for those who should specially distinguish themselves. On the other front, Totila, trying to delay the charge of battle until two thousand Goths who were still lacking should come up, arrayed himself in gorgeous armour and paraded between the two armies his skill in horsemanship and in throwing the javelin. At length he desisted, changed his brilliance for the outfit of a common soldier, and led his troops to the attack, hoping to find the Romans off their guard.

But Narses was ready. The fight went on all the rest of the day, till at dusk the Goths began to fall back before the superior armour of their opponents and were soon in full and disorderly retreat. No quarter was allowed by the victors; very many of

[55] Bury, *Lat. Rom. Emp.* II, p. 264.   [56] VIII, xxixff.

the fugitives yielded themselves to capture, only to meet execution a little later on.

Totila himself was dangerously wounded, but fled in the dark some fourteen miles to a place known in ancient days as Caprae. Its exact site is now unknown, though it may be the modern Caprara.[57] Here his men did what they could for his wound, but death came upon him before long, and they hastily buried him there in that same place. Procopius mourns so unworthy an end for so successful a career, even accusing the Gothic King of cowardly action in this last struggle. He tells us that the Romans learned of Totila's death from a woman of the Goths, and refused to believe it till they had dug up the spot and brought to light his body. Then they buried it again where it had been found. Another account of the disaster is also given by Procopius—that Totila in his disguise as a private soldier was fatally wounded and obliged to retire, and that the Goths turned to flee in their utter dismay at his loss.

The joy of Narses at this complete victory knew no bounds. In his accustomed self-restraint, however, he made it one of his first acts to dismiss the savage Lombards with a generous reward of money to their own lands. They were celebrating conquest vigorously by wholesale destruction of homes and rape of women.

The fleeing Goths elected the General of Totila, Teias, as their King. Under him they retreated to Ticinum and set to work to organise themselves into another army of defence. Meanwhile those of their race who were still holding Rome after its re-capture by Totila in 549 did their utmost to defend its walls when Narses now approached. But their strength was too feeble to withstand the onrush of the Roman power, newly invigorated by success. Thus in this same year, 552, for the fifth time during the reign of Justinian, Rome fell, this time

[57] Hodgkin, IV, p. 724.

before the rapid action of Dagisthaeus, an officer ordered by his Chief to attack the ramparts in an undefended place. Their extent was so great that no one could guard them at every point. Once again, as Belisarius before him, Narses despatched its keys in triumph to the Emperor in the East.

The Goths worked what revenge they could, marking their retreat by killing ruthlessly all the Romans they met in their path. Roman nobles who now set out for Rome, emboldened by the news of its passing into Imperial hands once more, were slaughtered as they travelled. Worst of all, perhaps, was the brutal murder by Teias of three hundred of the flower of Roman children, collected by Totila from various cities as hostages. To fortify his desperate position he did as Totila before him and sent envoys to the King of the Franks, promising much money in return for aid. But, as Procopius drily observes, "the Franks, I think, keeping in mind their own ends, wanted to die neither in the interest of the Goths nor of the Romans. If they were to submit to the dangers of war at all, they were minded to secure Italy for themselves." [58]

With Rome again securely in his hold, Narses went south into Campania to crush the last remnants of the Goths in the valley below Mount Vesuvius, near the town of Nuceria (Nocera). These for a while protected themselves on the inaccessible heights of a neighbouring mountain, known as Mons Lactarius, now Monte Lettere. Soon, however, finding themselves in critical need of food and thinking it better to die in clash of battle than in starvation, they marched down upon the enemy in a furious attack. Its hero was Teias, the Goth, who fought for hours in the first line of his men, overcoming all who were bent on confounding his cause by slaying him, its leader. At last for a second he forsook his guard and was instantly killed.

[58] VIII, xxxiv, 17f.

Yet even then his soldiers did not flee, though confronted by the dreadful sight of their King's head triumphantly brandished on a pole. They held their ground till darkness set in, and all through the night remained encamped upon the field. Again a second day they fought stubbornly from sunrise till sunset, and only when darkness again came on them, realizing "that their contending was against God," sent envoys to Narses in quest of peace. Narses allowed them to depart safely from Italy on condition of their promise never again to molest Roman soil or attack Roman men. A tiny number still held out and succeeded in inducing a force of Alamanni and Franks to invade Italy on their behalf. The attempt was crushed by Narses in another battle at Capua.

For thirteen years from this time Narses was in command of Italy.[59] But the delight that had attended deliverance from the Goths in the hearts of his subjects soon changed to misery when Justinian sent peremptory orders that revenue be collected from this troublesome land. Narses, the commander renowned for generous and pious acts, was gradually transformed into Narses, the superintendent of enforced levies of money, and his very name before long was a mark of universal fear and hatred.

In 565, the same year which saw the death of Belisarius in humble retirement, the Emperor Justinian also departed this life. We have noted much of his legacy. It remains to add the better part: the record of his famous codifying of laws and statutes; of his making of churches and palaces; of his building and rebuilding the glorious Cathedral of Saint Sophia.

He was succeeded by his nephew, Justin the second, a man of strong ambitions and little prudence, constantly under the influence of his wife. The Empress Sophia was a niece of Jus-

[59] Our principal authority for the following period is the *History of the Langobards* by Paul the Deacon, written at Monte Cassino circ. 792.

tinian's wife, Theodora, who, as we have seen, had died some years before her husband. It was Sophia's power which now ruled the Empire, but without vision or virtue.

One of the first acts of this partnership was the recall of Narses to Constantinople, in an attempt to appease the inhabitants of Italy, now openly rebellious. "It were better," said they (so the story runs), "for the Romans to be slaves of Goths rather than of Greeks, when Narses the eunuch orders us about and treats us as serfs, and our most righteous ruler knows nothing of these things. Either, Sire, free us from his hand, or surely we will surrender the city of Rome and our own selves to the pagan Goths." [60]

It may have been, as the complaint declared, that enforced extortion became at length pleasant in the eyes of Narses, for his own profit. Justin professed himself much vexed, and replaced the erring eunuch by a governor named Longinus. His Empress is said to have sent Narses a message, saying "that he was no man, and she would set him to distributing portions of wool for the women in her Palace when he got back." We are told that Narses retorted: "I will begin a web for her which she shall not be able to set aside all her life long!" [61]

There is also a tradition, dubiously regarded by historians, that in his resentment Narses encouraged the Lombards to invade Italy; [62] it is far more likely that they took advantage of the excitement attending his departure to make up for their reluctant farewell to its lands fifteen years before. But, according to tradition, he never returned to Constantinople, and spent his last days in Italy.

The Lombards were now ruled by Alboin, son of King

[60] *Gesta Pont. Rom.* I, pp. 157f.
[61] *Hist. Lang.* II, 5; cf. the slightly different version of "Fredegarius," *Chron.* III, 65.
[62] "Fredegarius," III, 65; *Hist. Lang.* II, 5; Isid. of Seville, *Chron.* ed. Mommsen, in *Chron. Min.* II, p. 476; *Gest. Pont. Rom.* p. 158. See Foulke, trans. *Hist. Lang.* p. 60, for this ancient evidence.

Audoin. Alboin was of high repute for valour, and in consequence Chlothar, King of the Franks, had given to him his
daughter Chlotsvinda in marriage. After her death he had
married Rosamund, whom he had carried off as captive from
the people of the Gepidae. He had also killed in war her father
Cunimund.

In 568 this Lombard King led a host of his men to invade
the north of Italy. Soon he had made nearly the whole of
Venetia his own, ravaged Liguria, and sealed these preliminary
victories by the capture of Milan. Subsequent campaigns
added to his achievements the cruel siege of Ticinum, the occupation of the lands bordering the River Po, the crossing of the
Apennines and the invasion of Umbria. There is a tale that
after the people of Ticinum had stubbornly resisted for three
years, Alboin vowed that he would put them all to death for
their obstinacy when once he should enter their walls. But as
he was at length doing so, his horse fell, and could not be induced to rise through spur or blow. Finally, on being reminded
that he had sworn his dreadful oath against a Christian people,
he renounced his purpose and promised mercy to his captives.
Then the horse immediately arose, and the people of Ticinum
drew a new breath of hope.[63]

But his last hour was at hand for Alboin himself, brought
to him of his own doing. As the story goes, he had made from
the skull of his dead enemy, the Gepid King Cunimund, a
drinking-cup for his feasts. One day, at the height of the
revelry of a banquet at Verona, he ordered his wife Rosamund
to drink from the cup, telling her in his drunken jest to take a
draught merrily with her father. The Queen had long been
burning to avenge her father's death. In a natural fury of passion she sought the help of Helmechis, armour-bearer and
foster-brother of Alboin, and the King was murdered in his

[63] *Hist. Lang.* II, 27.

Palace. One version, probably a legend, tells that she forced the deed by making one of the royal courtiers the unwitting recipient of her embrace, and then told him on his horrified discovery of his guilt that he must now either slay the King her husband or be slain by him.

Punishment came quickly. In reward for his work Rosamund now married Helmechis, and he tried hard to seize the Kingship of Lombardy. But its nobles were loyal to their late head, and the pair hurried to Ravenna to seek aid from Longinus, now installed under the title of Imperial Prefect of Italy.

He proved only too kind to Rosamund, and she yielded soon to his suggestion that she should marry him and become Lady of Ravenna. Her historian tells us, indeed, that "she was ready for every iniquity" if this glory might be hers.[64] Helmechis was to be despatched from life with all speed, and it was Rosamund herself who held out to him strong poison as he came from his bath under the pretence of refreshment. He drank unwarily, but proved himself her equal in his revenge, When he knew he must die he drew his sword and forced his murderess to drink to her death in the rest of the cup.

Upon the news of Alboin's death the Lombards elected from their warriors one called Cleph as their King. He gained some success against the Romans, but soon fell before an assassin's dagger. Then in 574 a general Lombard Assembly at Ticinum, the Lombard headquarters, determined that henceforth there should be no Lombard "King," but that the power of government should be shared between its thirty-six chieftains, known as the "Lombard Dukes."

The history of the next twenty-five years is full of the struggle between the enfeebled Roman grasp of Italy and the increasing dominion of these Lombard warriors. They ruled with a

[64] *ibid.* 29.

heavy hand both the Italians, whose lands they had invaded, and the alien immigrants, who had accompanied them on their march in the hope of permanent homes and the following of their old traditions in a new country. Nothing could stay the rising tide of Lombard advance, neither barbarians nor the Roman Prefect Longinus, vainly trying to rule Italy in the name of Constantinople, nor even Constantinople itself. Emperor succeeded Emperor in the East, while Italy slipped steadily from their hands. First the nervous mind of Justin, stricken by continued disaster to his arms, flickered out in insanity. Of him we read in one chronicle that he was given to all greed, a despiser of the poor, a robber of the rich, and suspected of heresy.[65] We shall meet presently with another writer who sang his praise.

For a while his colleague, Tiberius, administered the Empire as Regent, and then succeeded to full power of rule on Justin's death in 578. He was credited with all the virtues, including unimpeachable orthodoxy. Four years later Tiberius in his turn was followed by his son-in-law, Maurice, who was still holding the Byzantine throne when the sixth century closed. In vain he held out golden inducement to the Franks to invade Italy and to try to keep back the Lombards streaming down from the North. The King of the Franks received his gifts, it is true, and advanced into Italy with soldiers countless in number. But once there, he prudently preferred to exchange presents and terms of peace with those whom he had been bribed to attack. Maurice demanded return of his money, and received no answer.

Meanwhile the divided and discordant rule of the Dukes over their Lombard subjects was not turning out a success. It seemed best to renew the Kingship, and in 584 by consent

[65] *ibid.* III, 11. For a terrible description of Justin's later years see John of Ephesus, *Eccles. Hist.* III, 2f. But Justin had persecuted the followers of the Monophysite creed which John professed.

of all the election fell on Authari, son of Cleph. The change
soon proved its wisdom. Authari knew how to control his tur-
bulent underlords, and his people honoured him and his suc-
cessors-to-be with the surname of "Flavius," an official title
borrowed from the Flavian line of Roman Emperors. His
marriage, too, was to mean much to history, by his choice of a
Queen devoted to the Catholic faith, Theodelinda, daughter
of Garibald, Duke of the Bavarians. We are told that the
young King wanted to see for himself what the lady was like,
and journeyed in disguise as his own ambassador to her father's
court. And when she pleased him, for she was very fair to look
upon, he asked that she might give him wine to drink. As he
returned the cup, he touched her hand in sign of secret greeting, which her nurse told her only a King himself would dare
to do. He was made known afterward to the Bavarian nobles
by smiting a tree with an axe and crying aloud, "Such a blow
is Authari wont to strike!" Doubtless he pleased the girl, for
he was in the pride of his youth at this time, tall and hand-
some with his yellow hair.[66] At all events, she fled to seek him
in Italy some time later, when Bavaria was disturbed by an
inroad of the Franks, and they were married with much pomp
near Verona.

During all this time not only the Emperor at Constantinople,
but also the Pope in Rome had been striving hard to protect
the Italians against their Lombard masters. Constant entreaties
for aid were sent from the Holy See to the Emperor Maurice by
Pelagius the second, Pope from 579 till 590. More interesting
are the efforts toward peace made by the famous successor of
Pelagius, Gregory the Great. Smaragdus, on whom Maurice
first conferred the title of Exarch of Italy, followed Longinus
as Prefect, and was followed by Romanus in the same dignity.
The King of the Franks, thinking better of the Imperial cause,

[66] *Hist. Lang.* III, 30.

despatched an army which ravaged Northern Italy for months without any lasting gain.

In 590 Authari died. Rumor declared that he, too, perished by poison. As he left no heir, the Lombard nobles agreed that Theodelinda should still be their Queen and should take a second husband, one of their number who might lead them in battle. She yielded to their will, and her choice fell on Agilulf, a chieftain sprung from a Thuringian race and himself Duke of Turin. In the same year Gregory the first, known after as the Great, became Pope of Rome.

The new King held his rule for fifteen years after the end of the century. Under him Catholicism gained the allegiance of the Lombards, largely through the devotion of Theodelinda, united with the great power of Gregory. Under his Papal rule the Frankish invasions ceased. The story of his negotiations with Lombard dominion belongs to the chapter of his life; here it will be enough to say that in 599, when the Exarch Romanus had been succeeded by Callinicus, a treaty of peace was at length struck between Callinicus and Agilulf the Lombard King in the name of the Roman Empire and of the Lombard invaders. As history knows, it was the beginning of the Lombard rule in Italy.

CHAPTER II

THE GOTHIC RULE IN ITALY: CASSIODORUS, SECRETARY OF THEODORIC THE GREAT

AGAINST this background thus briefly sketched we can now set up some of the chief writers of this sixth century. At its beginning Italy was enjoying a brief respite of comparative calm. The rule of Theodoric the Great was now firmly established, and his energy was turned to its supreme end, the transforming and yet continuing of the Roman Empire in this country under the control of Gothic barbarians. That his noble ambition failed through lack of an adequate successor to his rule is one of the greater things in history one could wish otherwise arranged. Under him and his heirs of the male line, so he dreamed, in a succession of Amal Kings claiming as proud an ancestry as the Romans themselves could boast, Rome would once more be the mistress of the world. The fresh blood of her conquerors from Northern and Eastern Europe would pour new life into her, and they themselves would willingly reckon themselves her subjects in culture and tradition, glad to lend her their physical strength in return for her wise guidance in things of the mind. Rome would forget that long century dark with the agony of invasion and death. She would rise again in one vast Empire, old in wisdom, young in vigour, to promote once more the splendour of peace on earth. It was the hope once again of Vergil and of Claudian for their beloved City, with this difference, that now barbarian and Roman were to be united in one civic body, differing in administrations as they differed in gifts, but bound together in one spirit of loyalty to their common Lord and State.

That hope has often been summed up for us in the key word of Theodoric's dream—*civilitas*—the word so often recurring in the records of his reign. It meant a character born of a union in ideal and practice of the best things: of justice and humanity in word and in deed, of virile force and polished culture, of massive substance and delicate beauty in form. Thus the Empire, once reestablished under one Head of many nations united in one commonwealth and bound by solid ties of treaty and kinship with other barbarian peoples, would progress steadily to greater heights of glory—*nobis cordi est in melius cuncta mutare.*[1] All its varied activities, reset in motion on a firm basis, were to function smoothly throughout this State of dual tradition. Civil and military discipline were to be developed in every detail under its King and his many officials. Stern administrative control, blended with the widest toleration, were to mark the new era. Arian and Catholic would worship in harmony the One God and Father of all. East and West would be bound together once more in a dignified relation of sovereignty, and the Emperor at Constantinople was to be a brother, if an elder brother, to his fellow monarch in Ravenna.

But if this vision of Pisgah was glorious, the labour of its attaining must have loomed gigantic to the Gothic King in his less optimistic moods. How was he, a barbarian busy now these many years in fighting for his homeless people, to deal with all the diplomatic routine, the official correspondence, the courtly etiquette demanded of a royal Palace in Italy herself, crusted with the old traditions of past splendour? He had had little leisure for the study he must have wistfully at times desired, and aptitude with book and pen was the last thing his

[1] Hodgkin, *Letters of Cassiodorus,* p. 183.

Gothic warriors looked for in their Chief. We are told that
the King could not even write his own name, and had to
use for the Royal assent to documents—expressed in the word
LEGI, "I have read"—a thin sheet of gold stencil, cut with
these letters in open outline. Around this he would laboriously
trace his way with a pen.[2] The story seems somewhat doubtful
when we think of the ten years of his youth spent in Constantinople. But certainly his education was of the simplest kind.

Occasion rose to answer the need, with a character the very
opposite in literary training of this high-souled barbarian. The
choice of Theodoric, seeking for a Secretary in whom his unskilled mind could rest secure, fell on a member of a great
Roman house, whose fathers had served Rome from generation to generation. Cassiodorus had inherited all their pride
in her magnificence of old, and, in common with all their
sons, had been born to sorrow in her fall. Now there opened
before him a new hope. Better Rome supreme in civilization,
in government and in culture under the Goths, than Rome
dying or dead! Moreover, his passion, next to Rome herself,
was culture. He adored books and their writing, rich long
phrases and sentences, turns and quips, words dark and words
brilliant. It was a splendid prospect, to be entrusted with the
careful composing of State epistles and documents for all
occasions. In these, as on a broad canvas, he might paint with
free use of colours all the devices and decorations, all the lights
and shades he could invent for the lustre of his office and of his
State.

His name befitted his character—Flavius Magnus Aurelius
Cassiodorus Senator, shortened in his writings to Cassiodorus
Senator or simply Senator.[3] It calls up before us the picture of

[2] *Anon. Vales.* 24(79).
[3] For the life of Cassiodorus see his *Letters* and the *Anecdoton Holderi;*
also Mommsen, preface to his edition of the *Variae, M.G.H. Auct. Ant.*
XII.

a courtly official of Italy's bluest blood presenting day by day for his barbarian master's signature countless letters, fruit of happy ponderings with his pen, full of pompous periods, written to flatter, to propitiate, to rebuke and to instruct correspondents of every place and rank. Yet, in spite of all his rhetoric, it is to Cassiodorus and his twelve books of *Letters* that we owe much of our knowledge of the administration of Rome in the West by the Ostrogothic Kings.

There was little, indeed, of technical originality in this administration. Theodoric declared to the people of Rome that by the help of God he would faithfully observe all that the Roman Emperors had enacted in the past, and his laws show little departure from previous rulings. The interest of these writings lies partly in the adapting of Roman code to barbarian practice, partly in the picture they give of the character of Cassiodorus himself. He came of a family notable in civil and military distinction. His great-grandfather had defended the region of the Bruttii in Southern Italy and Sicily from Vandal invasion shortly before Gaiseric conquered Rome in 455. His grandfather had been tribune and notary under Valentinian the third, was a friend of his minister Aetius, and in company with the son of Aetius had been entrusted with a special mission to King Attila of the Huns. His father had held civil office under Odovacar; but as Governor of Sicily had helped the cause of Theodoric on his invasion of Italy and had won over the Sicilians to this new lord. For this service he was rewarded by the governorship of Lucania and of the region of the Bruttii—an exceptional honour, as this region was his native land, and the Imperial laws had frowned on native-born citizens as governors.[4]

In the province of the Bruttii, then, at Scyllacium, the modern Squillace, the Cassiodori had a family estate, and here

[4] Mommsen, ed. p. viii.

Cassiodorus Senator was born about 480. His description of the surrounding country, given in his *Letters,* tells of an earthly paradise. Its plains smile with rich pastures, rising high with their forest of vine-poles, grazed by all manner of sheep and kine and sturdy horses. Deep in cool woods the beasts seek refuge from the sting of summer flies. Now and again we read of hills and clear mountain streams, of hospitable shores and busy ports, receiving and sending out in turn the wares of nations. There is inland marketing, too, as at the Fair of Leucothea held in Lucania on Saint Cyprian's Day, to which all the folk of industrious Campania and the wealthy Bruttian land and Calabria send their products for sale at prices marvellously cheap. You can see them, says Cassiodorus, piled up in booths woven of boughs and leaves. Even youths and maidens are offered for hire by their parents, eager for more attractive service in the cities of Italy; all are dressed in holiday clothes and sing merrily over their bargains. The Church also reveres the day. Hard by there is a well of water, transparent as air, and on Saint Cyprian's Eve Baptism is administered by its side. Then as the priest begins the office lo! a miracle, and the water rises up in a leap to revere the holy Sacrament.[5]

Cassiodorus, therefore, was yet a boy when Theodoric marched down on Italy. Soon enthusiastic adherence to the Gothic cause won for his father honour after honour of increasing distinction. We hear of him as Count of the Private Estates, whose duty it was to take care of the private domains of the King; as Count of the Sacred Largesses, who supervised the distribution of public monies; as Governor of provinces; as Praetorian Prefect of Italy, the highest official under the King in the governing of the land; as Patrician, after the fulfilment of the duties of this last ministry.

The son began his official career as an assistant in legal business to his father, the Prefect. While he was still a youth he

[5] *Variae,* VIII, 31-33.

attracted the notice of Theodoric by some speech in praise of
the King, and was given the office of Quaestor.[6] From this
date we may follow his career best by examining the volume
of correspondence which he published in 537 as the literary
fruit of his administrative life, known as the *Variae* or *Various
Letters*.[7]

The Preface to this correspondence begins as a dialogue
between Cassiodorus and his eager friends. "All men know
your merit as Praetorian Prefect," they urge, "a position upon
which public works attend as handmaids—the financing of
the army, the feeding of the people, the heavy burden of the
law-courts. . . . All men know your hard tasking as Quaestor,
when you had to help out so many other officials who could not
manage their own affairs . . . and those frequent conferences
with the King on public matters which have taken up so much
of your time. Surely it would be sad that all the very many
labours for which you have spent your energy, skill and knowledge should be lost without record for the benefit of men to
come. Doubtless, as you complain, Sir, leisure is scarce. You
ask us with reason how a man is to write decently among the
distractions of office, interruptions of petitioners, quarrels of
citizens and complaints of the hungry, who heed rather the cry
of their stomachs than the needs of their ears. True; but
should not a permanent portrait gallery be left in literature of
the apt speeches in which you, Sir, with sincere praise and with
something of the historian's brush have described those honoured by the Empire in your day? Should not future generations be edified by these examples? And is it really right that
you should hide from the world, as it were, the mirror of your
mind?" "Speech," persist these admirers, "is the true child
of character. What a loss if yours should never be revealed!"

---

[6] *Anec. Hold.* ed. Usener, 1877, p. 4.
[7] The *Letters* were written during the period 507-537. Mommsen places
the publishing of the whole collection in the autumn of 537, when Belisarius
was blockaded in Rome by the Goths. See his edition, pp. xxixf.

We will look first at a number of *Formulae* preserved in the
sixth and the seventh books. These are formal announcements
of the conferring by the King of different offices and distinc-
tions of the State, to be embodied in letters sent to those who
should receive such honours in the future. The object of Cassiodorus here was to help his successors in the Royal Cabinet,
whose pens might not be so ready as his for the business of
Writer to the Throne. Through these ready-made congratula-
tions the task of secretaries to come would be immeasurably
lightened. His hope was fulfilled, and in the Middle Ages
the *Formulae* were constantly used as models for official messages.

Under Theodoric's Gothic rule the State magistracies of the
Roman Emperors were continued, with modifications and
additions. It is natural to begin here with the Quaestorship
of the Sacred Palace, the office held by Cassiodorus himself
under Theodoric from about 507 to 511. To the Quaestor at
this time fell the work of drafting of laws and decrees for submission to the approval of the King and the Senate. For the
King he composed answers to petitions, formal letters to State
Ministers, to distinguished foreigners, to recipients of office.
As the royal secretary his position was primarily a private one,
but of importance. And so Cassiodorus places upon the lips
of the King these words as a suitable *Formula* for a Quaestor-
elect: "We embrace the Quaestorship with our whole heart,
for we regard it as the voice of our own tongue. Its holder must
be privy to our own thoughts, that he may say rightly that
which he knows we feel. If in aught we hesitate, we seek aid
from the Quaestor, who is the treasury of the State's fair fame
and the armoury of its laws. Other officials may seek the comfort of collaborators; your dignity, O Quaestor, ministers counsel to the Sovereign. Persuaded, therefore, by the repute of
your prudence and eloquence, we hereby confer on you the

Quaestorship: the glory of letters, the shrine of civilized living, the mother of all honours, the home of temperance, the seat of all virtues." [8]

We may smile at the high-sounding words, especially when we remember that the writer was Quaestor when quite a young man. In his thirties, when he could look back upon his period of quaestorial duties now ended, he wrote for the King a letter introducing a new Quaestor, Honoratus, to the Senate: "In the case of other offices we confer benefits, from our Quaestor we always receive them. He is the happy sharer of our anxieties, he enters the door of our thoughts." [9] Evidently the Quaestor's office demanded long hours of confidential discussion in the royal study.

As Quaestor Cassiodorus was a member of the Senate. Admission to this House under Theodoric was given to holders of the greater State ministries, including several to be mentioned hereafter: the Count of the Private Estates, the Count of the Patrimony, and the Vicar of the City of Rome. It was divided into three great classes, bearing the titles of *Clarissimi, Spectabiles,* and *Illustres*—"Most Excellent," "Admirable," and "Illustrious." The "Most Excellent" formed the lowest class, and every senator held at least this rank. The *Formula* conferring it declares: "It is a great witness to a man's life that he should be called, not simply *Excellent,* but *Most Excellent,* since scarcely anything but the best is believed of him who is addressed by the superlative of such a splendid title." The "Admirable" consisted of lower and assistant officials, the "Illustrious" of the highest dignities of the State. When Cassiodorus published his *Letters* he had been admitted to both the lowest and the highest of these divisions.

[8] On State offices under Theodoric see Mommsen, *Ostgothische Studien,* pp. 387ff.; Dahn, *Die Könige der Germanen,* III; Hodgkin. *Letters,* pp. 85ff.; Bury, *Invasion of Europe,* pp. 186ff.
[9] *Variae,* V, 4.

In 514 he became *Consul Ordinarius*.[10] This office held now
in itself but a shadow of its former distinction, though it was
eagerly sought because each year was dated afterward by the
name of its Consul. The chief qualifications at this time were
noble birth and great wealth; the Consul's business and pride
was to glorify the State by pageants and entertainments on a
grand scale. There were still two of these officers, but they did
duty for the whole Roman Empire; one for the East, the other
for the West. A letter from Theodoric to Anastasius, Emperor
at Constantinople, dated by the consulship of Felix in 511,
shows that the two sovereigns combined their authority in
appointing Consuls, each nominating one. "Do you unite your
vote with mine," writes Cassiodorus in Theodoric's name:
"Felix is worthy of being chosen as Consul for the West by the
judgment of us both." "Enjoy yourself," are the words thought
suitable for the King to say in his letter to a Consul-elect. "We
have the labours, you the joys of your office. Wear your purple
robe, mount your curule chair, ennobled with staff and gilded
shoes. But do not be sparing of your private fortune. Other
officials we appoint on our own initiative. Consuls alone we
invite to come forward voluntarily, that only those may offer
themselves for these acts of bounty who know themselves to be
equal to so great expenses." [11] It is not surprising that Justinian in 541 allowed this office to lapse.

When Amalasuntha became Queen-Regent for her son in
526, she found Cassiodorus holding the position of Master of
Offices. From the letters which he wrote in tenure of this position we may infer that he held it from about 523 till 527. Some
time between his ministry of Quaestor and this of Master of
Offices he had retired for a season to his old home in Southern
Italy as Governor (*corrector*) of Lucania and the region of

[10] See *Anec. Hold.* and the title-page of the *Variae*.
[11] *Variae*, II, 1; VI, 1.

the Bruttii, an honour, we may recall, which his father had held before him.[12]

As Master of Offices his responsibility, according to the *Formula,* was now great. In his hands lay the superintendence of the minor Court officials, the controlling of the soldiers of the King's household, the escorting of Senators and of foreign legatees into the King's Presence, the regulating of the foreign business of the State. His it was to appoint Governors of provinces and at his will to revise their decrees; to oversee arrangements for the public mails, for the buying of food and other supplies for Rome, for the entertainment and pleasures of its citizens. In fact, he was of so high dignity that the members of his military staff at the end of their term of office were given leading rank in the praetorian cohorts, which even Cassiodorus thought hardly fair to the praetorians!

Under the direction of the Master of Offices stood the *comitiaci,* identified by Mommsen with the *agentes in rebus,* an older name for this body of lesser officials of the State.[13] They were sent on secret and confidential errands and acted generally as the vigilant eyes of the administration, reporting to their Chief how all things in the provinces were working; thus headquarters were kept informed of the conduct of officials throughout the Imperial domains. These numerous agents had been employed under the Roman Emperors in Italy and were taken over by the Ostrogothic rule. Under the same Master, also, we find still in Theodoric's time the four great divisions of State clerks, who had written official letters and drafts and documents of all kinds and had kept account of engagements day by day for the Crown in Imperial days.[14]

---

[12] *ibid.* XI, 39; I,3. See Mommsen's preface, pp. xf. for dates in the life of Cassiodorus.

[13] *Var.* I, 12 and 13; XI, 35 and 38; Mommsen, *Ostgoth. Stud.* pp. 408f.

[14] The four bureaux (*scrinia*) were called *memoriae; epistularum; libellorum; dispositionum.*

It was not till 533, shortly before Amalasuntha herself became Queen by the death of her dissolute young son, that Cassiodorus attained the dignity of Praetorian Prefect of Italy, the highest administrative officer under the King. It is interesting to read the letter written by him as Royal Secretary to himself as Praetorian Prefect-elect, reviewing his past dignities and his merits in each! [15] The *Formula* for the Praetorian Prefect tells of this minister's functions and of his glory, so splendid that Mommsen aptly names him the "Alter Ego" of the sovereign in all civil affairs. He distributes the public monies, pays the salaries of State officials, controls the Governors of provinces, is the Supreme Judge, and superintends supplies and equipment for the army. He rides in purple through the city on his official chariot, bears the name of Father of the State, and receives bows of reverence to the very ground as he enters the Palace gates, an honour accorded to him alone among State ministers of Italy. In fact, "it is a kind of priesthood to fulfil worthily the high office of Praetorian Prefect." This great man resided in Ravenna, delegating work in Rome to his representative there, called *agens vices praefecti praetorio.*[16]

At the beginning of Theodoric's reign this was the only Praetorian Prefecture still left; those in control of Illyricum, Africa, and the Gauls had ceased to function. When, however, under the eyes of Clovis he had laid hold on Provence, shortly after the defeat of Alaric the second by that grasping monarch of the Franks, a Praetorian Prefect of the Gauls was once more appointed, and we have a letter written by Cassiodorus in the name of Athalaric bestowing this office on a certain Liberius.[17] There is also a notice written by him for Theodoric to a Senator called Gemellus in 508, a little while after the seizure of Provence, appointing him as deputy Governor of the Gauls, *vicarius praefectorum.*[18]

[15] *Var.* IX, 24.
[16] *Ostgoth. Stud.* p. 398.
[17] *ibid.* pp. 398f.; *Var.* VIII, 6.
[18] *Var.* III, 16 and 17.

There was, indeed, another lower Prefecture, that of the city of Rome. The dignity of its holder was but little below that of the Praetorian Prefect, and within his own sphere he was independent of that chief official. His *Formula* tells us that he presided over the Senate and was the supreme administrator of the city's laws. His authority also extended outside her walls. "Not only is Rome entrusted to your charge," says this statement, "though in Rome all things are contained, but our ancient laws have ordained that you should hold your authority one hundred miles beyond her site." The letters announcing the elevation of one Artemidorus to this office are noteworthy, inasmuch as they tell that he was a foreigner who had come from Constantinople to the Court of Ravenna. Theodoric chose whom he would as his ministers.[19]

Side by side with the City Prefect worked another official with minor but independent authority—the *vicarius urbis Romae.* He was honoured by a special robe, the military *chlamys,* rode in a special carriage, held courts of justice of his own, was a member of the Senate, and exercised power for forty miles outside the city, according to the description in his *Formula.*[20]

As Praetorian Prefect Cassiodorus governed Italy till 537, under Amalasuntha, Theodahad, and Witigis. It was perhaps toward the end of this time that he received the distinction of enrollment in the Patriciate.[21] This was an honour of title, not of office, bestowed on those who had held high positions of the State; in this collection of letters we find it given to one Importunus just after his consulship. Its possessor enjoyed precedence

---

[19] I, 42f.

[20] VI, 15. In addition to the two Vicariates here mentioned, of the Gauls and of Rome, at the end of the fourth century there was a Vicariate of Italy. There is reason to believe that this was not in existence under Theodoric, though the matter of Vicariates at this time is a disputed one. Cassiodorus gives no *Formula* for a Vicar of Italy. Mommsen (*Ostgoth. Stud.* pp. 395ff.) here opposes C. Diehl, *Études sur l'administration byz.* p. 161.

[21] See Mommsen, preface, p. xi.

over all officials except the Consul, even over Prefects. Moreover, it was held for life.[22]

So much for the offices held by Cassiodorus himself. There
are also found in these *Letters* formal declarations of the bestowing of certain other charges. Cyprian, of whom we shall
hear in connection with Boethius, is made Count of the Sacred
Largesses, as the father of Cassiodorus long before. To him
fell the care, not only of the Royal gifts and bounties, but also
of the State Treasury, of the Mint, of the State mines and of
taxes, including customs dues. According to the *Formula* of
bestowal this Countship carried with it in the time of Theodoric the position of *primicerius,* whose privilege it was to make
and confirm the selection of candidates for office.[23] Senarius
receives the dignity of Count of the Patrimony, or Imperial
Estates, those which fell to the Crown by conquest.[24] As such
he shared the labours of another minister, the Count of the
Private Estates, a title also once enjoyed by Cassiodorus the
elder.[25] The *Formula* for the Count of the Patrimony bids
him be independent in his attitude to his subordinates on the
Crown lands, to be calm and moderate in his decisions, and,
especially, to please the sovereign and his foreign guests by a
plentiful supply of good things for the Royal table! Let him
be on his guard; the Imperial eye will be upon him. Marcellus
is entrusted with the investigation of claims made upon the
Imperial exchequer, under the title of Advocate of the Treasury.[26] Let him not look to the number of his successes against
complainants, but rather to the cause of justice. "Sometimes
let the Imperial Treasury have a bad case, that you may show
the goodness of the Crown." Venantius hears in a laudatory

---

[22] *Formula, Var.* VI, 2.
[23] V, 41; VI, 7. This seems to be the *Primicerius Sacri Cubiculi,* as the
other *Primiceriatus,* that of the Notaries, is provided for in another *Formula* (*Var.* VI, 16; *Ostgoth. Stud.* pp. 400f.).
[24] VI, 9.   [25] VI, 8; IV, 3.   [26] I, 22.

letter that he is made a Count of the Domestics.[27] These were in name body-guards, attached to the Imperial Palace. They were theoretically of Roman race, and their Count was certainly a Roman. But since the Romans under Theodoric had nothing to do with military affairs, this office seems to have been at this time purely a title of esteem. It is significant that its *Formula* and the letter to Venantius both speak of it as *vacans*.[28]

Among other lesser dignities one Bacauda receives at Milan the Ministry of Public Entertainments as a prop of his scanty income in his old age. He thus becomes censor of the theatre and supervisor of spectacles in the Circus.[29] We may also notice here the Grand Chamberlain (*praepositus sacri cubiculi*), in charge of all the officials connected with the ordering of the Royal Palace itself; the Prefect of the Corn Supply, to whom his *Formula* declared that Pompey earned the title of Great by his merit in this office; the Count of the Chief Physicians, a magnificently named dignity. He is also magnificently advised. Let him give his time to the study of his art, and beware of asking his patients silly questions, such as: "Has the pain left you?" or "Did you sleep?" The quickest and best way, he is told, of arriving at a correct diagnosis is to let the sick man do the questioning.[30] Then there are the Palace Architect, who was honoured by a golden staff of office, and walked in processions directly in front of the King; the Count of the Aqueducts; two Prefects of the Guards, one of Rome and one of Ravenna; the President of the Lime-kilns; and the Master of the Mint, who is warned to keep the proper weight in the coins or he will suffer disgrace.[31]

We pass on to consider a few of the letters written by Cassiodorus in Theodoric's name to his ministers. Agapitus, Prefect of the City, is admonished to be the guardian of its peace; a

[27] II, 15 and 16; VI, 11.
[28] *Ostgoth. Stud.* p. 403.
[29] *Var.* V, 25; VII, 10.

[30] IV, 51; VI, 18f.
[31] VII, 5-8; 17; 32.

quiet populace is his particular glory. The same official is
requested to procure mosaics for a great Basilica in the city
of Ravenna: "It becomes the King to take thought for the
adorning of buildings, so that, as we do not fall behind in the
happiness of our age, we may not be found inferior to ancient
days in the beauty of our cities." [32] Another City Prefect,
Artemidorus, is congratulated on his diligence in reporting dishonesty: "We are glad that you did not try to conceal your
friend's theft of the money set apart for building walls at
Rome. For you yourself would have been guilty as his accom-
plice, and his feeling of security would have led him on to still
greater crime." [33] Instructions and admonitions greet even
the Praetorian Prefect of Italy. A certain Jovinus, a leading
citizen of the curial class from which civic officials were chosen,
has killed in a fit of rage a man of his own standing in his small
town of Southern Italy. As he has fled for refuge to a church,
reverence forbids that he be put to death. Let the Praetorian
Prefect, one Faustus at this time, see, therefore, that he be sent
into perpetual exile on the Lipari islands, to live in the region
of never-ceasing flames, like a salamander. Physical details
about the salamander and bits of history about the Lipari islands
drip off the pen of Cassiodorus during the rest of this letter. [34]
Another Praetorian Prefect, Abundantius, is bidden to chastise
Frontosus, who has promised ever so many times to repay money
he has stolen. Frontosus is like a chameleon; for he changes
his words as the chameleon changes his colours. Two more
important letters to this same Praetorian Prefect deal with the
building of a fleet for Italy: "Since our mind has often been
troubled that Italy, so well supplied with timber, has no ships
for the purposes of export, of importing corn supplies for the
public, and, if need should arise, of meeting a hostile fleet, by
the inspiration of God we have decided to contract for the
building of a thousand swift cruisers." [35]

[32] I, 32 and 6.   [33] II, 34.   [34] III, 47.   [35] V, 34; 16; 17.

Other letters on administration deal with the prompt payment of the soldiers who guard the frontiers of Italy: "Special thought should be given to those who for the common peace are labouring to keep out barbarians"—a curious sentence, as Hodgkin observes, to put in the mouth of Theodoric the Gothic invader; with the rewarding of services: "It is our wont to give more to our servants than we receive from them, not to consider that equality is equity in this respect"; with all sorts of business matters, such as the postal service of Italy, the potteries, the iron mines, the traffic in corn, timber, and lard.[36] Many rebukes are found. The King is much concerned because the Praetorian Prefect, Faustus again, is accused of wresting property from a certain Castorius: "A Praetorian Prefect is not permitted to run riot in assaulting the lowly." Another petition is heard against a Praetorian Prefect accused of using his official power for wreaking revenge on one called John. "But," writes Theodoric to this John, "we will fence you round against such illegal presumptions." Sloth is repeatedly castigated. The tardiness of the Prefect of Rome is only allowed to escape with a warning because it is his first offence. Delay of that same Praetorian Prefect Faustus in forwarding corn from Calabria meets with a sharp reprimand. So does the laziness of the official charged with preparing the famous purple dye.[37]

A number of letters enforce the payment of taxes. To Venantius, a provincial Governor in Southern Italy, Theodoric remarks: "Justice requires that his proper due be demanded of each man, and that public monies be promptly exacted, lest his neglect land the debtor in greater difficulty.[38] Other letters mercifully order remission of payment, because of unjust assessment, or of damage done by enemies in fighting, or by physical forces, such as the eruption of Mount Vesuvius. "We

[36] II, 5; Hodgkin, *Letters,* p. 174; *Var.* I, 29; II, 23; III, 25; I, 34; II, 26; IV, 8; II, 12.
[37] III, 20 and 27; IV, 29; I, 35 and 2.
[38] III, 8. Cf. I, 14; II, 4; III, 25; V, 7, 14, and 31.

desire to increase our resources by the treasure of righteousness, and we detest gains won by the iniquities of oppressors," the King maintains, and declares in a letter to the Cravassiani and the Pontonates that under him their taxes shall drop to the lower figure in force in the time of Odovacar. In the same spirit the Senators are admonished to pay their proper quota of taxation, lest the poorer citizens be oppressed by too heavy a burden: "The Senate sets the rule of life for the people. You, O Senators, have been called Fathers in order that those who in a way are your sons may follow your lead. . . . We have heard from the report of the magistrates of the provinces, made to the Praetorian Prefect, that little or no contribution at the first assessment has come in from Senatorial houses, and that therefore the poor are heavily taxed on account of this falling short. . . . Please pay your own fitting dues that those who can scarcely meet their own obligations may not be crushed beneath the burdens belonging to other men. For the task of the State is as much yours as ours"—an important admission. The words are, of course, the words of Cassiodorus, but we may see in them the ideal, at least, of his barbarian King.[39]

And, in general, Theodoric treated the Senate with special respect and courtesy, as was prudent for one of alien race whose rule had been gained by invasion. If he himself retained supreme power in his own hands, he paid the Senate the deference of referring his actions to their notice. The State officials were presented to the Senate on their appointment in a formal letter of introduction which regularly contained words of praise. So, when Artemidorus was made Prefect of the City, Theodoric wrote to him: "For your merits you shall now preside over that body to which you know reverence is due from all men. Would you compare the ruling of palaces or of private houses with this?"

[39] I, 16; II, 38; IV, 38 and 50; II, 24f.

Candidates for admission to the Senate must be severely scrutinized. "Let some other Order receive average men; the Senate refuses to admit without scrupulous testing. Its members must be as noble of character as they are aristocratic of blood." At the same time the King also prudently appointed to high office under his new sovereignty men not of the elect, whose fathers had never sat in the seats of the mighty.[40]

As near to Theodoric's heart as magistrates of all ranks were all civic matters pertaining to Rome and Italy. Rome, mistress as ever of the world, must be its most glorious city. "Let nothing," Cassiodorus writes, "be unused which may add to the beauty of Rome." "Let the citizens themselves impel us by their own eagerness to magnify their city; for no one can admire a city which its own citizens do not love." "It is even more important to maintain than it is to build. Let bricks be furnished for repairing the walls of Rome." A letter addressed "To All the Goths and Romans" bids them bring forward for the repairing of the city stones of any kind lying in their fields: "The worthy building of a city is a King's work, and the repairing of ancient cities is the honour of each age." "We suffer nothing commonplace in Rome."

The same care is given to other cities. Ravenna is to be adorned with marble columns and marble tombs; money is to be paid out for repairing the walls and towers of Arles, as "the loveliness of the city's fabric will be a sign and token of her renewed prosperity." Temples, aqueducts, baths are to be kept in preservation in Rome as elsewhere; granaries must be guarded from decay; the sewers of Rome must be vigilantly protected from ravages of time, for "in them is seen the greatness of Rome herself."[41]

Not only the buildings, but the bodies and minds of those

---

[40] I, 42; VI, 14; I, 41; V, 41.
[41] *Var.* II, 7; I, 21, 25, and 28; III, 9, 19, 44, and 31; V, 38; III, 29f.

who use them share equally in the royal consideration. "It may seem a humble thing for a King that he should deal with public entertainment," Theodoric writes to two Patricians, "occupied as he is by the illustrious matters of State; yet for love of Rome he wills to provide for this in any way he can. His people's joy is the blessing of his reign. By the graciousness of God we see now the fruit of our labours, in that the rank and file of citizens realize that they do have time for recreation." Constant appeals are made against quarrels among rival parties in the Circus. "Let the Roman people," the King requests, "behave like Romans, not like foreigners. Insults neither beget joy nor are begotten of it. He who insults a Senator shall be brought to trial before the Prefect of the City. Even if fickle favour does veer round from the Green Party to the Blue and vice-versa, enthusiasm is no reason for discord. The games in the Circus drive out serious habits, invite trifling quarrels, expel decency, and are a welling spring of strife." [42]

Yet common sense must be applied in these matters. "Who would expect men to be dignified at the games? We don't expect a circus full of Catos. Quips made in hilarity are not really insults. Senators must, of course, be dignified, but they need not get upset by idle remarks of ordinary citizens." Special grants of money are made to famous charioteers in Rome and elsewhere on the ground of merit and need: "We rejoice when the pages of our account-books are filled with these items." Generosity, above all, should be shown to those who fight with wild beasts. On this subject Theodoric, or rather Cassiodorus, waxes violent with indignation: "The people do not wish such contenders to escape alive. It is a loathsome business, destruction before death for the victim, devoured alive by his brute foe. Such a spectacle was devised in honour of Diana who delighted in bloodshed—no wonder

[42] I, 20 and 31f.; III, 51.

primitive people called her Queen of nether Darkness! Alas
for blind humanity! If there were any thought of justice, men
surely would spend as much for living mortals as they seem to
want to pour out on their deaths." [43]

A description of the Circus and its athletes is given in one
letter written to compensate a charioteer called Thomas.[44] We
are told here that twelve gates at its entrance correspond to
the twelve signs of the Zodiac. The colours of the four parties
represent the seasons: green for spring, blue for cloudy winter,
red for flaming summer, white for the hoar-frost of autumn.
A white starting line is drawn, and a race consists of seven
roundings of the goal-post. The signal for starting is given,
as of old, by flinging forward a napkin, a custom explained
here by a story of Nero. When he was lingering over his lunch
and the people were frantic that he should hurry and finish, he
told his servants to throw the napkin which he was using to
wipe his fingers out of the window as a sign that the races might
begin. The chariot-race is run in twenty-four heats, equal to
the number of hours in day and night. Each rounding of the
goal-post is marked by the raising on high of an egg (really
a huge egg-shaped object made of wood), by which Cassiodorus wishes us to understand a token of the birth of an event.
There follows some lively description of the excitement of the
populace: "The Green rushes past, some of the spectators wail.
The Blue dashes ahead, and in a twinkling the great multitude
are cast down. Wildly they cheer, but for nothing! They are
grievously wounded, at nothing! In vain contentions they
struggle as if they were distressed at the fate of their suffering
fatherland. Surely such extravagance is an offering to superstition. But we support these things of necessity, constrained
by frivolous minds."

Other letters deal with law, education, and religion. Law-

[43] I, 27 and 30; II, 9; V, 42.   [44] III, 51.

yers are warned that trials must not last forever in long-drawn
debate. Dishonesty and murder occur frequently in these
records; slaying of a father by his son, of a master by his servants, of a lover by an injured husband. This last deed is
allowed. Much indignation is expressed at the theft of an
ancient statue from Como, "inasmuch as we are daily trying
to augment the adorning of cities."

In the cause of education Valerian and Filagrius, both *Viri
Spectabiles,* gain their petitions that a son and a nephew may
be ordered to remain in Rome after they themselves have
retired to Syracuse from their duties there: "No one should
object to living in Rome, for she is foreign to none." [45]

Special interest marks the letters written on affairs relating
to the Church. Property given by the Crown to the Church
may by special decree be exempted from taxation; other gifts,
however, are not allowed a like immunity. "Taxes are the
property of the purple, not of the military cloak," is the admonition bestowed on some offender, presumably a soldier. Property stolen from the Church must be restored, in Italy, Gaul,
or elsewhere. Injury to property done by the royal army on
the march is compensated by money sent to the Bishop of the
district. "What better choice for the administering of justice
than he who is adorned with Holy Order, who loves the right
and judges for the common good, not for his own selfish ends?"
We shall see presently that Cassiodorus, who composed these
letters, was a fervent Catholic. But his master endorsed the
following words, written in a letter protecting the Church in
Sicily: "Though we wish none under our gracious protection
to suffer injury, because the peace of his subjects is the glory
of their King, yet we desire especially that the Churches be
free from all harm. For when justice is rendered them we gain
the mercy of Heaven." [46]

[45] I, 5; II, 14 and 19; I, 37; II, 36; I, 39; IV, 6.
[46] I, 26; IV, 17, 20; II, 8 (cf. IV, 36); II, 29.

On the other hand, wrong-doing on the part of bishop or priest is met with reprimand as in the case of secular officials. "The nearer to divine grace, the further should nobles of the Church be removed from earthly greed. John accuses your Holiness with tears of never paying for sixty casks of lamp oil received from him. Pay him promptly if the accusation is just. You do not sin in great matters, see that you do not in little ones." This is written to the Bishop of Salona. The Venerable Bishop Aurigenes is called to task because certain men, servants of a celibate prelate, have assaulted the wife and injured the property of one Julian. "Will the Bishop examine into the matter, and if it be proved administer prompt punishment to the offender?"

With this letter we may compare another written to a Bishop Peter, concerning the complaint of Germanus that the Bishop has defrauded him of part of the property left him by his father. The King requests the Bishop to hand over the property without delay if this complaint is rightly made. Accusation against a bishop should be left to the judgment and decision of the accused himself, since justice is rather to be expected than exacted from one of his office. If, however, the Bishop Peter does not decide the matter in justice, the suppliant's case will be brought to the Royal Court.[47]

These two letters do not mean that bishops or their clergy were exempt from secular tribunals when accused of offence against a layman. They show rather that, in deference to the reverend office of the person addressed, the bishop is advised to settle the complaint privately out of court before the accusation comes before a secular judge, as it would if persistently neglected by him. There is no question here of necessary exemption from secular trial.[48] A third letter, of importance in this connection, shows that the King did leave the judgment of

[47] III, 7, 14, 37.
[48] Hodgkin, *Letters,* pp. 204, 216f.; Dahn, III, p. 194; Pfeilschifter, *Der Ostgotenkönig T. der Grosse und die katholische Kirche,* pp. 238ff.

clerical offences in which no lay individual was concerned to the bishop or archbishop, as a mark of respect to the Church. Here Theodoric writes to Eustorgius, Bishop of Milan, that the accusation of traitor to his country brought against the Bishop of Aosta has been proved false. Let the Bishop therefore be restored to all due honour, not by secular authority, but by his Metropolitan of Milan. His accusers are to meet with the lawful penalty. But as they themselves are reverend clergy, the Bishop of Milan will deal with them, "he whose office it is to guard judgment in matters of the Church." [49]

Once a horrible accusation against a priest is brought by Theodôric before the notice of Annas, a Senator. It is said, declares the King, that the priest Laurentius has been searching among the graves of a cemetery for "fatal riches," and that "he who ought to preach peace to the living has been disturbing the dead." His findings are to be seized, if the report is true; the offender, as a priest, is left to a jurisdiction higher than that of Theodoric. [50]

As an alien ruler who had gained his throne by power of Gothic arms, Theodoric's position between Roman and Goth was a delicate one; under him the two nations lived each its own separate life in outward harmony one with another through the King's personal tact and skill of government. Nevertheless the division between them was very deep. Only Romans were citizens of the Empire; they alone could hold the dignity of Consul, Prefect, Master of Offices, Quaestor, and others of the chief civil positions in the State. They alone could attain to the rank of Senator or of Patrician. The Goths in this time were held as soldiers of a foreign nation, resident

[49] *Var.* I, 9; Hodgkin, *Letters,* pp. 149f.; Dahn, p. 191. Pfeilschifter (p. 244), guided by a corrected text, argues against Dahn for the regular jurisdiction of Bishops over clerical offenders of this time.

[50] *Var.* IV, 18. It is doubtful whether these words refer to the judgment of Heaven or of the Church on earth; Hodgkin (p. 245) favours the former theory, Pfeilschifter (p. 242) the latter.

in the Roman Empire and under the jurisdiction of her laws, but possessing in the administration hardly any official status of their own. Procopius represents the Gothic warriors as declaring to Amalasuntha that Theodoric would not dream of cowing the warlike spirit of Gothic youths by lash of discipline at school. With an occasional exception, therefore, as in the office of Count of the Patrimony, the honours enjoyed by the barbarians were military.[51] The army, officers and men alike, was composed of Goths, to whom fell the duty of defending the Empire in the West, as to the Romans was assigned the distinction of administering it. Under the King as Commander-in-Chief (*magister militum*) the army was ordered by the same barbarians who had won it for him; its officers were termed *Prior* or *Comes*.

Among the civic exceptions some light is thrown on the position of the Goths under Theodoric by the *Formula* for the appointment of a Gothic "Count of the Goths" over a particular district. This office was instituted by the King for the deciding of quarrels between two Goths or between a Goth and a Roman. In the latter case a Roman lawyer was to be called in for consultation, but the final decision rested with the "Count," a distinction, for once, in favour of the alien race. Doubtless this resulted in much wrath on the side of the Romans. The *Formula* reveals the aim of the King for both races under his rule: "Let each people hear our desire. As the Romans are neighbours of the Goths in land, so let them also be united to the Goths in affection. And you, Romans, should esteem the Goths very zealously, for they add numbers to your populace in time of peace and defend the whole State in time of war. Therefore obey the magistrate appointed by me and fulfil his biddings for the good of my government and for your

---

[51] *Hist. Wars,* V. ii, 14ff.; Bury, I, pp. 456f.; Mommsen, *Ostgoth. Stud.* p. 402.

own advantage." Unhappily this excellent desire was little realized, while the two peoples lived side by side distinct and discordant, ready for the struggle which broke out after Theodoric's death.[52]

Another official frequently mentioned, though inferior in rank, was the *Saio*. The *Saiones* were employed on personal missions by the King. In all probability they were Goths, on the evidence of their names, and fulfilled on the Gothic side the same purpose as the Roman *agentes in rebus*. Their duties were very many and varied. They summoned the Goths to fight for the State, called criminal offenders to justice, supervised the erection of strongholds for the Goths, rounded up Goths who neglected payment of taxes, controlled barbarian troops on the march, marshalled sailors to a given point when needed, procured timber for the formation of a fleet, drilled soldiers. It was their duty, also, to gather in the Goths on the occasions when Theodoric augmented the ordinary pay of his soldiers by "largesses," a custom surviving from the days when he rewarded his nomad followers after some victory in the plains of Europe. A proclamation to "All the Goths in Picenum and Samnium" bids them appear before Theodoric on the sixth of June to receive in formal manner the royal gifts. "Although," Cassiodorus writes in his sovereign's name, "our bounty is always most welcome to all men, it is certainly much enhanced when bestowed in our Presence. The man who is not known to his Lord is almost as one dead. But be sure you do not damage any harvests or meadows as you hurry on your way to Rome!" The relation of the *Saiones* to the Emperor is shown by the description "Man of Devotion" by which they are frequently addressed.[53]

Another special duty fulfilled by *Saiones* was *tuitio*, the serv-

<hr />

[52] *Var.* VII, 3; Dahn IV, pp. 157f.; Bury, I, pp. 457, 459.
[53] *Var.* I, 24; II, 13; III, 48; IV, 14; V, 10, 19f., 23, and 26f.; IV, 47.

ice rendered by a Goth as personal guard of some wealthy
Roman who needed protection against attack. Sometimes the
fierce retainer went a bit too far and nearly murdered the
enemies of his charge, and at last the rich Roman was obliged
to deposit a sum of money on engaging his protector, as a fund
from which to make compensation for any damage he might
do. Such a transgressor was condemned to lose his pay. On
one occasion the *Saio* actually attacked his own employer,
rushing upon him with drawn sword so violently that he
wounded him in the hand, and only an intervening door saved
it from being entirely cut off. Theodoric writes of his horror
at such betrayal of trust, especially as the *Saio* has demanded,
and received, his usual reward. He is sentenced to hand over
double that amount to his employer and is dismissed from his
post.[54]

As free men, however, no servile burdens are to be imposed
upon the Goths. A relic of special Gothic legislation has been
thought to remain in the permission given to a Gothic husband
to punish his wife for a crime of violence by his own authority
as her husband.[55]

To the other barbarians who dwelt in the Roman Empire
Theodoric showed uniform tolerance and mildness. In sending out to those settled throughout Pannonia a governor named
Colossaeus, the King urges them to fight the enemies of Rome,
not each other, to put aside their swords and live humanely as
brethren in a civilized world. Colossaeus himself is exhorted
to instil Roman manners into his charges, that their hot tempers
may learn to live gracefully.

The King's fair-mindedness is especially evident in the matter of differing religions. An Arian himself, he was as eager
to allow differing creeds in his State as he was to combine

[54] VII, 42; IV, 27f.; Bury, I, p. 458 note.
[55] *Var.* III, 38; V, 29f. and 32; Dahn, IV, pp. 149f.

nationalities. When he made his first formal visit to Rome in 500, Pope Symmachus, victorious over his rival Laurentius, received him outside the City gates with the Senate and people in all joy, and the King made pilgrimage to the Church of St. Peter "most devoutly, as though a Catholic himself." [56] He was scrupulous in his treatment of the Jews, so despised by the Romans in earlier days. Theodoric desired their conversion; yet permission is given to those in Genoa to repair their synagogue. "Why," he adds, "do you want that which you ought to flee? We truly allow your petition, but, as we ought, we disallow the desire of your erring hearts. We cannot *command* obedience to any religion, because no one is compelled to believe against his will." Their ancient rights are confirmed for the Jews of Genoa in another letter. At Milan Christians and Jews alike are not to act "incivilly" against each other, and the Jews are to be protected against the frequent assaults of which they complain: "But why, O Jew, dost thou beg for the peace which lasts but in time, if thou canst not find the repose of eternity?" Once, when Christians had burned down the Jewish synagogue in the Trastevere at Rome as an act of revenge, the King ordered prompt punishment for the offenders. Even the "adherents of the Samaritan superstition, brazen in their bold front," are to have justice done them in their conflict with the "sacrosanct Church of Rome." [57]

From toleration we come to the social amenities. The correspondence of Theodoric with foreigners of royal state is naturally significant. The letter which opens the collection is written to Anastasius, successor of Zeno as Emperor of the East and over-Lord of Italy. It is interesting, therefore, to see that its tone, full of courtesy as it is, as meet for a letter which seeks to reestablish harmony between Rome of the East

[56] *Anon. Vales.* 17(65).

[57] *Var.* II, 27; IV, 33 and 43; V, 37; III, 45; R. W. Church, *Church Quarterly Review*, X, pp. 305f.

and of the West, does not reveal any sense of inferior position. The words are rather those of a sovereign addressing his elder brother in rule: "We believe that you will not allow any discord to remain between two States which always formed one body under the Emperors of the past, States which ought not only to be united by love in theory, but ought also to aid one another in practical ways. Let there be one will, one aim in the Empire of Rome." The King of Italy declares, however, that he follows the leadership of Constantinople: "Our realm is patterned after yours, the form of a goodly model, the copy of a unique sovereignty. In so far as we follow you, we surpass other peoples."

This letter seems to have been written in an attempt to settle some quarrel between Ravenna and Constantinople which had arisen subsequent to the amicable arranging of their relationship. For in 497 Anastasius had forgiven the presumption of Theodoric in taking on himself the royal power in Italy without waiting for his consent, and had returned to him all the crown jewels and ornaments which Odovacar had transferred to Constantinople.[58]

Important correspondence was carried on with the various royal kinsmen of the King of Italy. His connections by marriage were numerous: with the Kings of Burgundy, of the Visigoths, of the Franks, of the Thuringians, and of the Vandals.

To Gundobad, King of Burgundy, whose son married one of Theodoric's daughters, Theodoric sent the gift of a water-clock by aid of Boethius; to whom he wrote: "We must not scorn friendly requests from our royal neighbours; often pleasant courtesies procure what arms of battle cannot. Let us work for the State even in play." To the same monarch was addressed

---

[58] Bury, *Invasion of Europe*, p. 186; Hodgkin, *Letters*, pp. 23, 143; *Anon. Vales.* 16(64). Mommsen (ed. p. xxxi) places the date of the letter circ. 508, as occasioned through the ravaging of Italian coasts by the Byzantine fleet.

one of a group of letters written in a most earnest attempt to prevent that conflict, mentioned before, between Clovis, King of the Franks, and Alaric the second. The appeal failed, and the war that followed caused defeat and death to the Visigothic King. He was son-in-law of Theodoric, who warns him not to encounter the Franks: "The spirits of fierce peoples become soft through long continued peace; beware of putting to the test those men of yours, who now for a long time have had no experience of war. So far there is only a small contention of words between you and Clovis. Stop! and let me send ambassadors to him. Do not let harm come to one of you by defeat, since you are both my kinsmen." A similar entreaty is sent to Clovis, brother-in-law of Theodoric, forbidding him "by the right of a father and a loving friend" to cast into war two most noble Kings, men in the prime of their age. The Kings of the Heruli, of the Guarni, and of the Thuringians are begged by letter to join Theodoric in sending a mission on behalf of peace to Clovis: "He who has made himself victor in a hateful struggle believes that he is master of all. You know this. So send your legates with mine." [59]

Another remonstrance, sent to Clovis at about the same date, was backed by greater chance of success. He was in full cry after conquest and had utterly defeated the Alamanni for the second time. The unhappy people had fled to Raetia and to Pannonia, into the protection of the Roman Empire, and Clovis had requested Theodoric to yield them to his will as their conqueror. Theodoric had no intention of doing so: "It is enough," he wrote, "that you have roused the Franks again to victory and have subdued a mighty people. That is a memorable triumph for you. Therefore be kind to them, now they are driven to beg for their lives and are hiding in terror within my domains. Listen to me, for I am much experienced

[59] *Var.* I, 45f.; III, 1-4.

in these matters. My campaigns have won me success when I have waged them *with restraint*." [60]

The Kings of the Heruli and of the Thuringians have also each a second letter in our collection. The former is signally honoured: "According to the law of nations I beget you herewith for your soldierly prowess as mine own son in arms. Sons born of nature often disappoint their parents; do you take the horses and swords and shields which I send you of my gift, and use them for your good and mine." Hermanfrid, King of the Thuringians, is given Amalaberga, niece of Theodoric, in marriage, "that you who are of royal descent may now be even more illustrious through the splendour of Amal blood." The lady is "well read in letters," a doubtful recommendation to the Thuringian King! There are also two letters to Thrasamund, King of the Vandals in Africa and husband of Theodoric's sister Amalafrida. The first rebukes him sternly because he has given aid to Gesalic, an illegitimate son of Alaric the second. Gesalic had claimed the kingdom of Alaric after that King's untimely death at the hands of Clovis, though the rightful heir was Alaric's son by marriage, Amalaric. The second letter is full of peace, because Thrasamund has repented his fault. [61]

At length Theodoric the Great departed this life, though not in peace, as we shall see presently, and Cassiodorus turned with a sigh to compose the letters of the eighth and the ninth books, written by him in the name of Athalaric and his mother, the Queen-Regent Amalasuntha. The formal announcing of the King's accession to the Emperor Justin, successor of Anastasius at Constantinople, opens with a note of deference: "Neither the robes of my ancestors" (so Cassiodorus wrote for Athalaric's signature) "nor my own royal throne so ennobles me as your favour extended to me far and wide. Add therefore your love;

[60] II, 41.   [61] IV, 1; V, 43f.

let strife be buried in the grave of the dead. It was you who
honoured Theodoric, my grandfather, with curule office in
Constantinople, you adorned my father with the consulship
in Italy, you accorded to him the joy of adoption as your son."
This election to the consulship of Eutharic, Athalaric's father,
one of the Gothic race, was a definite exception to the rule,
made only by the express favour of Constantinople. A declara-
tion written by Cassiodorus to the Senate tells that Athalaric
has become King with general consent and solemn oath of
loyalty, both on the part of Goths and of Romans. The Senators are cordially urged to ask what they desire for their own
advantage. The Roman people are told in a third letter that
there is to be one common body of law for Goths and Romans,
and that the only difference is that "the Goths undertake the
toils of war for the general welfare, while the Romans gain
might of numbers through peaceful residence in Rome." Both
Senate and people are assured that things shall be as they were
under Theodoric.[62]

Military administration under Athalaric shows at once an
enforced change. As the present King in his tender years cannot hold supreme command of the army, this charge is now
confided to the Gothic General Tuluin, renowned for great victories under Theodoric. These are rehearsed in a letter to the
Senate announcing that Tuluin has been raised to the Patriciate, a rank held hitherto by no Goth except Theodoric himself,
who had been thus honoured by the Emperor of the East.[63]

Legislative work of this reign, as compiled by Cassiodorus, is
seen in the *Edict of Athalaric,* dated by Mommsen 533–534.[64]
This deals with the seizure of property; with alienation of

[62] VIII, 1-3.   [63] VIII, 9-11.

[64] IX, 18. This is an appendix to the more important *Edictum Theo-
dorici,* of which, however, Cassiodorus was not, in all probability, the
compiler. For the text of the *E.T. see M.G.H. Leges,* V, pp. 145ff.,
and, for comment, *ibid.* and Dahn, IV, pp. 1ff., where the *E.A.* is also
discussed.

affection of a married person, the punishment for which is the
forbidding of marriage to the offender himself; with adultery,
for which the penalty declared by Theodoric is to remain,
death for all concerned; with bigamy, punished by the confiscation of all possessions; with illicit unions, either with a
free woman, in which case she and her children are to be bound
in slavery to the wife of the offender, or with a slave woman,
who is to be handed over to the injured wife for any punishment save shedding of blood. The practice of black arts is
specially condemned, and oppression of the poor. We have
also evidence for the thought of Cassiodorus under Athalaric
for education, in an interesting letter to the Senate bidding an
increase in the salaries of teachers in Rome. His sentiments
have a curiously modern sound: "It is being whispered that
the professors at Rome are not receiving the due rewards for
their labours, and that their pay is being reduced by unfair
bargaining. This we hold impious—that the teachers of young
men should be defrauded, when they should rather be persuaded to their splendid work by increased recompense. Rhetoric, their profession, is not the study of barbarian kings; it
is found only among civilized rulers. So kindly provide for the
pay of your professors regularly, that it may not depend on
what their employers choose to do. If we pay actors on the
stage for amusing us, surely we should reward promptly those
responsible for our morals and our education. Let us hear
no more complaining from our professors that they ought not
to be worried with two burdens at once, how to teach and how
to live." [65]

Ecclesiastic procedure is illuminated here by several letters.
One, addressed to the Senate, expresses the satisfaction of the
Government at the election of Felix IV as Pope in 526: "We
declare it right well pleasing to us that you have followed the

[65] *Var.* IX, 21.

judgment of our glorious Lord and Grandfather in the election
of your Bishop. It is no shame to have been overruled by the
King in this matter. For even if the faithful have not obtained
the particular individual they desired as Pope, yet in having
a Pope they have all they need."

The letter is of importance with regard to the manner of
the Papal election at this time. Evidently Pope Felix IV was
chosen by the nomination of Theodoric shortly before his death,
possibly after a dispute with regard to the choice. The matter
may have been referred to the King, as in the case of Symmachus and Laurentius.[66]

In another letter, written to Pope John the second in 533,
Athalaric forbids any promise of payment to the poor on the
part of candidates for the Papacy. The ordinance was called
forth by corrupt practice, carried on in the electing of this
Pope John as successor to Boniface the second. Another letter,
written at the same time to Salventius, Prefect of Rome, also
confirms the decree of the Senate on the same subject, made
about the time of the death of Boniface.[67] Such great contribu-
tions had been promised, the King complains, that it is said
that even the holy vessels themselves have been advertised for
sale in order to meet these obligations. The amounts that may
be promised to the poor by Popes or Patriarchs are herewith
fixed, and a warning is given against simony. The Prefect of
the City is ordered to see that these royal commands be en-
graved and posted at the doors of the Church of Saint Peter.

Thirdly, Athalaric ordained about 527, in a letter to the
clergy of the Church of Rome, that any one desiring legal
redress from one of their number must bring his complaint
before the Papal Court. There the matter was either to be

[66] VIII, 15. See Dahn, III, pp. 238f.; W. H. Hutton, *The Church
of the Sixth Century*, p. 93; Duchesne, *Lib. Pont.* I, p. LXIII; p. 280;
Mommsen, ed. *Variae*, p. xxxviii.
[67] *Var.* IX, 15f.; Duchesne, p. 283, note 16; Mommsen, *ibid.*

decided by the Pope himself, or referred by him to some expert for settlement. If it should happen—perish the thought!— that the plaintiff remain unsatisfied, he may then take his quarrel to the secular courts, if and when he shall have proved that his petition has been despised by the aforesaid See. Any plaintiff who has recourse first of all to the secular courts is to be fined ten pounds in gold, which shall be donated by the Pope to his poor.

As Hodgkin remarks, the plaintiff in these cases would usually stop short of accusing the Holy See of injustice.[68]

Athalaric, no less than his grandfather, appears in bold relation to his fellow-monarchs. Cassiodorus addressed for him in 526 or 527 an indignant protest to Hilderic, now ruler of the Vandals. He had dared to put to death Amalafrida, that sister of Theodoric who had married Hilderic's predecessor, Thrasamund, deceased some three years before. The lady had been accused of conspiring against Hilderic—truthfully, perhaps, from the tone of the remonstrance. The Vandal King in his answer to Ravenna denied the act altogether, and declared that this ex-Queen had died a natural death. But there is no doubt about the slaying, and the pen of Cassiodorus bubbles over in expressing the wrath of Athalaric's mother, the Queen-Regent. Unfortunately Amalasuntha had to be content with wrath; her own troubles did not permit of a Vandal war.[69]

When Cassiodorus at length obtained office as Praetorian Prefect in 533, he launched out into exuberant praise of this Queen-Regent, its bestower.[70] She is pictured as a miracle of learning, full of eloquence both Attic and Roman, a mar-

[68] *Letters of Cass.* pp. 372f. Mommsen dates this letter (VIII, 24) circ. 527.
[69] *Var.* IX, 1. See also, for Amalafrida, Procopius, *Hist. Wars*, III, ix, 3ff.; Victor Tonnennensis, *Chron. Min.* II, ed. Mommsen, pp. 196f.
[70] *Var.* XI, 1.

vellous ruler, of surpassing goodness, and a real woman and mother to boot. Behind the rhetoric we may discern truth. But even this courteous Secretary cannot mete out much praise to her royal son, who at this moment was hastening death by rioting and drunkenness. He has to fall back on excuses: "It is difficult for a young man to hold the Kingship; scarcely does restraint in morals come with gray hairs. . . . You remember, Senators, that most apt saying of Symmachus: 'I do not praise these beginnings of Athalaric, because I am content to look forward to better things later on.' We must hope on, remembering that he is his mother's son."

He died, however, the next year, and we find then the letters written by Cassiodorus for Queen Amalasuntha herself as reigning Queen, in that desperate act of folly, her partnership with Theodahad. The Secretary had already written letters in Theodoric's name to this nephew of his, and of no complimentary nature. Theodahad had ordered his servants to rob distinguished citizens of their properties: "What has meanness of mind to do with splendour of birth?" runs a rebuke. "Vulgar ambition is not fitting for a descendant of the Amals, whose forerunners have worn the purple." [71]

We now see both Theodahad and Amalasuntha announcing their alliance to Justinian, Emperor of the East since 527. Theodahad writes of Amalasuntha, as "his most distinguished Lady and Sister." He was, of course, her cousin, as the son of Theodoric's sister, the ill-fated Amalafrida, and a husband she had married prior to Thrasamund. It is significant that both send messages to be delivered privately in Justinian's ear, telling, no doubt, of their willingness to yield power to the East. In a letter to the Senate Amalasuntha glorifies her new partner: "The Lord, of His great mercy, in taking away from me my son in early youth thought to provide for me the love of a

[71] III, 15; IV, 39; V, 12.

brother of ripe age." Among her compliments there is a rather pathetic stress on Theodahad's cultured mind, so likely to attract this Gothic Queen in her enthusiasm for all things civilized and Roman: "In books his natural prudence has found wisdom; his martial courage has learned strength of soul. And indeed, no fortune can exist in this world which the glorious knowledge of letters does not magnify." [72]

There is also a greeting from Amalasuntha to Theodora, Empress in the East: of interest in connection with the statement of Procopius, in his malicious *Secret History,* that the jealous mind of Theodora was plotting the death of this Queen in Italy. We do not know that this story is true.[73] But the wife of Theodahad, Gudeliva, was also full of ambition. We can read a letter written to Theodora by her, too, about this time, praising that ambassador Peter whom Theodora had sent to the Court of Theodahad, with the object (so says Procopius) of inducing him to put Amalasuntha to death. Toward the end she adds: "With regard to that person concerning whom an itching whisper has come to us, you must know that that has been ordered which we thought would suit your purposes; for we desire that by the intervention of our good-will you should issue your orders no less in our kingdom than in your own empire." Another letter of Gudeliva to Theodora may very possibly hold a similar dark hint in its mysterious wording: "You must know, most sagacious Empress, how keenly I long for your good favour, as does my Lord and yokemate. Of course, this is very, very precious to him, but to me it is the greatest thing in my life. . . . So I send your Serenity an eager greeting of respect, and commend myself to your affection, hoping that your wonderful sagacity may give me greater confidence in you than ever. There should be no disagreement between the Roman kingdoms, and, besides, such

[72] X, 1-4.   [73] X, 10; *Hist. Arc. (Anecdota)* XVI, 1ff.

a thing has happened as should make us dearer to your sense
of justice." Theodahad writes to Theodora in an equally
guarded manner: "We have learned from your ambassador
Peter that you have approved that which is known to have happened in this State." One wonders with what sort of feeling
the royal Secretary Cassiodorus wrote these words. Mommsen
in his edition dates all three letters in the year of the murder of
Amalasuntha, 535, and it is tempting to see in them veiled
rejoicing over the removal of a hated rival. The wife of a
reigning King must have found it hard to bow before another
woman as his Queen.[74]

King Theodahad, meanwhile, was sharply remonstrating
with Roman Senators, smouldering with resentment at his
rule: "It is reported to us that the city of Rome is stirred by
foolish agitation, and acting in such a way that, were we not
mild of temper, real danger would come to it from its un-
founded suspicions. . . . Please return to your former loyalty
to the throne, and aid me in my cares for the commonweal."
So to the citizens at large: "Do not let me find in my day
anything which may arouse my wrath. It is not meet that
the Roman people should be fickle or crafty or full of sedi-
tions." [75]

When he, too, had passed, five letters came from the pen
of Cassiodorus for King Witigis. The Secretary tries now to
adapt his style to suit the mind of a bluff barbarian warrior.
In the first Witigis announces to his own Gothic race that he
has been raised upon the shield as King of the Goths in Italy:
"Not in the small space of a room, but in wide open plains was
I chosen as your King. Not amid delicate flatteries, but the
blare of trumpets, was I sought. Put away fear of losses, cast
aside suspicion of expenses to come. We have learned in many

---

[74] *Var.* X, 20, 21 and 23. See on this matter Gibbon, ed. Bury, IV,
p. 325; Bury, *Lat. R.E.* II, p. 167, note; Hodgkin, *Letters,* p. 433.
[75] *Var.* X, 13f.

wars to love brave men. I have seen, too, the deeds of each
of your warriors, done in my sight as your fellow in battle.
No arms of the Goths shall be broken by my fickle promises.
Everything which we do shall be for the good of all the Goths;
we will have no private love. Finally, in all things we promise
to maintain such a State as it befits us to have after the example
of glorious Theodoric." An appeal is sent to Justinian in Constantinople: "We ask peace from you as though no one of you
had done us harm. We have endured such things as may even
offend those who have done them: assaults without cause,
hatred without fault, loss without debt, and this not only in
the provinces, but manifestly in the very Capital City itself.
Such a thing has been wrought upon us that even the whole
world is talking. If vengeance for King Theodahad is sought"
(Witigis had already put him to death), "I deserve your esteem. If you are mindful of Queen Amalasuntha of blessed
memory, remember now her daughter. Your efforts rather
than mine should have brought her to the throne." Matasuntha, as we have seen, was most unwillingly the wife of this
Gothic King. Cassiodorus also made a grand speech at the
enthroning of Witigis. We have still a fragment of it, somewhat inconsistent with the words of its speaker in the past,
praising the martial spirit of Witigis to the detriment of Athalaric and of his mother: "Her motherly affection may well
excuse the wrong she did." [76]

   The character of Cassiodorus as Prime Minister to the Goths
is, indeed, a mixed one. Why did Theodoric leave it to Amalasuntha to reward his minister's co-operation, if he valued it so
greatly, with this honour of the Praetorian Prefecture? The
Faustus to whom Cassiodorus writes so frequently as Praetorian
Prefect during Theodoric's reign was not a very righteous official. Naturally, so Roman a Secretary was anathema to the

[76] X, 31-35; Mommsen, ed. *Variae*, p. 473; Bury, *L.R.E.* II, p. 221.

more determined of the Goths in Rome.[77] But was he allowed
to retire for a season to the Bruttian district as its Governor
because Theodoric and his Court were sick to death of his
long and courtly phrasings? Did Queen Amalasuntha turn
to him in the desperation of her helplessness? Did she look to
him to train her boy in Roman learning and save him from
Gothic barbarism, holding this prop to her side by the awarding
of the highest office in Italy?

More serious is the thought that Cassiodorus, sincere patriot
and lover of Rome as he was, flavoured his official writings
from time to time to suit the different sovereigns under whom
he worked. He puts forward the grossest rhetoric of praise in
presenting Theodahad to the Senate; he fills with pious and
high-sounding sentiments the letters of Theodahad himself.
This King appears in the official *Letters* exactly the same angel
of mercy and grace that was Theodoric, when Cassiodorus did
duty as mouthpiece under him. While Amalasuntha lived,
she was praised to the skies. But we have seen that *peccare*
expresses before Witigis the fault of her training of her son.
Under Witigis it is glory of arms, rather than the learning
extolled so long before, which is the theme of the Secretary's
panegyric.

At the same time, it was loyalty to the fading dream of Rome
that kept the Secretary at his post. Bury has well described the
isolation of the Ostrogothic crown in Italy after Theodoric's
death.[78] Of the four great nations with whom he had carefully connected his power by marriage, the Visigoths had lost
their King Amalaric, Theodoric's grandson, placed by him on
the throne after Alaric's death; both they and the people of Burgundy were too hard beset by the Franks to think of Amalasuntha and her troubles; the fear was only too great that the

[77] Cf. van de Vyver, *Cassiodore et son œuvre, Speculum,* VI, 1931,
p. 250.
[78] *L.R.E.* II, p. 161.

Franks would turn the rising flood of their energy against Amalasuntha herself. With her own death there sprang into life the terrors throughout Italy of the Gothic War. We cannot but commend Cassiodorus that he did not at once forsake the trust which the Great King had left, we may think, in his hands, the supporting of the feeble rule of a woman and a child.

And his words, fulsome and at times insincere, brought nevertheless their recompense to him and his Gentile lord. The anonymous writer "Valesius" also tells how Theodoric loved buildings, how he restored cities both to power and to comeliness, and wrought many other benefits: "He so pleased neighbouring peoples that other nations, desiring him as King, gave themselves to him by covenant. Traders from different provinces hastened to him. For there was so great order under his rule that any one who wished to bury gold or silver in his own open field did so with as much trust as if he were inside the walls of a city. It was said of him throughout Italy that he gave gates to no city, and in his time no gates were closed. Each man did his appointed work at the hour and on the day he wished." And the record goes on to show that food was cheap in Theodoric's reign.[79]

In all these things Cassiodorus loyally took his share, by suggestion, by support, and by practical service. It was only when increasing age, clouded by despair of war and its tumult and wretchedness, bade him retire at last from the world and its political emptiness that he turned to serve more directly the cause which for long must have been beckoning to his heart, even while he served a failing purpose under masters barbarian and heretic.

The devotion of Cassiodorus to the Catholic Church we shall see hereafter in discussing his later works. But the letters

[79] *Anon. Vales.* 22(71).

which he wrote as Praetorian Prefect under his own name show something of it. In the midst of the complacent singing of his own praises, when he announces his election as Praetorian Prefect, he writes to Pope John the second: "May public affairs find in me that same man as judge whom the Catholic Church sends forth as her son. I am, it is true, the Judge of the Palatine, but I shall not cease to be your disciple; for I do my duties well if I hold fast to your rulings." So also to "various Bishops": "Do you, my spiritual Fathers, pray earnestly for me to God, the Holy Trinity, that He may make to shine brightly my candlestick set in the midst." In keeping with these letters is the announcing of many promotions to his Praetorian staff on the joyful Feast of Christmas, and the general pardon granted to prisoners at the time of another great Festival, probably Easter.[80]

As it is the historian who values these productions of loving toil, it is disappointing that Cassiodorus, obedient to the spirit of education in this age, chose for publication the letters we possess from his correspondence on the ground of their "literary" merit, not, primarily, of their historical worth. Therefore he did not trouble to date them, and the names of consuls and ambassadors are not given. He explains in his Preface that he has given the name of *Variae* to his selection because good writing demands that different styles shall be used in composing letters for people of different degrees of culture and education, "so that sometimes it is a kind of skill to avoid polished writing." Three kinds of style are distinguished in this Preface: the lowly, the medium, the elevated; they are to be applied severally, each to the person for whom it is suitable. This explains the letters written for King Witigis.

But their composer far preferred a free hand, and no account of these letters could fail to mark the extraordinary bypaths

[80] *Var.* XI, 2, 3, 17, and 40.

in which he allowed his pen to wander at its will. In writing State epistles for Theodoric he dallied in describing all manner of things: the origin of purple dye, discovered, we are told, when once a famished dog crunched in his jaws the shells lying on the Tyrian sands; the mysteries of arithmetic, controlling things above and things of earth; the intricacies of a water-clock; the marvellous properties of certain hot springs, so chaste that they wax hotter in fury if entered by a woman; the power of music, banishing from the mind all thought save of itself, and the legends of its fascination. Instructions on the repairing of aqueducts are enlivened by mythical accounts of the discovery of lead and brass; orders to build a fort are interrupted by the provident measures by which birds and animals protect themselves; a mention of rebate on taxation, allowed to the Campanians for damage done by Vesuvius, is accompanied by a long description of the erupting mountain. Even the young Athalaric is supposed to indulge in such discussion, though here Cassiodorus would seem to be infringing his own rule that the style should fit the writer. In the letters composed by his Secretary, Athalaric relates the story of the devising of letters of the alphabet by Mercury as he watched the Strymonian cranes in their manœuvres; he illuminates talk of sewers by rhapsodizing over the merits of water; he illustrates directions for mining by the habit of a mole. But perhaps the most remarkable digression is found in one of the letters written in the name of Theodahad. It tells of the elephant. The elephant lives more than a thousand years, Theodahad is supposed to tell his correspondent. It reveres righteous kings, but is unmoved by tyrants. It surpasses all other four-footed beasts in intelligence, because it kneels in instant adoration before the Lord Ruler of all.[81] Here the writer outdid the elder Pliny, whom very probably he

[81] I, 2, 10, and 45; II, 39f.; III, 31, 48, cf. 53; IV, 50; VIII, 12, 30; IX, 3; X, 30.

copied in some details. He was writing to order the repair of figures of elephants on the Sacred Way.[82]

Almost as marvellous are sundry derivations of words: as of *pugna* from *pugni,* since battles began with the fists; or of *bellum* from Belus, because he first introduced the iron sword![83] Such feats of imagination explain the eagerness with which their perpetrator turned later on to that sacred pastime so well loved in this age, the enwrapping of the lamp of truth in the embroidered veil of allegory.

[82] *Hist. Nat.* VIII, 1ff.; Hodgkin, *Letters,* p. 443.
[83] *Var.* I, 30.

CHAPTER III

THE GOTHIC RULE IN ITALY:
JORDANES AND ENNODIUS

CASSIODORUS was not always writing letters; now and again he left the royal Presence and retreated to his study. It was the diving into ancient records that delighted him at this time, especially the archives of his own clan. We have only a fragment of his *Family History of the Cassiodori,* and this itself is made up of excerpts from the original work. The ancient compiler tells us that it was addressed to Rufus Petronius Nicomachus: Consul, Patrician, and Master of Offices. We learn from other sources that this gentleman was also called Cethegus, and was consul in 504. Its dating before or after 537 depends upon the question whether we may include in its genuine text a mention of the *Various Letters* of Cassiodorus.[1] The fragment, as we have it, gives a short account of Symmachus, of Boethius, and of Cassiodorus; it has been conjectured from this that the three were in some way related.

His natural pleasure in his own most illustrious family, however, never allowed him to forget his allegiance, first and foremost, to Rome. So we find still another work, called *Chronica,* dull and dry, mostly a list of names of Assyrian and of Latin Kings, of Kings and Consuls of Rome, from the very time of Adam to 519. It flattered mightily the pride of the Ostrogoths, and was published to please Eutharic, consul and son-in-law

---

[1] Mommsen accordingly dated the fragment after 537. Usener, who edited it (*Anecdoton Holderi*) ruled out mention of the *Variae* as spurious and dated it 523, as the latest event mentioned in that case is the consulship of the sons of Boethius in 522.

of Theodoric. The sources on which Cassiodorus relied here were
chiefly the chronicles of Eusebius and St. Jerome, of Aufidius
Bassus, of Victor of Aquitaine, and, more especially, the histories of Livy. Indeed, the principal interest which the
Chronica has for us to-day comes from light it throws on lost
portions of this work, when Cassiodorus from time to time adds
some short narrative to his bare list.

When it comes to contemporary times, it tells that Theodoric
slew Odovacar in fear of attack upon himself, draws another
bright picture of the Gothic King, and ends with a burst of
praise of Eutharic as consul in 519. Marvellous games were
held by him, so grand that even an ambassador from the court
of Constantinople, who was then visiting Rome, was astonished
at the exhibition of wild beasts hitherto unknown in the city.
Special features were brought all the way from Africa, and so
thrilled were the spectators that the show was repeated at
Ravenna in the presence of Eutharic's royal father-in-law. It
was the year in which the Great Schism between Rome and Constantinople ended, after the death of the Emperor Anastasius
in 518. He had kept alive the rift between Pope and Patriarch
by his favouring of the Monophysite heresy, but his successor,
Justin the first, was a zealous Catholic. In the general *rap-
prochement* Theodoric had secured consent from the East for
the succession on his own death of Eutharic to the Kingship of
Italy. But three years before Theodoric departed this life
Eutharic was dead. It was a bitter disappointment.[2]

Even in this concise record Cassiodorus has something to
say of himself. Against the year 514 he notes, referring to the
death of Symmachus and consequent ending of the long quarrel of the Papacy: "Under myself as Consul welcome peace
returned to the clergy and people of the Church of Rome."

[2] *Var.* VIII, 1. For the *Chronica* see Mommsen, *Chron. Min.* II. pp.
109ff.

There remains one more mention of writing from his secular pen: a work which introduces us to another author of Gothic times.

In the letter written for King Athalaric in which Cassiodorus sums up his own services to the State, now rewarded by the Praetorian Prefecture, he remarks: "Cassiodorus led forth from their ancient lurking-places the Kings of the Goths, hidden in long oblivion. He restored the Amals in the glory of their race, showing clearly that we, the Goths, have a royal line extending back for seventeen generations. He made the origin of the Goths part of Roman history, gathering as it were into one wreath every blossom which had once been scattered here and there in the fields of books." [3] The work mentioned before, *The Family History of the Cassiodori,* also tells of Cassiodorus that he wrote at the bidding of King Theodoric "the history of the Goths, of their origin, their homes and their customs, in twelve books." [4]

Undoubtedly, in his desire to unite the Goths and Romans in one Empire, Theodoric thought it well to represent the Goths of a lineage as aristocratic as that of the Romans. He planned to show in written witness that the Goths, too, had part in the glorious tradition of Greece and Rome.

This work of Cassiodorus is now lost. But we may gain much information concerning it from a book written by a disciple of his. This is also in itself of some importance: partly for a romantic cause, as it is the earliest historical writing which has come down to us from a Goth, partly for practical reasons, as it gives us information which we do not find elsewhere. The name of its author is properly Jordanes, as it is recorded in the best manuscripts, as well as by the *"Geographer of Ravenna"* in the seventh century, and by writers of the Middle Ages. [5]

---

[3] *Var.* IX, 25.   [4] *Anec. Hold.* end. Cf. *Var.* Preface, 11.
[5] It was formerly written **Jornandes**.

He compiled from that *History of the Goths* of Cassiodorus, which has not survived, a history which bears the title *The Origin and Deeds of the Goths*, and is still extant. So is another work of his, a brief, dry and unworthy chronicle of Roman history. Mommsen, whose edition of both works is the standard one, has conveniently named them *Getica* and *Romana*.[6]

Most matters concerning the life of Jordanes are subjects of dispute among the authorities. He himself tells us he was a Goth: "No one must think that I have added anything to what I have read and received as true concerning this Gothic people, through partiality to it on the ground that I myself am sprung from it."[7] That seems conclusive. But because the word here translated "on the ground" is *quasi,* it has been thought that he may have been of mixed blood.[8] Mommsen finds evidence for holding him born of one of the tribes loosely known as Goths, dwelling in Moesia and in Thrace.[9]

Of his family Jordanes also gives some account: "Now the Scyri and the Sadagarii and certain of the Alans, with their leader Candac, received Lesser Scythia and Lower Moesia. As long as Candac lived, Paria, my grandfather, father of my own father Alanoviiamuth, was his secretary. Also I myself, although an uneducated man, was secretary, before my conversion, to Gunthigis, also known as Baza, Master of the Soldiers, and nephew of Candac (sister's son). Gunthigis was son of Andag, who was son of Andela of Amal descent." From this we learn that Jordanes was a man of respected position as a secretary (*notarius*), and descended from one who had held the same office. His employer Gunthigis has been identified as son of the Andag described by Jordanes himself as slaying the Visigothic King Theodoric the first, ally of the Romans,

[6] *M.G.H. Auct. Ant.* V.   [7] *Getica*, 316.   [8] Schanz, p. 118.
[9] ed. pp. vif., p. xii. Mommsen suggests he was an Alan; cf. Schütte, *Our Forefathers,* I, p. 70.

in the battle of the "Mauriac Plain" against Attila the Hun in 451.[10]

The words "before my conversion" have been interpreted variously as meaning: from paganism to Christianity, from Arianism to Catholicism, from secular life to the monastic profession, from mundane occupations to an ordered life of prayer in the world, from lay rank to Holy Order.[11] The last theory is more generally approved, and Jordanes is tentatively put down as Bishop of Crotona. For the preface to the *Romana* is addressed to "most noble brother Vigilius," and the Vigilius who was Pope from 537 till 555 mentions in his condemnation of the erring Bishop Theodorus a Jordanes, Bishop of Crotona, who was with him during his exile in Constantinople in 551.[12] The best MS. authority of the *Romana* also describes Jordanes as *episcopus* in the title of the work.[13]

Opinions also differ as to where he wrote: whether in Constantinople while sympathizing with Vigilius, or whether in some cloister of Moesia or Thrace.[14]

The date of his works is fortunately proved by internal evidence. Both were written in 551.[15] The *Romana* was begun first, at the request of Vigilius; it deals briefly with history from the Creation, giving a bare list of patriarchs, and of the kings

[10] *Getica*, 266; 209; Mierow, *Gothic History of Jordanes*, 1915, p. 181; Mommsen, *ibid.*

[11] See Ebert, *Gesch. d. Lit. des Mitt.* p. 557, note 2; Mommsen, ed. pp. xiiif.; Mierow, pp. 5f.; Manitius, p. 211.

[12] *PL* LXIX, 62. Mommsen, adhering finally to Jordanes as monk, does not believe that the Vigilius here mentioned was Pope, as a monk would not presume to write to the Pope "te ad Deum convertas." Yet from a Bishop to the most unhappy Vigilius in exile the words seem fitting in their context: *quatinus diversarum gentium calamitate conperta ab omni erumna liberum te fieri cupias et ad deum convertas, qui est vera libertas;* cf. the ending words: *nobilissime et magnifice frater.*

[13] Inferior MS. testimony in the title of the *Getica* describes him as "episcopus Ravennas." This has been shown to be incorrect by Muratori, *Scriptores*, 1723, I, 189.

[14] Mommsen, ed. p. xif.

[15] *Romana, praef.* 4; sections 363 and 383; *Getica, praef.* 1; sections 104 and 314. Mommsen, ed. xivf.; Mierow, pp. 12f.

of Assyria, of the Medes, and of the Persians. Then come
Alexander the Great and the Ptolemies, followed by the history of Rome in some small detail, both Republic and Empire,
as far as the times of Justinian. The course of events does not,
however, follow smoothly in due order. The sources from
which the writer drew include the Eusebius-Jerome *Chronicle,* Orosius, Eutropius, and Marcellinus Comes. The book
was used as a compendium of history in later times, but need
not detain us a moment.

The *Getica* is worth reading, since its original is lost, for the
borrowed light it throws upon the history of the Gothic race.
Occasionally, too, it has a touch of originality. In the first
place, Jordanes continued the record as his own for nearly
twenty years after the point where Cassiodorus ended.[16] Sec-
ondly, the position of the Goths under Jordanes was very different from what it had been when Theodoric and Amalasuntha were striving for their ideal combination of Romans and
Goths in a united Empire. By 551 Belisarius had done his victorious work in Italy; Constantinople was now far stronger
there than in the day of Cassiodorus. And so the Emperor
Justinian must be glorified by Jordanes even at the expense
of the Gothic race, and the Goths must expect to realize their
hopes under the Eastern Empire rather than under a Western
King.[17] Thirdly, Jordanes lived in the East, not, as Cassiodorus, in the Court of the ruler of Italy. Of necessity, and especially if he did live in Constantinople itself, his work would be
permeated by an Eastern spirit.[18] Nevertheless, even if Justinian was the great Lord, and even if the tone of the *Getica*
did reflect the East, yet Jordanes cherished in his heart one
splendid solution for Italy's problems. Might not Roman and
Goth once more be united, and the glorious days of Theodoric
return, under the rule of Germanus?

[16] Mommsen dates the publishing of the *Gothic History* of Cassiodorus
as under Athalaric, ed. p. viii.
[17] *Getica,* 316; cf. Schanz, p. 116.   [18] Mommsen, ed. pp. xliiif.

This prince at the time was a little child. His father, Germanus, nephew of Justinian, had been expected as successor to this uncle on the throne of the East. He had been appointed, as we may recall, Commander-in-Chief in Italy against Totila; but he had died in 550, before even reaching Italy, and his son had been born after his death.[19]

The preface to the *Getica* tells us that Castalius, a friend of Jordanes, has requested him to reduce to a small book the substance of the twelve volumes of Cassiodorus on the origin and deeds of the Goths. The request is not astonishing. Jordanes consented, but tells us that he had not these volumes before him at the time of writing, and therefore borrowed them for three days from the steward of Cassiodorus to refresh his memory. The *verba ipsissima*, therefore, of Cassiodorus are not to be looked for, though Jordanes hopes he has reproduced faithfully the matter and the spirit of his original. He has made, moreover, certain additions on his own account from Greek and Latin history, and has added "a beginning and an end, and many things *passim* of his own composition."[20]

So he reports. But much of this large claim to his own writing may well be dismissed. Modern scholars have noted the resemblance, too striking to be accidental, between his preface to the *Getica* and that of Rufinus to his translation of Origen's commentary on St. Paul's *Epistle to the Romans*. We may reasonably suspect that most of his quotations from authorities were borrowed from sources second-hand, especially, of course, from Cassiodorus.[21]

Probably he added to his original some geographical details, introduced at the beginning from the authority of Orosius. Then, following Cassiodorus, he glorified by heroic legends and

---

[19] Of course the hope of Jordanes was never fulfilled. The theory that he was writing here a definitely political pamphlet with this aim (see Ranke, *Weltgeschichte*, IV, 2, 315ff.) is not supported by the amount of space he gives to the idea. See Bury, *L.R.E.* II, p. 255.
[20] *Get.* 3.　　　　　　　　[21] Mommsen, ed. p. xxiii, pp. xxxf.

vain imaginings the Gothic race from which he himself claimed descent. The Goths and the Getae he called the same people, also on the strength of Orosius. He identified them, too, with the Scythians, allowing his patriotic pride to see them roaming freely in early days over the modern Balkan States and Russia. According to the story reproduced here, they contended before Troy against the Greeks, they fought with Cyrus and Darius, Kings of Persia. Of the people of the Goths were also the Amazon women and their leaders, Hippolyte and Penthesilea. But we need not trouble to follow the saga by which Cassiodorus delighted the Ostrogoths and tried to soothe the wounded pride of their Roman subjects. We may rather note that we owe to this copying of Jordanes, later on in the work, no mean part of the historical tradition of the Goths, East and West, during the fourth and fifth centuries after Christ.

It is a very simple narrative. It tells of Hermanaric, Gothic King in the fourth century, "most noble of all the descendants of Amal," of his many conquests, of his prudence, and his prowess in war. At length the Huns "blazed forth" against the Goths and brought death to Hermanaric and the submission of his warriors to these dreadful assailants, "more savage than any terror known." Again we find interweaving of classic legend, as Jordanes describes how Hermanaric was sorely wounded by the brothers of a barbarian woman whom he had given over to death by the fury of wild horses, angered by her husband's disloyalty to him. Henceforth the Ostrogoths, the Goths of the East, were obedient for a season to the Huns.

The Visigoths, Goths of the West, in their panic at the coming of the Huns made alliance with the Romans, at that time ruled by the Emperor Valens. Here Jordanes strikes an individual note, in his denunciation of the Arian creed. "Because at that time Valens, duped by the treachery of the Arians, had shut the doors of all our churches, he sent to the Goths preach-

ers who favoured his adopted cause, and they poured the venom
of their lies straightway into these unskilled and ignorant men.
That is why the Visigoths became Arians instead of Christians."
It has been well remarked that Jordanes did not find this strong
language against the Arians in his master's work. Cassiodorus,
Catholic as he was, had no desire to offend the Arian spirit of
Theodoric the Great.[22]

In the record of the fifth century we are grateful for some
vivid pictures, the originals of which are lost to us. One of
these is the description of Gaiseric, the great King of the Vandals, who led his people to invade Africa in 429 and wrested its
northern part from the Roman Empire in the succeeding years.
Jordanes tells us that the Vandals were invited to attack Africa
by Boniface, Count of the Roman Empire in that province,
because he had a grievance against the Emperor Valentinian
the third and could only avenge himself at the cost of the State.
Gaiseric appears here as "of medium stature, lame because of
a fall from his horse, a man of deep intent but few words, the
despiser of luxury, passionate in his anger, eager for possessions, zealous in trying to win barbarian nations to his cause,
ready in scattering seeds of quarrels and in stirring up feuds."[23]
The immediate source is probably Cassiodorus.

The Vandal King was truly a barbarian of deepest dye. We
read that he sent presents to Attila, King of the Huns, asking
him to make war on the Visigoths; for he went in fear of Theodoric, the Visigothic King, whose daughter had been married
to Gaiseric's son Huneric. He had reason to be afraid. As the
chronicle of Jordanes puts it: "Cruel even to his own children,
just for a bare suspicion that she had plotted poison against
him, he had cut off her nose and slashed her ears, spoiling her
beauty, and sent her back in this state to her father in Gaul."[24]
The real reason for this atrocity was that Gaiseric wanted his

[22] *ibid.* p. xliii; *Get.* 132.　　　[23] *Get.* 168f.　　　[24] *ibid.* 184ff.

son to marry Eudocia, daughter of Valentinian the third, Emperor of the West. This marriage did take place, after long delay, when Gaiseric had taken Rome in 455.

Later on there is a detailed story of the descent of Attila and his Huns upon Romans and Visigoths allied. This time Jordanes drew his information largely (through Cassiodorus) from Priscus, a Thracian, who went with Maximin, general of Theodosius II, on a mission to Attila and wrote in Greek a full account of his adventures. Through his diligent copying Jordanes now serves to fill up gaps left in our fragmentary possession of Priscus, and we get an interesting description of Attila himself: "a man born into the world for the shaking of nations, the terror of all lands, who in some strange way affrighted all things by the panic of his fame spread abroad. For he was haughty in his walk, darting his eyes hither and thither, so that his power seemed mightier through his very movements. A lover of wars, but temperate in action, most forceful in counsel, merciful to supplicants, gracious to those who submitted to his rule." His appearance was certainly not attractive: "short, broad of chest, a rather large head and very small eyes, a beard scanty and streaked with gray, a flat nose and a swarthy skin, showing the marks of his race." [25]

The battle of the "Mauriac Plain," in which Attila met the Romans and the Goths, is described with detail borrowed, it would seem, also from Priscus. [26] Here stood Aetius, the great general of Valentinian III, with his allies, the Visigoths, under their King Theodoric the first. Sangiban, commander of the Alans, was placed in the centre, as his fidelity was judged weak-

---

[25] ibid. 182.
[26] Hodgkin (Italy, II, p. 125) prefers Cassiodorus as source here, because of the "Gothic colour of the narrative." But Jordanes mentions Priscus three times during his narrative of Attila, and the elaboration of his record in this part, so different from his usual style, agrees well with the fragments still preserved of the history of Priscus. See Mommsen, ed. pp. xxxivf., and for Priscus, Bury, L.R.E. I, pp. 272ff.

est. Opposite him the centre line of the enemy was held by
Attila and his boldest Huns, though Jordanes drily remarks
that the King took good care to guard himself by taking his
stand in the midst of his best warriors. On the flank were the
three famous Ostrogothic brothers of Amal race: Walamir,
Widemir, and the second and most renowned, Theodemir,
father of Theodoric the Great. Thus Goth fought against Goth.
Jordanes holds them "nobler than the King Attila himself," for
the might of their Amal blood.

And now Attila exhorted his men in a stirring harangue:
"To arms, O Huns! smite the Alans, fall on the Visigoths! This
plain shall see our promised victory. I first shall hurl my spear
against the enemy. Whoever can rest idle while Attila fights,
that man is already dead and buried." Soon blood swelled the
river on the plain, Theodoric was unhorsed and crushed beneath the feet of his own soldiers, Attila was forced to flee to
the slender fortress of his own camp. The battle yielded victory to neither side. Yet, the story continues, on the next day's
dawn "Attila did nothing mean or cringing, but with loud noise
of arms sounded the trumpet and made for attack, as a lion
pressed hard by the hunting-spears neither dares to leap forth
nor ceases to strike panic by its roars." Then the Goths and
Romans held counsel and decided to starve him out from his
refuge by blockade; while he, so they tell (says our author),
determined to set fire to his shelter and perish in the flames,
"that no one might triumph in wounding him, and that the
Lord of so many peoples might not come into the power of his
enemies." [27]

The Visigoths, meanwhile, were honouring their King Theodoric with the ceremonial due to the dead, even in the midst of
battle. His son, Thorismund, longed to carry on the fight as
an act of vengeance, but was persuaded to withdraw by Aetius.

[27] *Get.* 197ff.

This Roman general, we read, did not want to destroy the Huns entirely, as he hoped they might be of service to the Empire later on. Thorismund, then, retired to Toulouse and ruled the Visigoths for a short time in succession to his father, while Attila, not daring at first to put his head outside his camp, after long hesitation "bethought him of the fortune foretold for him of old." Thus encouraged, he sallied out again to the attack, marched into Italy, and laid siege to Aquileia. When the blockade had lasted long and the Huns were growing weary, their King took fresh heart by marking the storks, as they bore their young ones away from the houses of the city into the fields beyond. So would the citizens of Aquileia be doing shortly, he concluded. The omen proved in truth a happy one; Aquileia was taken by a vast effort, and Rome lay open to the Huns' advance.

Jordanes cites Priscus as authority for the story that Attila's soldiers dissuaded him from attacking Rome: "fearing the fortune of their King, and reminding him of Alaric the Visigoth, who did not long survive the destruction of Rome." He was actually hesitating when suddenly Pope Leo himself came out from Rome with a prayer for peace.

The two, Pope and barbarian chieftain, met on the reed-fringed banks of the River Mincius at a spot where "the stream is crossed by travellers to and fro." It was the river Vergil had known and loved. Jordanes does not tell us what Leo said, but it must have been convincing. For we do read that Attila "forthwith laid aside his usual fierceness and returned the way he went beyond the Danube with covenant of peace." Yet he was persistent in one threat, in his ambition to possess himself of the Lady Honoria, sister of the Emperor Valentinian, daughter of Galla Placidia and of her second husband, the Patrician Constantius, who for a brief while was Constantine the third.[28]

[28] *ibid.* 219ff.

The lady herself had stimulated his desire. Out of her close guarding she had appealed to Attila to save her from the hateful marriage of respectable sobriety which was being forced upon her by her family, fearful of her ambitious plots and plans. Jordanes, following, perhaps, his originals, comments briefly: "An unworthy act indeed, to compass her own wanton will at the price of harm to the State."

The retreat of Attila is followed here by a definite victory over his army, won by Thorismund the Visigothic King in a second struggle on the "Mauriac Plain." No other authority tells of this second encounter and we may well doubt that it ever occurred.

Through Priscus, also, we gain in Jordanes a vivid description of Attila's end: "He had taken as wife a beautiful girl called Ildico, having previously wedded countless other women according to the practice of his race. At his marriage festivities he became very drunk and afterward lay overcome with wine and sleep, till suddenly a rush of blood, unable to escape through his nose as on former occasions, poured on its deadly way from his throat and choked his life. So drunkenness gave a shameful end to this king renowned in battles. Late on the next day the royal servants, foreboding some evil from his silence, called to him with all their might in vain. Then they broke open the great doors and found Attila unwounded, but dead through this loss of blood, and the girl sobbing with eyes downcast beneath her veil.[29]

According to the custom of their tribe, his warriors tore their hair and marred their faces with deep wounds, that this soldier might be mourned, not by women's laments and tears, but by the blood of men. And now a marvel took place. For Marcian, Emperor of the East at this time, in his constant terror of such

---

[29] Marcellinus Comes in his *Chronicle* states against the year 454 that "he was slain at night by a knife in a woman's hand, though some say he died of haemorrhage": *Chron. Min.* II, ed. Mommsen, p. 86. Jordanes read his story, no doubt, in Priscus: Bury, *L.R.E.* I, p. 296, note.

a savage enemy dreamed a strange dream. He thought that a god stood beside him on the night of Attila's death and showed him the bow of Attila broken in pieces. This, so Priscus declared, was a true story ; Attila was such a menace to kings that the gods mercifully declared his death to them.

"Let me not," Jordanes continues, "omit to tell briefly how his departed spirit was honoured by his people. His body lay in state in the centre of the plain under a silken tent, and round it the most famous horsemen of the Huns rode intricate measures like games in the Circus and told his deeds in this funeral hymn :

" 'Attila, Chieftain of the Huns, born of Mundzucus, Lord of the bravest peoples, with might unheard of before his time hath possessed alone the realms of Scythia and Germany. He, even he, hath terrified the twofold sovereigns of the Roman State and captured their cities. He, lest all things that remained should be given to plunder, suffered their prayers and accepted from them yearly tribute. Now, having wrought all these things by the outcome of good fortune, not by wound of the enemy, not by treachery of his own men, with no hurt to his people, rejoicing in the midst of his own joys and untouched by pain, he hath fallen dead. Who then would think this to be death? Who would think this meet for vengeance?'

"After they had wept with these laments, they celebrated with high revelry above his grave the funeral feast, the *Strava,* as they themselves call it. In turn they drew together in grief at death, then spread abroad in a common gladness, till in the dead of night they buried his body in the earth. And his coffins they strengthened, the first with gold, the second with silver, the third with the unbending grip of iron, showing by such device that for the most powerful King all these things were fitting : iron, because he had tamed nations, gold and silver, because he had gained glory from the two Empires, of the East and of the West. They added arms taken from those who had fallen in battle, trappings rich with varied gleam of jewels, and emblems of diverse kind devised for honour in a royal Court. Lastly, that the greedy desire of men might know nothing of such great riches, they slew in dreadful repayment those who had been assigned to the work of burial." [30]

Such was the end of Attila, an end of great meaning to the world of the fifth century. Otto Seeck puts it tersely: "Ein unzeitiges Nasenbluten lenkte das Schicksal zahlloser Völker in neue Bahnen." [31]

And now Theodoric the Great comes on the scene of this chronicle: born to Theodemir, so Jordanes says, of a concubine, Erelieva by name. They dwelt in Pannonia, and to Theodemir had fallen the territory between the Plattensee and the Danube. About the year 454, when his brother Walamir had won a great victory by his own arms over the Huns, the messenger bearing the glad news to Theodemir's house was greeted by the rejoicings over the birth of this son. No slur seems to have been cast on his name because of his mother's humble birth. Another authority tells us that she was a Catholic and that her baptismal name was Eusebia. [32] The child was always honoured as his father's heir, "a boy of good hope."

When he was seven years old, Jordanes continues, he was sent as a hostage of goodwill to Leo, successor of Marcian as Roman Emperor in Constantinople. There had been some trouble because Marcian had promised to make tribute— "New Year's Gifts" they euphemistically called it—to the three Amal brothers, and the dues had not been forthcoming

[30] *Get.* 255ff.
[31] *Gesch. d. Unterg. d. ant. Welt,* vi, p. 314; cf. Bury, *L.R.E.* I, p. 297.
[32] *Anon. Vales.* 14(58). Here her pagan name is Èreriliva. Cf. her praises, told by the Bishop Ennodius: ed. Vogel, p. 208; Gibbon, IV, p. 191, note.

at the appointed time. Moreover, another Chieftain, also called Theodoric, son of Triarius, a Goth not of blue Amal blood, had received too much attention from Marcian. So the three brothers gathered their forces and ravaged Illyricum, which soon brought an excellent understanding and the co-operation they desired. Theodoric's father hated to send the little boy, but the strong representations of his uncle Walamir prevailed on behalf of a peace with the Eastern Court.

In Constantinople Theodoric grew up from seven to seven-teen, though by the time he arrived Marcian was dead and the Eastern Court was ruled by Leo the first, "from whom, because he was a charming child, he won royal favour." At the age of eighteen he was returned to his father, laden with gifts, a man able to assert his own power of arms.

It was about 471 that he became sole Lord of the Ostrogoths. Jordanes gives an interesting version of the starting of Theodoric and his people toward a new home in Italy. We saw in a previous chapter that one view represents the first step in this matter as taken by the Emperor Zeno in his eagerness to gain Italy for his own advantage and find a settlement for these threatening wanderers. Jordanes relates: "Theodoric, as he was enjoying alliance by treaty with Zeno's Empire and all good things in Constantinople, heard that his people, now settled in Illyricum, as I said, were neither sufficiently nor happily supplied with needs. So he did what one might have expected of his character, and chose to seek support for his people by his own toil rather than to enjoy lazily the blessings of Rome and let his own race go hungry. After much thought he spoke thus to the Emperor: 'Although nothing is lacking to us who serve your Empire, yet, if your Piety thinks it meet, hearken to the desire of my heart.' And when permission to speak freely had been granted him, as was the Emperor's wont, he said: 'How comes it that the West, ruled hitherto by the governing of your race and your predecessors, with that city,

the Head and Mistress of the world, is now wavering under
the tyranny of the King of the Thorcilingi and the Rugi? Send
me thither with my people, if you think it right, that you may
not only be freed from heavy expense here, but that also, if by
the aid of the Lord I prevail, the glory of your Piety may blaze
forth. For it is good that I, your servant and son, if I conquer,
should possess that realm by your gift, not that that man whom
you do not know[33] should oppress your Senate with his tyrant's
yoke and part of your State with the bonds of slavery. If I
conquer, I shall hold the land of your gift and of your bounty.
If I am conquered, your Piety loses nothing; nay rather, as I
said, it is freed from expense.'

"When the Emperor heard these words he was grieved at
the thought of Theodoric's departure; yet because he did not
want to disappoint him he granted his request and sent him
on his way enriched with great gifts, commending to him the
Senate and the people of Rome."[34]

Thus Theodoric in this narrative went into Italy at his own
petition. Jordanes goes on to tell that he "took away the life"
of Odovacar,[35] assumed royal state under Zeno, and married
Audefleda, a Princess of the Franks. He mentions also a previous union of Theodoric with a concubine, who bore to the
King two daughters, married in due time: one to Alaric, King
of the Visigoths, the other to Sigismund, son of Gundobad,
King of Burgundy. Other record speaks of these girls as the
daughters of his lawful wife.[36]

The reign of Theodoric is shortly told, summed up at the
end with the brief comment: "There was not one people in
the West which did not serve Theodoric while he lived with
either friendship or submission."

As an old man soon to die Theodoric here gathers around him
the Gothic leaders and holds out to them his grandson, bidding

[33] Odovacar.   [34] *Get.* 290ff.   [35] *ibid.* 294f.
[36] *Anon. Vales.* 15(63), where the names are Augoflada, Areaagni and
Theodegotha (known to us as Arevagni and Theudegotha).

them "to cherish their King, to love the Senate and the people of Rome, to serve for peace and goodwill the Emperor of the East next after God." It is only Jordanes who adds for us to the longer story of Procopius the exact detail of Amalasuntha's slaying on her island fortress: "There the unhappy queen lived only a very few days of misery before she was strangled by men of Theodahad in her bath." [37]

His narrative from this point is his own, as the *History of the Goths* by Cassiodorus has now ended. It was his own longing for a united Italy that caused him to hope for her happiness, if only Roman and Gothic blood might be united in that descendant of both races, Germanus Postumus.

The style of this "unlearned" chronicler is simple; some more elaborate patches reveal the borrower. His Latin definitely savours of the early mediæval, with its strange declensions and conjugations and its variations in syntax from the classical norm. Novel meanings are given to words, and at times a loose rendering of the sense is the only one possible. [38]

It is as far from Moesia and Thrace to northern Italy, where our third writer of the Ostrogothic rule awaits us, as it is from the simplicity of Jordanes to the inextricable labyrinth where the reader of the Bishop Ennodius must stumble, picking here and there a little flower of historical value among the rank and overgrown weeds of rhetoric. The very name of this courtly ecclesiastic is anathema among students of this time. Yet it is fair to give him his due; as one of his editors remarks: "In the darkness of the history of the fifth century Ennodius shines as a misty star of the murky night."

His proper style was Magnus Felix Ennodius, [39] Bishop of Ticinum in northern Italy, the modern Pavia. He was at the

---

[37] *Get.* 306.
[38] See Fr. Werner, *Die Latinität der Getica des Jordanes*, 1908.
[39] See for his life Vogel, ed. (preface): *M.G.H. Auct. Ant.* VII. Ennodius has also been edited by Hartel, *C.S.E.L.* VI; for Sirmond's edition see *PL* LXIII.

centre of the learning and culture of his life-time, from c. 473 to 521, and partly through his own energy, partly through good fortune, was concerned in much of its history. For Ticinum was unhappily prominent in the age of Odovacar and of Theodoric the invader, and Ennodius took a leading part in its ecclesiastic strivings. Trouble beset him from his childhood, which he spent in Liguria under the care of an aunt and, almost certainly, in Ticinum. As an orphan he had been brought there from Gaul; for his parents were of Gallic nationality, and he seems to have been born in Arles.

The family was of high standing, and could boast of the consular fasces in its records. We are to imagine young Ennodius drinking in all the grammar and literature he could absorb till he was about sixteen years old and trouble swept upon him again. His aunt died, and the Ostrogoths came down upon Italy, bringing poverty in their wake. There was no money for the lad's education or even his support. Once more fortune smiled, this time in the face of a young lady belonging to a pious and, luckily, well-endowed household. Our student proposed marriage, was accepted, approved, and given comfortable board and lodging in his betrothed's home. However, the rising tide of invasion soon brought bankruptcy upon this happy circle, and a third time Ennodius found himself homeless. In the dilemma he turned to Mother Church for counsel, and was admitted to minor orders by Epiphanius, Bishop of Ticinum. But the Church had no approval for the marriage of her clerks, and his fiancée was persuaded to enter a convent, where, says Ennodius, weak woman though she was, she excelled him in holy vigour! [40] Whether lack of money was the moving factor in his ordination we do not know; his

---

[40] The words of Ennodius (Vogel, ed. p. 304): *quae mecum matrimonii habuit parilitate subiugari,* the reading of its *Cod. Bruxellensis,* which has supplanted the previous corrupt *parilitatem,* might mean that the two had married. Yet we never hear of a wife or children, and Vogel interprets *habuit* as *habuit in animo,* with the resulting sense of *nuptura fuit* (ed. p. vi).

editor thinks probably not. Yet he himself writes in his "Thanksgiving to God for his life": "Thou didst rule that I should perforce be healed of my trouble by the office of Levite, and that the burden of the honour placed upon me should remove the weight that did beset me." This "Thanksgiving," which, as Vogel remarks, might more aptly be called a "Confession," modelled as it is on Saint Augustine, was the fruit of a serious illness which he suffered long afterward in 511. We may dismiss it here with a word, for it is of value chiefly for detail regarding his early life.[41]

Much more important is the *Life* written by him in 504 of the Bishop who first set him on the path of the sacred ministry, Epiphanius of Ticinum. The editors of Ennodius justly call it his best work, and it is of interest for its picture of one of the noblest Bishops of the fifth century. Naturally, its portrait-album is touched up here and there by bright colours of the miraculous. One of its first leaves shows us the little Epiphanius surrounded by heavenly radiance in his cradle at Ticinum, his native city, a sign of the holy life now beginning. At the tender age of eight he was admitted to the office of Reader in its Cathedral by Crispinus, its Bishop. Ennodius describes him as a fair, sunburned boy, pleasant to look on and pleasant to talk with, modest, happy, and wise beyond his years. He was trained in shorthand for secretarial work and did it very well, till at eighteen he entered in earnest the ladder that led to the priesthood. While yet a subdeacon he was assigned to settle a dispute with regard to a boundary of land, raging between the clergy of Ticinum and a certain Burco. Burco's temper got the better of him, and he dealt a heavy blow on the young man's head. Epiphanius was quite calm, but all the people of Ticinum were terribly excited at this sacrilege, and Burco's pious mother looked on her son as already a dead man!

[41] *Eucharisticum de vita sua;* cf. Paulinus of Perigueux, *C.S.E.L.* XVI, 1ff.

Later on Crispinus made him his private secretary and almoner of the diocese. The Bishop felt his strength ebbing within him and secretly longed to train this favoured youth for the ruling of his See. Thus for eight years Epiphanius toiled. He administered the house of the Church without extravagance and without meanness, was reckoned right marvellous in begging for his poor, sternly disciplined his own body and mind, but endeared himself to all by his happy cheerfulness. And so, when Crispinus fell victim to an attack of jaundice, all the clergy and people rushed with one accord to hasten the consecration of Epiphanius as their Bishop. Those who lived in neighbouring cities were jealous, we read, of little Ticinum; *their* Bishops did nothing but glory in the grand-sounding title of "Metropolitan"!

Ennodius pictures the words of the first address which Epiphanius gave the priests of his diocese, assembled in convocation: "Bear my burden with me, and do not think it an insult that a boy in years speaks to men, ripe of age and his fellow-priests, concerning temperance and righteous living. It is our conversation, not our years, which reveals our youth or our age. Do you examine the minor workings of my life, and fear not to admonish the ruler of the Church if you perceive aught that is unworthy." Then all the assembly rose to its feet and shouted as one man, "Hail, noblest Father! hail one and only Bishop! our election showed thee good; thine own words prove thee best of all!"

Then the new Bishop, twenty-eight years old, went home and sat down to make a stern rule of life for these dangerous years of honour. He must never visit the public baths, haunt of impurity, never indulge in luncheon. But lest he should be tempted to boast or be thought a miserly Bishop, he decided that he would dine in company with others, though his nose and his palate were to accept patiently whatever offered itself —except spicy seasonings! His food, so far as possible, was to consist of vegetables, and not too much of them, served with just a little wine, for he remembered what Saint Paul said to Timothy. Then he would get up betimes, he resolved, and be ready in his church for Mass even before his readers, as a good fatherly example. Once there, too, he would remain still and immovable, standing with foot pressed hard against foot till the consummation of the mystic rite. With all this should continue constant service for the poor and only the barest amount of recreation for his health's sake.

His ministry was not confined to his Cathedral and his diocese. Some four years later, in 472, Italy was distressed by discord between the reigning Emperor, Anthemius, and Ricimer, the "Kingmaker," who had lifted him to the throne of the West in 467. Anthemius had been the candidate of Leo, Emperor in the East, and had badly needed a supporter in Italy. No one had been more suited to give efficient aid than Ricimer, and his backing had been secured by Anthemius at the price of his own daughter, married to Ricimer as a reward.

Then the harmony had begun to fail, and failed more and more till it was feared that there would be civil war in Italy between Ricimer in Milan and his father-in-law in Rome. At last the Ligurian nobles came in a great company to Ricimer, begging him to make peace with Anthemius. "But, if I do send an ambassador," said Ricimer, moved by their tears, "who is there equal to the burden of this mission?" Then all the nobles shouted aloud for Epiphanius, "more skilled in persuasion than a snake-charmer or a tamer of wild beasts!"

To Rome, then, Epiphanius went, and all the citizens stared and stared because of his renown for holiness. But Anthemius barked out: "Just like that crafty Ricimer to send such a spokesman to persuade me, after all his insults! Bring in the man of God, and let us see this famous figure." When the Bishop entered the royal presence, the Emperor might as well have vanished out of sight. All in the assembly were soon overcome by his eloquence, and even Anthemius, after bitter complaints, was compelled to promise reconciliation. Epiphanius, his task accomplished, immediately hurried off homewards, for Easter was near at hand. Most of his companions he left behind en route; "they could neither keep up with his fasting nor his energy."

Unfortunately, all was not yet well. Ricimer, in spite of his oath of peace, set up Olybrius on the throne of the West, besieged Rome, and caused the defeat and death of Anthemius. Olybrius in his turn was succeeded by Glycerius, both Emperors of no importance in Rome. But Glycerius has some place in this narrative of Ticinum. Certain of its citizens offended the Emperor's mother, and Glycerius was only stayed from revenge by the calm dignity of the Bishop's intercession.

After a few months Glycerius was deposed, and Julius Nepos succeeded him in 474. Then once more Epiphanius was chosen as mediator, this time in a quarrel between Nepos and the Visigothic King, Euric, whose warriors persisted in attacking Roman territory across the Alps. In 475 the Bishop set out for Toulouse, Euric's capital, in a journey of indescribable hardships. These he increased by his own persistence in reciting the Hours and other prayers, while he halted for a while in the shade of trees by the roadside.

Again his genius for persuasion prevailed. Euric did not understand one word of the Bishop's Latin, but he "growled out something barbaric" and promised by his interpreter to do as Epiphanius wished. He did more. He invited his visitor to a banquet. But the Catholic Epiphanius was not going to feast with Arian clergy, and so he pleaded necessary haste as excuse for declining. Toulouse was almost deserted of its citizens as they poured out to see the Bishop safely on his way. He visited Lérins as he travelled: "low-lying mother of the highest mountains." A sudden radiance in the sky greeted his return to his people. But Euric, alas! held himself released from his promise a year later and renewed his attacks.

We are told, however, that the Bishop's present triumph was too much for the devil, ever restless in his evil mind, and he began to ponder how he could best annoy the holy man. And therefore, so Ennodius declares, he aroused the soldiers of Italy against Orestes the Patrician with secret sowing of accusations and discord. He excited the minds of corrupt men to aim at revolution, and he raised up in Odovacar the ambition of becoming their King. Furthermore, the devil decided to wreak his wrath on Epiphanius by selecting Ticinum itself as the scene of conflict.

Ennodius is especially valuable here, as he adds to our meagre records details of the horror of the capture of this city. When at length it yielded to Odovacar, his men rushed within, hunting Orestes. Grief, panic, and death walked the streets. Churches were plundered in vain hope of treasure, based on the well-known generosity of the Bishop. Noble ladies were seized, among them the nun Honorata, the Bishop's sister. All districts blazed with fire. The citizens to a man fought to protect Epiphanius, and he himself did heroic work. At last Orestes was captured and killed near Placentia, and the tide of ravaging slowly died down into peace.

By Odovacar, we read, Epiphanius was held in special reverence. The Bishop at once began the labour of raising churches where now only ashes remained. He also cared for distressed men as well as broken walls, by sending messengers to Odovacar to beg for relief, and in this way obtained for his people exemption from tribute for five years.[42]

And now, in 489, Theodoric descended upon Italy. Epiphanius went out to meet him in Milan with calm and coura-

[42] Ennodius himself supported Theodoric.

geous front. The King was much impressed. "By this mighty wall," he declared to his officers, "the city of Ticinum is safely fortified. . . . Here a man may well bestow his mother and his family." No doubt it was not only the military advantages of Ticinum but also the high repute of its Bishop which induced Theodoric to settle here in winter quarters, when reverses caused by the desertion of his general Tufa decided him to delay a while his progress into Italy. His barbarians swarmed into the city with their wives and children, bivouacking throughout the houses and even on the open ground. Here, also, for three years the Gothic chieftain left in safety those of his multitude whom sex or age held from fighting. Among these unwelcome intruders the good Bishop toiled as steadily as for his own people, with no discrimination between friend or enemy, till both Odovacar and Theodoric were compelled to respect a breadth of charity that could rise above patriotism itself.

But worse was in store. When finally the Ostrogothic host, old men and children, soldiers and women, had streamed out to a better settlement, now won them by their victorious chief, invaders from the Rugians, a truly barbaric nation of East Germany, occupied Ticinum in their turn. For nearly two years Epiphanius had to endure these marauders, "men," as Ennodius describes them, "who thought a day lost which by some accident had not seen its evil deed." Yet even they were conquered by the Bishop's care for all mankind.

After Theodoric had gained control of Italy, he sought revenge for his struggle of three years by ordering that all who had aided Odovacar, even of necessity, should no longer be allowed to act as witnesses in the law-courts or to bequeath their property by will. Again it was Epiphanius who departed on one more mission of pleading, and again his words prevailed.

Theodoric did even more than remit penalties. He actually

gave money from his treasury for the ransoming of captives, carried off from northern Italy by the soldiers of the Burgundian King Gundobad when they had swooped down to invade its fields. Epiphanius was overjoyed at being entrusted with this errand to Gundobad and promptly set out, with Victor, Bishop of Turin, as his chosen companion. In their company travelled also Ennodius himself on this occasion, and, therefore, he is again a reliable witness here. It was March, he tells us, and the Alps were frozen fast. At Lyons adroit words were spun on either side till the prisoners were freed, and a great multitude streamed back in gladness to their Italian homes. Gundobad had no objection to exchanging captives for harmony and rich store of gold. When the money contributed by Theodoric was exhausted, certain residents of Gaul gave of their wealth, among them Avitus, that literary Bishop of Vienne.

Twice more Epiphanius came to the rescue of his diocese. He wrote to Theodoric asking for help for these returned captives; at another time he travelled to Ravenna to plead in person for remission of taxes in their distress. The petition was granted to the extent of two-thirds of the tribute due.

It was the Bishop's last journey, though none but he himself thought it. At Parma on his way home he was suddenly attacked by catarrh in its gravest form. He paid scant attention to the trouble and hurried on to Ticinum, where the rejoicings of his people soon turned to tears. He lingered a week and then died, a martyr to his labours of charity, in the fifty-eighth year of his life and the thirtieth of his ministry as Bishop.

The *Life of Epiphanius* was written by Ennodius long after he had left the town of Ticinum where we saw him last, working as a humble cleric under this diocesan. He departed from Ticinum for Milan while still a youth in his twenties to serve on the staff of its Bishop Laurentius. These times were exciting for the clergy, and Ennodius now broke out into writing during the Papal struggle of 498 to 506 between two rival claimants for the Holy See, Symmachus and another Laurentius.

Perhaps we had better recall briefly the story of this schism.[43] Upon the death of Pope Anastasius in 498 Rome was distracted by strife between two factions, each claiming its own nominee as successor. The candidate of the orthodox party, which upheld the Catholicism of Rome in all its integrity, was Symmachus, a deacon, born in Sardinia and a convert to the Christian creed. In the Lateran he was elected and consecrated Pope. On the same day, under the leadership of the Senators Festus and Probinus, a minority who held other views elected Laurentius, an Arch-Priest, in the Church of S. Maria Maggiore. These men favoured a closer alliance with the Eastern Church and with the Emperor of the East, Anastasius, by a liberal attitude with regard to the *Henoticon* of Zeno. Over Laurentius, also, a ceremony of consecration was celebrated, and he was held rightful Pope by those supporting him against Symmachus.

In this embarrassment both parties appealed to Theodoric, who, as an Arian, might be expected to prove impartial. The King, after hearing both sides at Ravenna, decided that Symmachus rightly held the Papal Chair, as he had been elected somewhat before his rival, and by a greater number of votes. Laurentius seems to have acquiesced in this judgment, and was given by the victorious Pope the Bishopric of Nuceria in Campania. Some of his supporters, however, declared that the election of Symmachus had been promoted by bribery.[44]

[43] For ancient authorities see also the *Acta Synhodorum habitarum Romae sub rege Theodorico,* ed. Mommsen, *M.G.H.* xii, pp. 416ff.; Duchesne, *Lib. Pont.* I, p. 260; *Fragmentum Laurentianum, ibid.* pp. xxxf., and 44ff.; *Anon. Val.* 17f. Among modern writers see especially Pfeilschifter, pp. 55–111; Sundwall, *Abhand. zur Gesch. d. ausgehenden Römertums,* pp. 201ff.; Vogel ed. Ennodius, pref.; Hodgkin, *Italy,* III, pp. 445ff.

[44] *Frag. Laur. Lib. Pont.* I, p. 44.

That bribery was rampant is shown by the fact that Symmachus called a Synod for March 1, 499, to draw up new regulations against offences in regard to Papal elections.

The peace which followed was short, and strife broke out again between the two parties over the date of the keeping of Easter. But this was not sufficient for the defeated Laurentians, and grave accusation of immoral conduct was now put forward against the Pope. The Court was resident at the moment in Ariminum, and Theodoric invited Symmachus to come there for a discussion of the matter, intending to subject him to a formal investigation in the interests of justice. The Pope went as requested, but never experienced the purposed ordeal; whether reverence on Theodoric's part finally allowed him to return to Rome untried, whether, as a writer on the side of Laurentius declared, the Pope fled in terror before the trial began. The story went that with some of his priests he was taking a walk by the sea and suddenly caught sight of some women travelling past. Immediately he divined that they were going by royal command to Theodoric's Court as alleged witnesses and accomplices of his guilt. He therefore hurried back in the darkness of that night to Rome with one companion, saying nothing to his staff of what he had seen. At all events, the Pope shut himself up in St. Peter's in Rome, and new accusations were brought against him that he had wasted the property of the Church, and in consequence was subject to the penalty of excommunication ordained for this offence by a Synod of 483.

So the Laurentians clamoured that a Synod should be summoned to try Symmachus on the secular charges preferred against him, and that a special Visitor should be appointed to judge him regarding the keeping of Easter at the wrong time. The matter came before the King, who after consulting Symmachus and obtaining his consent assembled a Synod of Bishops. He also appointed a Visitor, Peter, Bishop of Altinum in northern Italy. The Bishop, however, speedily proved a great disappointment; for he showed himself grievously partial to the side of Laurentius. By this time the Laurentians had taken possession of many churches in Rome.

The Synod met after Easter, 502,[45] and held during the year three sessions in Rome, productive of nothing but indecision on the part of these Fathers of the Church, faced, indeed, with the terrific problem of a charge against their Head, the Pope. We may still read, in the official *Proceedings* of the Synod, their petition to Theodoric to be allowed to return home, as unable either to bear further troubles of body in their frail health or to contend in their simplicity any longer with the cunning craft of their adversaries. We have still three stirring remonstrances from Theodoric, the Arian layman, endeavouring to incite these Catholic Bishops to settle the affairs of their own household. On August 27 he writes: "The Church demands peace from her own priests. Before God and men we commit all things to your judgment and absolve from responsibility our own conscience, as is meet. It is intolerable that when by grace of God our Empire is at peace without, Rome alone should not enjoy tranquillity." On October 1st he declares that the Synod should have ended its debates long since. Let its Bishops make up their minds without more ado and give peace to the clergy and people of Rome. It is not for him, he affirms, to law down rules for the government of the Catholic Church. Let them get on with the Lord's business, fearing neither King nor any man.[46]

And so a fourth session of the Synod was called for October 23, the famous *Synodus Palmaris*.[47] This decided at last that

[45] So Pfeilschifter, Vogel, and Sundwall; Mommsen and Duchesne date it 501.

[46] See the *Acta*, ed. Mommsen.

[47] Mommsen (*M.G.H.* XII, pp. 417f), after mentioning meanings of *Palmaris* derived from sites in Rome, *Palma* in the Forum or *ad Palmata*, the porch at St. Peter's, decides that probably *Palmaris* means here "triumphant," as the decisive session after three inconclusive ones.

Symmachus was innocent on all counts, that he was the rightful Pope and should enjoy undisturbed possession of all Church property accruing to the Papal See. The decisions were confirmed by the signatures of seventy-six Bishops, headed by the name of the diocesan of Ennodius, Laurentius of Milan.

On the sixth of November, 502, another assembly of Bishops,[48] held in St. Peter's under the presidency of Symmachus, once again the victor, annulled the proceedings of the Synod of 483.

We come now to the writing of Ennodius. It was put forward in answer to a pamphlet published by the Laurentian faction in the bitterness of their defeat, entitled *Against the Synod of the unseemly acquittal* (*i.e.*, of Pope Symmachus).[49] The document is now lost, but we can gain some view of its contents from this retort which Ennodius gave out early in 503, on behalf of the Bishops who voted at the *Synodus Palmaris*. A complete understanding of what Ennodius or his opponents did or said is scarcely possible; for the gist of this little work, called *A Pamphlet against those who have presumed in writing to oppose the Synod,* lies hidden in a dense fog of ellipses, rhetoric, declamations against the Laurentians, and texts of Scripture, in season and out of it. If only Ennodius had stuck to his sound words in the Preface: "He who makes useful statements scorns fanciful speech coloured by an artist's brush!"

Much of his wrath is called forth in loyalty to the Bishopric of Rome. It was impious, he declares, that a Visitor should be called to the Holy See at all, far more so one caught in the coils of the Laurentians. It was impious that a Synod, even a Synod of Bishops, should dare to bring the Holy Father to trial, even were he guilty: "It may be that God has willed to decide accusations against other men by the agency of their

---

[48] Either a fifth session of the Synod, if dated 502, or a calling of a new Synod, if the *Synodus Palmaris* be dated 501.

[49] *Adversus Synodum absolutionis incongruae.*

fellows; the Chief Bishop of this See of Rome He has reserved without question for His own judgment. He has willed that the successors of Blessed Peter the Apostle should look for proof of their innocence to Heaven alone. By the voice of the Saints the dignity of this See has been revered in all the world. In the words of the Prophet: 'If this be laid low, to whom will you flee for aid, and where will you leave your glory?'" [50]

How, then, did the Bishops justify the Synod? Because, as Ennodius emphasizes, Symmachus himself had given them the requisite authority, and so "he had converted the Laurentian menace into his own desire." It was this alone which had made the Council lawful in the eyes of the Church. So strong was this feeling among the supporters of Symmachus that Ennodius felt himself constrained to devote a special section to praise of the impartiality and justice of Theodoric the King as chief agent in this unhappy affair.

The work winds up with swirling streams of words, in which, first, Saint Peter entreats the rebellious Laurentians to abandon this irreverence in seemly homage to their rightful Father in God, Symmachus. He talks so long that at last he feels obliged to apologize, and is then succeeded by Saint Paul. He speaks only a short piece, for his tears flow too fast. Finally, the Lady Rome pours out the story of Rome, now cleansed from heathendom and glorious in Christianity. The former children of her fruitless womb—Curius, Torquatus, Camillus, and their ilk—are now in the torments of hell, unregenerated of the Church. For nought did Fabius save his country or Decius cover himself with renown; theirs is the same fate. Even Scipio, most observant of human justice, ranks but as a criminal in heavenly count, for he knew not Christ. But in these days of Theodoric the sons of Rome are offering their prowess in worldly

[50] Cf. Hartmann Grisar, *Hist. of Rome and the Popes in the Middle Ages*, II, p. 245.

things for the greater glory of God; thus, indeed, success in this world may redound for grace to their souls. Let not the Laurentians, therefore, destroy the new happiness of the City in this golden age.

A third among these longer writings of Ennodius is a *Panegyric of Theodoric,* composed between 504 and 507.[51] This also is painfully difficult to read, though as a narrative and not an argument its course is somewhat plainer. It is of some value to history in dealing with events known to its writer during his own life.

The picture of Odovacar is drawn, of course, in the darkest colours. "Prodigal of his resources he did not so much expect to swell the treasury by legal taxes as by plunder." On the other hand, Odovacar was afraid of his army; he knew that the soldiers remembered his humble birth and saw him as one not born to a throne. "Shivering with terror he issued his orders to his legions, for obedience rendered to unworthy commanders is uneasily received by them." It is all in keeping with the avowal that Satan himself had stirred up in Odovacar's heart the desire to invade Italy, and must be read as the narrative of a partial panegyrist. It is a pity that Ennodius lacks comparison in his undocumented time.[52] In this description Theodoric started for Italy with his mighty horde, "gathered from innumerable peoples." They camped in caravans by night, and their oxen carried stones to crush the grain they needed for food. Mothers bearing tiny babies, women great with children yet unborn, went forth, forgetful of their sex, all to do their share in preparation of food. The cold was intense, and icicles wreathed the clothing and the hair of the travellers.

On the way the migrant swarm was beset by an army of

---

[51] It does not mention the war between Clovis and Alaric the Visigoth (507), and it ends with the reception of the Alamanni under Ostrogothic rule.

[52] Cf. Dumoulin, *C.M.H.* I, p. 437.

Gepids, and Ennodius tells of a fierce battle by "the River Ulca, fortified by this tribe." [53] The passage of the river was forced in the teeth of the enemy, but the Goths who reached the farther bank were in desperate straits. Then Theodoric, with a shout to his men to follow him, drank off a cup of wine as sign of bold confidence and broke a path through the Gepid barrier.

Odovacar, with "all nations and so many kings," encountered him, only to be defeated at the Isonzo and at Verona. Ennodius draws here another picture of Theodoric, on the morning of the battle of Verona. He was arming himself for the attack when suddenly his mother and his sister came to him, nervous with anxiety, and he comforted them by appealing to their pride. "Bear hither your embroidered robes," he boasted, "the toil of your spinning, and let this battle see me more splendidly arrayed than aforetime on a holiday. Let my gorgeous dress attract the eyes of the ambitious. Let him who knows not my stroke in battle value me for my sumptuous robes. Therein I shall be a mark more to be prized. If men cannot see me fighting in their midst, then let them be astonished at my rich array as I lie before them in death." So speaking, he leaped on the horse that could scarcely wait still, as it heard the cry of the bugles for the start. At his coming the tide of battle changed from hesitation to certain victory, and the soldiers of Odovacar fled for refuge to the River Adige, swollen with corpses and bloodshed from either side. "Hail! most glorious River," cries Ennodius, "thou who hast washed away much of the filth of Italy!" [54]

Soon the pious biographer is confronted by the difficult task of veiling the horror of Theodoric's massacre of the soldiers of Odovacar throughout the land. He actually commends it, as a necessary act in punishment of the treachery of Tufa

---

[53] The river is unknown.   [54] *Panegyric,* c. viii.

and his followers. This officer of Odovacar had surrendered to Theodoric and had gained his confidence, so much so that Theodoric placed him in command of a force of men and sent him into battle on his own side. Then Tufa betrayed the King's trust, and deserted to his former Chief. "You shook out the flag of vengeance," Ennodius declares to the King he is praising here, "and made the people, already tested in loyalty, privy to your secret designs. Not one of your enemies chanced to find out what the greater part of the world was planning with you. A sacrificial act of slaughter was commanded throughout the district far and wide. Who ordained this except the will of Heaven, that the harvest of disasters that had marred the name of Rome over so grievous a length of time by the stroke of one moment should be swept away?" This happy peal of words must have rung very pleasantly in Theodoric's ear.

But the murder of Odovacar and his clan by act and order of Theodoric is swiftly passed over: "All was brought to an end in a war successful as it was fated to be. The presumption of Odovacar was cut off when guile gave him no aid." How, indeed, could Ennodius justify this, seeing that Theodoric had promised to his defeated rival safety from bloodshed? [55]

The last detail of history mentioned here is the settling of the Alamanni by permission of Theodoric in Pannonia about 507. We may remember that Cassiodorus also mentioned this event. It called forth from Ennodius a shout of joy: "Let my King rightly be named Lord of the Alamanni, even though a stranger bear this name." The last words may be a scornful reference to the Emperor Anastasius, who had added to himself the title *Alamannicus.*[56]

This *Panegyric,* as the other works we have noticed, was composed while Ennodius was serving under Bishop Lauren-

[55] Cf. here *Anon. Vales.* 11 (51) and 13 (55).
[56] *Panegyric,* cc. XV, XVII; Cass. *Var.* II, 41.

tius in Milan. Many of the letters we still possess from his pen belong to the same period, though they were frequently written from other places during many journeys. We have two hundred and ninety-seven of these, arranged since the edition of Sirmond in nine books.[57] Writing of letters seems, indeed, to have been the chief recreation of our young deacon, not only for the pleasure of corresponding with acquaintances, but as an exercise in the rhetoric he loved so dearly. He composed them with an eye deliberately centred on form, and his remark in one of them: *lex est in epistulis neglegentia,* tells of an ease entirely studied. His friends were forever receiving these artificial concoctions, with earnest requests for a return in kind. Thus he speaks constantly of his "garrulity," and writes to Avienus, son of his special friend Faustus: "I allow that people have different aims, but my manner of life must unlock the fullness of my affection by the key of speech. I cannot bear that costly silence should creep over my relationships by getting out of touch with my friends. So, if your eminent self is like-minded, let your feeling for me be shown equally by frequent correspondence; let us see many letters."[58] Again to Faustus: "I love much writing;" and, to another: "Silent affection almost points to lack of love."[59] Among his correspondents were men of high rank: Pope Symmachus; Boethius and another Symmachus, the philosopher's father-in-law; Faustus, Praetorian Prefect under Theodoric, and also friend of Cassiodorus and supporter of Symmachus in the Papal strife; Avienus, son of Faustus and consul in 502, the year of the *Synodus Palmaris;* Hormisdas the deacon, to whom Ennodius prophesied his future as Pope;[60] Luminosus, another close friend of Symmachus; the brothers Olybrius and Eugenes, known also to us from the letters of Cassiodorus, both high in official position; Senarius, intimate with

[57] Paris, ann. 1611.
[58] *Epist.* III, 27.
[59] *ibid.* III, 21; I, 23.
[60] VIII, 33.

King Theodoric; Agapitus, a bad correspondent, but an old friend from Liguria, honoured by office during Theodoric's rule.[61]

Unhappily, Ennodius wasted his opportunities in his letters. One soon wearies of hunting in all this chaff for a grain or two of wheat—so much burden of chaff that we find repeated mention of a "private mail-carrier."[62] Personal details, naturally, occur often. The ordinary routine of the diaconate, in which "the loud calls of duty summon me to answer wailings and beseechings,"[63] admitted, he declared, of no leisure for the "flowers of rhetoric." The leaves, at any rate, shot out unchecked.

He tells that he defended clients of Stephen, Abbot of Lérins, in the Bishop's Court at Milan; that he taught rhetoric to young men in the city; that he was deeply interested in its school, presided over by his friend Deuterius. He writes in the manner of a College tutor: "I know you will be so glad to hear that your son is doing even better in his work (*in studiis liberalibus*) than you had hoped"; concerning young Paterius: "I am specially interested in his University training, since I am his godfather"; concerning young Arator, who is about to enter a trial of oratorical skill: "I shall be proud if he succeeds, for, under God, I have taught him all he knows about his art." Avienus, son of Faustus, was a pupil of his, and Ennodius shared with his father the pride of his accomplishments.[64] He was extremely keen about the education of his two nephews. One was Lupicinus, son of his sister Euprepia, who lived in the town of Arles, where conjecture has it that Ennodius and his three sisters were all born. Euprepia was apparently satisfactory neither as sister nor as mother; Ennodius reproaches her for not writing to him, and for neglecting her son. "Your

---

[61] See Sundwall, *Abh.* Kap. II.
[62] *Epp.* III, 6, 13, 14; VI, 21, 36. [63] I, 16.
[64] *Epp.* III, 4; VII, 24; IX, 32; *Dictio* 13; 22: cf. *Opusculum* 6.

mind has become as provincial as the place you live in, and so
I myself must be both father and mother to the boy." He did,
indeed, take care of him, and we have an address: "For Lupicinus on entering the school of Deuterius." Similar attention
was paid to Parthenius, son of a sister who had died. To him
Ennodius was both "parens et nutritor," though the office cost
him no little trouble. It is true that we have among his writings a "Thanksgiving to the schoolmaster, because Parthenius
has declaimed well." But we also have a strong admonition:
"I have heard from your father that you take no trouble at all
about your study. Know, son, that you can never reach the top
unless you keep on working. Knowledge flees on swift wings
from the careless, and you will lose all you have won by your
hard toil." So Ennodius complains to Faustus, to whose care
he has entrusted the lad: *Aetas illa peccatis amicior multos
repperit ad errata ductores.* It is the ever green cry of the
older generation! [65]

Names of great men of the time are noticeable by reason of
their presence or absence. The sickness of Laurentius, Bishop
of Milan, grips his young deacon with anxiety, as much for
his own soul's sake as for the diocese. To Faustus he throws
a question born of a trying hour: "Why *did* you drive me into
this dreadful ministry of Orders?" Leontius, Abbot of Lérins,
obtains from him by request a *Life of Saint Anthony,* a work
of Ennodius similar to all other *Lives* of holy men written at
this time, full of marvels of holiness. Felicitations are sent
Caesarius, Bishop of Arles, on his acquittal before Theodoric
at Ravenna on a charge of treachery.[66] Boethius, it would
seem, was related to Ennodius, and addressed a letter to him,
congratulating him on his writings. Ennodius was mightily
pleased, and wrote in turn a letter of praise to Boethius on his

[65] *Epp.* II, 15; III, 15; VI, 26; VII, 30f.
[66] I, 14; I, 7, and 4; IX, 33; *Opusc.* IV.

election to the consulship for 510.[67] He couples with his compliments a petition. Would Boethius be so very kind as to hand over a house of his in Milan? Boethius is not using it, and it really ought to be in the family. Ennodius would write a lovely letter of thanks (doubtless to remain on record as a published witness to the donor and the writer). Another letter, written in 510, reminds Boethius urgently of the prayer, which by this time he has promised to grant, and begs him to bestow the house as a *sportula consularis*. But both this and a third missive seem to have been equally fruitless. The letter of thanksgiving, therefore, is not to be found, but we do have some very rude verses by Ennodius about a certain Boethius, though they scarcely seem to suit the philosopher! [68] They show the kind of scribbling that amused our young cleric:

> Why bends the sword's taut rigour in decay?
> Why lies the steel inert as flowing streams?
> Boethius has lost his grip today,
> His spear is now a knitting-pin, it seems.
> A dancing-pole *your* pike, my popinjay!
> Quit serving Mars, for Venus holds your dreams!

Another mark of resentment against an acquaintance may lie in the strange lack of any letter to Cassiodorus. We do not know the reason, though it has been suggested that Cassiodorus may have offended Ennodius by opposing the cause of Symmachus.[69]

Certain points of interest to ecclesiastical historians have been remarked in these letters. From their evidence it is certain that money was used to promote the election of Symmachus as Pope, and probable that Symmachus already knew that formal accusation was awaiting him when Theodoric invited him to

[67] *Epp.* VII, 13.
[68] *Epp.* VIII, 1, 31, 36f., 40; *Carm.* II, 132; Vogel, ed. p. xxiv. On the futility of Ennodius as poet, see Raby, *Secular Latin Poetry*, I, pp. 118f.
[69] Vogel, ed. p. xvi.

Ariminum.[70] The attitude of Ennodius to religion appears definitely semi-Pelagian in a letter to Constantius, a dignity at the Court of Ravenna: "We owe it to grace that we are called; we owe it to grace that by hidden ways, if we resist not, life-giving savour is poured into us. But it is of our own electing that we follow the benefits pointed out to us." There follows an energetic denial of the doctrine on grace as taught by the "Libyan Doctor." [71]

It is scarcely worth our while to linger here over other compositions: the twenty-eight *Dictiones,* formal exercises in writing, certain prayers, verses composed for occasions both sacred and secular.[72] Their only interest is to show the mixture of man of the world with Christian clerk in the thought, or, perhaps, merely in the pen of their writer.

A comparison with Sidonius Apollinaris leaps to the mind, and makes one wish we knew more of Ennodius when he had ceased to be a young deacon. Sidonius, the cultured, leisure-loving student of southern Gaul, redeemed his younger years of ease by his faithful labours as Bishop during the encroachment of the barbarians and by his toils and captivity suffered under Euric the Visigoth, when he proved himself a very Father to his people in their need. It would be pleasant to know the same of this churchman of the sixth century.

We do, however, know a little to his credit. About 513 he left Milan and was consecrated Bishop of the See of Ticinum, where Epiphanius had left so great an example of episcopal labours. Two years after his election he was sent to Constantinople with other envoys by Pope Hormisdas, who had lately succeeded Symmachus, in an endeavour to heal the schism

---

[70] *Epp,* III, 10; VI, 16, and 33; V, 13. See Vogel, ed. pp. ixf.; Pfeil-schifter, pp. 57ff.

[71] Förster, *s.v. Ennodius, Realencyk. f. Theol. und Kirche,* ed. Hauck, p. 394.

[72] See A. S. Walpole, *Early Latin Hymns,* 1922, p. 160, for a hymn composed for Ascensiontide.

which now for so long had divided Old and New Rome. A second mission sent him there again in 517, this time with Peregrinus, Bishop of Misenum, armed with similar instructions and articles of faith to which the Emperor Anastasius was to assent.

But Anastasius was partial to the abhorred Eutychian heresy, and when the reverend legates proved firm against his words and his offer of money for their conversion to his way of believing, he flew into a passion and drove them out of his Palace by a little back door. Then he had them placed on a rickety old ship for their journey home, in charge of two officers instructed to prevent them from entering any city. By grace of God they escaped the dangers of the sea, and sent the articles which Anastasius refused to sign round to all the cities they could reach. This greatly perturbed certain Bishops who were in league with Anastasius, and they promptly sent information of what was going on to Constantinople, with copies of the articles which had come into their hands. So Anastasius flew into another passion and wrote with great wrath to Pope Hormisdas: "We desire to order, not to have orders given us." [78]

These were the last years of the Emperor and of the schism. Shortly afterward, in 521, as we learn from an epitaph, Ennodius died and was buried in Ticinum. The epitaph, which tells his praises in eighteen elegiac lines, is still to be seen, carved on a marble tablet of Saint Michael's Church in the modern Pavia. The Bishop was subsequently enrolled in the canon of Saints, and his Feast occurs in the calendar on the seventeenth of July.

His writings, then, tell us something of Kings and Churchmen in his time. They also show that the study of letters was

[78] See Thiel, *Epist. Rom. Pont.*, I, pp. 748ff.; Duchesne, *Lib. Pont.* I, p. 269.

still carried on in Italy under the rule of a barbarian King.[74]
Ennodius was not of those saints and bishops whose consciences
struggled so bitterly against their love of pagan learning; and
the fact that he has left us a mass of material almost unreadable,
curdled with mediaevalisms and swollen with a Latin style in
high ferment, is the fault as much of his age as of his own character. He loved too dearly the schools of rhetoric of these early
centuries. But he also delighted in brave and holy men and
their deeds.

[74] The influence of Vergil has been traced in his writings nearly 70
times. Then come Lucan with ten references, and Terence, Cicero, and
Horace with five each. Of Christian writers he recalls passages from Sedu-
lius and Sidonius. Symmachus was his special model in his letters, and
Ambrose in his hymns. For a study of his Latin see J. J. Trahey, *De ser-
mone Ennodiano,* 1904.

CHAPTER IV

PHILOSOPHY IN THE SIXTH CENTURY

IN THE preface to the eleventh book of his *Letters* Cassiodorus wrote: "After I had ended—and how glad I was!—the twelve books of my little work of *Letters,* my friends made me discuss the nature and virtues of the soul. To my soul I owed the writing of those many letters, and so it seemed proper to write on the soul herself."

Probably Cassiodorus wrote this short treatise *On the Soul* which he calls the thirteenth book of his *Various Letters,*[1] after he had resigned his office of Praetorian Prefect, and after the capture of Witigis in the year 540.[2] In its twelve chapters he assembled the fruit of his study of Claudianus Mamertus and of St. Augustine. Claudianus Mamertus, about 470, at the request of Sidonius Apollinaris and other literary Churchmen of Gaul, had written an answer to the argument of Faustus, Bishop of Riez, that the soul was corporeal. This work of Mamertus had drawn its material from Plato and the Neo-Platonists and Augustine, and had been lavishly praised by Sidonius.[3]

We need not spend much time, therefore, on the argument which Cassiodorus describes here at second-hand. The soul,

---

[1] See *PL LXX,* 1029.

[2] Mommsen ed. *Variae* p. xi. p. xxx. The date appears from the words in the preface of this work; *praecepta regum quae nuper agebantur.* The conquest of the Goths is shown in the words of the prayer at its end: *invidit (diabolus) pro dolor! tam magnis populis cum duo essent.* van de Vyver, *Speculum,* 1931, p. 253, thinks that Cassiodorus composed it before the end of this Gothic reign.

[3] *Epist.* IV, 3.

as created by God, is of spiritual, not bodily substance, able to discern and meditate on spiritual things, which it could not do were it corporeal. As a spiritual creation it quickens its body, which it loves most tenderly, grieving with the body's griefs and rejoicing in its joys. Though patient of suffering, it cannot die, but nevertheless dreads that separation from the body which is known as death. Through the senses of the body the soul learns, gaining wisdom through the body's power of sight, through its hearing of deep and solemn sounds, through its inhaling the sweet fragrance of earth. Sometimes it indulges the body and therefore gives way to sin. But, rightly speaking, the soul is as the sun to its body, vivifying and enlightening it, and when the soul leaves its habitation, the night of death falls upon its former home.

The soul is immortal, as being of a nature simple, not compounded, created in the image and likeness of God. After it departs from the body it enjoys even more freely power of the senses after a spiritual, not bodily, manner, seeing and hearing things as spiritually discerned, released from the burden of the flesh.

They err who have thought the soul part of God; for nothing in God can ever be turned toward evil. Nor is the soul of the nature of angels, for it is united with flesh; neither compounded of the elements, for it is not compound. Its spiritual substance may be illustrated by the parable of fire, which quickens by its heat and radiates a brilliance drawn from the Light that lighteneth every man. The soul is not endowed with form, being without body, and the story of the Rich Man in torment is a parable, meant for the warning of human minds.

The soul is possessed of the four moral virtues: justice, prudence, courage, temperance. These it exercises through threefold discipline: of contemplation, by which its sight is extended gradually to behold sacred mysteries; of judgment; and of memory. It is possessed, also, of five natural virtues: of the senses; of the motive power which drives the senses; of meditation at leisure when the senses are at rest; of natural vigour; and of natural appetite. These five powers are exercised by four means: by seizing, by retaining, by transferring, by expelling. The soul at creation is fully endowed with faculties of reason and spiritual understanding.

Why, then, are infants devoid of understanding, and why do people differ in their powers of reasoning and of spiritual comprehension? This is explained by bodily weakness, as a fire enclosed in a narrow-necked vessel cannot leap forth in all its brightness. Even the wisest man cannot exert his full intelligence when his body is stuffed with too much lunch! Souls, therefore, do not themselves grow in childhood. It is the power of using the faculties of understanding which may and does grow by means of meditation.

Where is the seat of the soul, its headquarters in the body, from whence it sends out its light and power through all the limbs? Some have thought that it resides in the heart, says Cassiodorus. He then gives with much energy the arguments for his own belief that it dwells, seated on high, in the head. For the head is the citadel of the body and the summit. Like mortal fire, we may think that this spiritual energy rises as high as it may. The brain, moreover, resides in the head, and a man can neither think nor act if his brain be harmed. Again, emotions trouble first and most the head, from which their effect passes to disturb other parts of the body. Thus we may think of the soul as on the dais of a tribunal, the ruler of appetites, judge of good and evil.

Cassiodorus leaves in mystery the origin of the soul, crying with Augustine, "Who hath known the mind of the Lord?" He cannot decide the question that exercised Jerome and

Augustine, the wavering between belief in separate creation of each individual soul and belief in souls of children generated from those of their parents. The latter theory, indeed, can explain to him the presence of original sin through entail of guilt, broken by our Lord.

Occasionally in this little work we find some thought of the writer's own contribution. This is not always worth while: as in the derivation of the word *anima* from ἄναιμα, bloodless, of incorporeal substance. But interesting in their way are the portraits of the good and the bad man, especially when we think with Hodgkin that Cassiodorus, no doubt, painted them from his observation in his magisterial office. Bad men are bad either because they do not hold the right faith and are foul with the rust of human error, or because they do not follow in practice the faith they own with their lips. Such a bad man, whether un-Catholic in creed or in character, is always afraid, nervously glancing here and there, ever suspicious, worrying what other people think because he cannot think for himself. He is always busy and never gets anything done. The foulness of his spirit is even palpable to the senses, and the delicate nose of the righteous soul can easily smell out a bad doer in its neighbourhood! So the wicked man can be recognized, too, by the strong spiritual perfumes with which he besprinkles himself to escape detection.

The good man, on the contrary, is always merry and tranquil, lean, of course, and pale through fasting, but strong withal and beautiful. He wears a long beard and speaks quietly and never hurries in his walk. The fragrance of his temperate and humble life delights all he meets; neither the words he speaks nor those he hears call for repentance. He has caught something of the vision of holiness and therefore knows his own littleness, and he loves all men save himself. Such a man converses with angels even here on earth, and miracles attend his work.

The pamphlet ends with a vivid description, based on the *City of God,* of the endless material torment of the wicked and the eternal joy of the redeemed in the world to come. There the damned shall dwell in the city of dreadful night, companying with the demons whom once they honoured. For the blessed there shall be for ever *quies operosa, opera quieta* —a work-full peace and peace-full works—in a blessed Heaven where they shall be wise without thought and shall feel without error. There they shall understand the mysteries of science in one everlasting holiday of happiness; there numbers and geometry and music and astronomy shall at last yield up their hidden tangles. There they shall see the vanity of all vanities under the sun in the true light of day; there they shall know how fruitless were the assaults of those without against God's One and Holy Church.

Part of the prayer which forms the close is perhaps worthy of quotation:

"Lord, since there is naught in us to reward, but in Thee there is ever abundance of giving, save me from myself and keep me safe in Thee. Destroy what I have wrought in myself, and save Thine own handiwork in me; for only then shall I be truly mine when I am Thine alone. Grant to me a road without wandering, truth without doubt, life without end. Grant it to me to hate things harmful, to love things that shall be for good. In Thee let me see my happiness, in myself my grief. Because I am nothing without Thee, teach me to be wise, that I may learn what with Thee I may become. Let me know what I am, that I may come to that which I am not. Without Thee I had never lived, without Thee I must profit nothing by my life; for all things sink to nothing which follow not in the obedience of Thy Majesty. But to love Thee is salvation, to fear Thee is joy, to find Thee is health, to have lost Thee is death. To be Thy servant is nobler than to rule a universe; for by Thee are we made sons from slaves, righteous from unjust, free men and innocent from prisoners held in bond."

The writing is simple, which is a welcome relief. Far greater relief, however, comes from the plain and clear Latin of the one philosopher of this reign of Theodoric who is still well-known to us, Anicius Manlius Severinus Boethius. His *Consolation of Philosophy* has been the meat of souls in distress, of minds in doubt, of editors, commentators and students in mediaeval browsings, all down the years from the sixth century to modern times. It was every whit as popular in the Middle Ages as Martianus Capella's famous text-book on the Seven Liberal Arts, and reaped a far more varied harvest of readers; it is still studied in our times, largely because of its influence upon Chaucer. But it loses some of its interest if it be not seen first in the picture of its own century.

For the name of Boethius has been the centre of many problems, as many as the varied sides of his extraordinary genius. He was skilled in mathematics and in logic, he was a musician and a poet; he was, above all, learned in the philosophy of Greece and Rome. So far all is serene. From this point scholars have started in the examination-paper they have set themselves to answer. Was Boethius a pagan? Or a nominal Christian? Or a convinced champion of the Catholic Church? Was he a martyr to his religious or to his political creed? Or did he fall justly in punishment for treason against his King? Did he write the *Theological Tractates* which have been ascribed to him? Above all, did he compose that confession of the Catholic Faith known as *Tractate Four?*

He was of aristocratic birth and tradition, of the great line of the Anicii, as his name tells. In 487, when he was about seven years old, his father held the consulship, but died not long after, and the boy, as he himself relates, was brought up and educated by the leading men of Rome.[4] Very probably his guardian was Quintus Aurelius Memmius Symmachus, destined to be his chief friend and his father-in-law, whom he describes as "the richest glory of the human race." Symmachus had himself been consul in 485, and it was his daughter Rusticiana whom Boethius married. A worthy lady, it would seem. Boethius calls her "modest, singularly chaste and pure—in a word, the image of her father." [5] Long afterwards she reappears in the pages of Procopius at that crisis in the Gothic War when the Romans were suffering agonies through Totila's siege of their city in 546.[6] This was twenty years after her husband's death, and Rusticiana was living in Rome. She had spent all her resources in helping the worst cases of misery, and now with other Roman citizens and even senators was driven by sheer starvation to beg for a little bread and other necessities from the barbarian enemy. Dressed as servants or country folk they would knock at door after door of the Gothic visitors after these had entered the city in triumph, so pressed by hunger that they could feel no shame. But the Goths one day seized her and carried her before Totila, with the charge that she had bribed the Roman generals to allow her to overthrow the statues of Theodoric in revenge for the fate of her father Symmachus and her husband Boethius. Let her be put to death, they urged. It is to the credit of Totila that he did not permit his soldiers in the first flush of conquest to hurt her or any other Roman woman.

---

[4] *Cons. Phil.* II, 3 (prose).
[5] *ibid.* II, 4 (prose). The story of a marriage of Boethius with a Sicilian lady, Elpis or Helpis, is pure legend.
[6] *Hist. Wars,* VII, 20, 27ff.

From his childhood Boethius was devoted to learning, and as he grew older was looked on as one of the rising men by intellectual and political circles in Rome and in Ravenna. Ennodius, in his *Instruction on liberal culture,* written about 511 for two young friends, Ambrosius and Beatus, speaks of him as a master and model for these disciples: "so young and yet he knows enough to teach." [7]

More significant were three letters written to Boethius by Cassiodorus in the name of King Theodoric. [8] Two are dated by Mommsen in 507 and show not only the high place Boethius had earned at the age of twenty-seven in the confidence of the King but also his achievements in intellectual work at this time. In one of them Theodoric asks him to send a water-clock to Gundobad, King of Burgundy, who has earnestly requested this favour. Cassiodorus writes thus for his royal master: "I know that you understand the inner workings of the arts which men commonly practice in ignorance, for your mind is packed full of learning. From afar you have entered the schools of Athens, [9] you have united in your learning the toga and the pallium, you have turned into Roman doctrine the dogmas of the Greeks. Now, thanks to your translations, Pythagoras the musician and Ptolemaeus the astronomer are read in Latin; the arithmetic of Nicomachus and the geometry of Euclid are heard just as if their writers were Italians. Now Plato discusses theology and Aristotle treats of logic in the language of the Quirinal; you have even restored to the Sicilians their mechanician Archimedes in a Latin form. And more. It is you, Boethius, who have entered into the famous art of noble disciplines through the fourfold doors of learning."

---

[7] *Paraenesis, Opusc.* VI, p. 409 H.   [8] *Variae,* I, 45; II, 40; I, 10.
[9] The words of Cassiodorus, *Var.* I, 45: *Atheniensium scholas longe positus introisti* have been wrongly understood as implying that Boethius actually studied in Athens itself.

The second letter asks Boethius to choose out a player on the harp, requested from Theodoric by Clovis, King of the Franks. Only Boethius could fulfil this office, writes the King, because he is skilled in music. The third, written at some time between 507 and 511, asks him to attend to a complaint from the infantry and cavalry of the Royal Household, who have been defrauded of part of their pay by receiving coins of illegal weight: "Let your sagacity, trained by your learned researches in philosophy, drive out this accursed falsehood from its partnership with truth." This request shows, it seems, that Boethius held at the time superintendence over the domestic payroll in virtue of the office of Count of the Sacred Largesses.[10]

Lastly, Cassiodorus gives us another glimpse of Boethius in the fragment we still possess of his *Family History of the Cassiodori,* the little collection of short notices describing members of his own clan and some "learned citizens" who had distinguished themselves by their writings. Here we read that Boethius "held the highest offices, and was an orator deeply versed in both Greek and Latin"; that "in translating works of logic and in mathematical studies he was so distinguished that he equalled or surpassed the writers of antiquity." [11]

In 510 Boethius held the consulship alone, and twelve years later, in 522, he had the supreme joy of seeing his two sons installed as consuls on the same day. There was a grand procession of Senators escorting the two young men from their home to the Senate House amid the shouting of the people who lined the streets. In the Senate House they sat in the famous chairs of their office while Boethius himself made an oration of praise and thanksgiving to Theodoric and earned great applause for his eloquence. Afterward in the Circus

[10] Schanz, p. 149.   [11] *Anecdoton Holderi,* ed. Usener, p. 4.

the crowd of citizens thronged around him as he stood between his two Consuls, repaying eager cheers of the public to the full by his splendid gifts of bounty.[12] In the same year the King promoted him to be Master of Offices and his cup of political prosperity seemed full.

But even patriotic and public life was not so dear as the meditations of his study. In one of his works he tells his readers of his aim in writing: "If God grant it me of His power and grace, my fixed purpose is this: The whole of Aristotle's writings, so far as they shall be accessible to me, I will translate into Latin and interpret by a commentary in Latin. All the subtlety of the logical skill of Aristotle, all the weight of his moral philosophy, all the keenness of his physical science as contained in his writings, I will arrange in due order, will translate and illuminate in some sort by observations. Furthermore, I will translate and comment on all the dialogues of Plato. And after finishing this I would not disdain, indeed, to bring the philosophy of Aristotle and Plato into some kind of harmony, to show that most people are wrong in maintaining that the two disagree at all points; that, rather, in most matters, and these the most important, they are in agreement with each other. These tasks, if sufficiency of years and leisure be given me, I would accomplish with great advantage and also with much labour." [13]

Of the work on Plato we possess nothing, and we may believe that the untimely death of Boethius entirely frustrated this part of the great plan. In the labours on Aristotle the work at least reached and included the writings on logic, in which Boethius was pre-eminently interested.

But first there must be preparation. He would approach his life-work through the "fourfold gates of learning." The

---

[12] *Cons. Phil.* II, 3 and 4 (prose) ; *Anec. Holderi, ibid.*
[13] Second Commentary on Aristotle's *De Interpretatione,* II, p. 79, Meiser.

sixth century was an age of compendious science, when students craved rather a view of universal learning, carefully and conveniently digested by some scholar, than the browsing for their own sake on the great works of antiquity. Were not these written by pagans? And, therefore, how could such avail for pilgrims following the star of Christianity through the dark desert of this present life? The development of the Christian life, whether in the world or, in its most prized degree, within the hermitage or the cloister, had driven from men's esteem the lingering joy of prose and poetry written by those who knew not the Catholic Church. Far better, surely, 'to absorb in comprehensive form and far swifter manner the cold substance of these heathen works, in order that the knowledge thus gained might be used for the glory of the Faith, not for the intellectual delight of the human mind.

Moreover, pagan ideals and Christian virtues were diametrically opposed. The old Latin tradition of independence, self-respect, and a sane enjoyment of this world's bounty could not be reconciled with a training in self-abnegation, in ascetic renunciation of temporal things for the fruits of eternity.[14]

Already in the days before Christ the condensing of science in encyclopaedic form had been begun. In the welter and hurry of political life the rising statesmen of Caesar's Rome, who were also her students, had gladly turned to Varro's *Nine Books of Disciplines,* dealing with the seven liberal arts as we know them and in addition with medicine and architecture. The two last were omitted in the far more famous handbook of Martianus Capella, written in the fifth century under form of an allegory to describe the "Nuptials of Mercury and the Lady Philology." Here the seven liberal arts

[14] See *s.v. Education, Encyc. Brit.*[14], p. 975.

attend the bride as maids of honour, and each in turn expounds the principles of her department of learning. Neither was this book of Christian character, though perforce it was eagerly read by Christian schools for the training of scholars who were to argue with skill and reason for the faith within them.

Boethius, then, was in sympathy with his age when he desired to educate young men in the liberal arts. We shall see later on that his friend Cassiodorus pursued the same ideal in the labours for education which filled his advanced years. But it was on the four arts which afterwards formed the higher division of culture among Renaissance scholars that Boethius chose first to write. The study of these would presuppose some acquaintance with the other three: the art of grammar, including literature, the art of dialectic, mainly concerned with logic, and the art of rhetoric, embracing composition both written and oral. To the influence of Boethius was due in great part the establishing in later days of the four arts of the higher course as an integral and fixed part of liberal education. It was to him, indeed, that we owe the famous name of this fourfold training: in arithmetic, music, geometry, and astronomy. "Among all the scholars in ancient days," he boldly declared, "who were renowned for reasonings of pure intellect as disciples of Pythagoras, it is certain that no one reached the height of perfection in the schools of philosophy except he had sought such noble prudence by what I may call a fourfold path (*quodam quasi quadruvio*). . . . By this fourfold path the student must travel whose mind, already endowed with promise, rises from the natural senses to the surer certainties of intelligence." [15] The name "Quadrivium" thus runs back to Boethius.

He began his work naturally with a treatise on arithmetic,

[15] *De institutione arithmetica*, I, 1, pp. 7 and 9, Friedlein.

"the first-fruits of my labour," he himself tells us.[16] It was
dedicated to Symmachus, to whose fatherly criticism he
earnestly commended his toil. There is little trace of originality in any part of the work on the "Quadrivium," and in
this first section the source was the Greek mathematician,
Nicomachus of Gerasa (probably the city in the Decapolis
of Palestine). Some time between 50 and 150 A.D. Nicomachus had won lasting fame by his *Introduction to Arithmetic,* and he was the obvious model for one who, like
Boethius, was no master in the field. So closely did Boethius
follow his lead that scholars have not hesitated to call this
Latin treatise a translation. And worse still, severe criticism
has been dealt him for marring his rendering by the repeated
omission of valuable portions of the original.[17] He declared
in the Preface that he was not "binding himself by the most
narrow law of translation but was roaming freely in the path,
not in the actual footprints" of his source, intending to con-
dense parts of his material and in other parts to make small
additions. This plan he carried out, though it is agreed that
the additions were of little, if any, value to later generations;
and his work only interests us here because through it many
of his own countrymen, and the vast majority of students of
mathematics in the Middle Ages, learned Greek principles
of arithmetic.

The same is true with regard to music, on which Boethius
wrote a treatise, *De Institutione Musica,* in five books, the
last of which lacks eleven chapters in its present state. Music,

[16] *ibid.* p. 5. For theories regarding this matter of chronology see
S. Brandt, *Philologus,* LXII, 1903, pp. 141ff. 234ff.; A. P. McKinlay,
H.S.C.P. XVIII, 1907, pp. 123ff. McKinlay, for instance, taking the evidence of style as test of date, believes that the *Arithmetic* and the *Music*
"were not written first of Boethius's works nor together."

[17] See the detailed discussion by M. Cantor, *Vorlesungen über Geschichte der Mathematik,* I,[4] 1922, pp. 579f., concluding: "Sein Grie-
chisch reichte aus zur Übersetzung, seine Mathematik nicht." For defence
of Boethius see *Nicomachus of Gerasa: Introduction to Arithmetic,* translated by Martin L. D'Ooge with studies in Greek arithmetic by Frank E.
Robbins and Louis C. Karpinski, pp. 132ff.

he begins, holds its special power, not only over the intellect, but over the character and behaviour of men of every age of life and of every class and race. That, therefore, which is of such universal importance, for which humanity possesses a natural affection, must not only be enjoyed from without, but must be learned and understood in its inner rhythms and harmonies. It must be learned, moreover, as a philosophical and mathematical science. Of the three classes into which Boethius divided students of music: those who play upon instruments, those who compose tuneful melodies, and those who understand the theory and harmony of this subject, only the third class, according to him, really deserves the name of musician. Those who play musical instruments are but the servants of scholars of musical science in his view, and composers of tunes are led, not by speculation and reasoning, but by some natural instinct.[18]

It was this stress upon music, as training in mathematics rather than as a practical art, which Boethius bequeathed to the Middle Ages. Martianus Capella had handed on the teaching of Aristides Quintilianus; Boethius summarized as best he could the wisdom in matters musical of Pythagoras, Claudius Ptolemaeus, Aristoxenus, and Nicomachus, whom he had used for his arithmetic. At times, it is true, he misunderstood his authorities, and so theoretical was his treatment that he tarried in his discussion to deal with matter long obsolete in actual practice.[19] But this legacy of his was meat and drink to humanity long after his death, prescribed by statutes of Europe's Universities as part of their fixed course of higher learning.[20]

[18] *De instit. musica,* I, 34.
[19] See Guido Adler, *Handbuch der Musikgeschichte,* 1924, pp. 30; 95ff.
[20] Rashdall, *Universities of Europe,* ed. Powicke and Emden, 1936, III, p. 155; Paul Abelson, *The Seven Liberal Arts,* pp. 128ff. The study was continued at Oxford till the eighteenth century: Rand, *Founders of the Middle Ages,* 1929, p. 147.

The next treatise of Boethius in logical order, that on geometry, has enjoyed its own dispute. Scholarship has been divided as to whether two books on geometry which we still possess under the name of Boethius are really by him. The consensus of opinion now holds them spurious.[21] That Boethius did translate Euclid into Latin we know from Cassiodorus,[22] and, indeed, Greek scholarship was naturally his model; Roman experts were not interested in the theory of geometrical mathematics and only used the science for practical purposes of surveying land. The question of the authenticity of the extant work in two books is of interest in connection with that noted mathematician of the tenth century, Gerbert, afterward Pope Sylvester the second. For this work, whether genuine or spurious, contains information regarding the nine Hindu numerals. If it was Boethius who told of these, they must have been known to the western world in the sixth century, perhaps before. If Boethius did not write the books, it would seem that these numerals were not known to the Christian world, at least outside trading circles, before the time of Gerbert, who was well acquainted with them. Gerbert tells, in a letter written by him as Abbot of the monastery of Bobbio in 983 A.D., that he has found "eight volumes of Boethius on astrology, and also some splendid books on geometry." If these were the work of Boethius, as has been thought, Gerbert could have obtained his knowledge of the matters mentioned above from him, as this knowledge is found in no other European authority before the end of the tenth century. But that Boethius was not the author is the more likely theory.[23]

[21] This work, under the title *Geometria quae fertur Boetii,* was included by Friedlein in his edition of 1867. Cantor, *op. cit.* ed. 4, 1922, pp. 587f., concludes that Boethius was not the author. See also Bubnov, *Gerberti Opera Mathematica,* 1899, pp. 161–196, and other authorities given in Schanz. Bubnov has given a number of fragments as relics of the real work, pp. 161ff.

[22] *De art. ac disc. liberal. litt. PL* LXX, col. 1213. Cf. also *Var.* I, 45.

[23] Bubnov, pp. 155ff., 188ff.; Letter 8 of Gerbert, Bubnov, pp. 99f.; Smith and Karpinski, *The Hindu-Arabic Numerals,* 1911, ch. V.

No eight books of Boethius on "astrology," or, as we should call it, "astronomy," [24] are extant, though from the importance which he attributes to the study of all four divisions of his "Quadrivium" it is highly probable that he did complete his introduction to philosophy by a treatise on this subject.[25] We have seen, also, that Cassiodorus writes of a translation of Ptolemaeus the astronomer, made by Boethius from Greek into Latin.[26]

We have now passed through the fourfold outer courts of mathematical science and can look at the more direct interests of Boethius in philosophy. Now, when he begins his labours in earnest, it is logic, above all, that attracts him. And, therefore, in accordance with his aim, he turns to the *Organon* of Aristotle. Here, again, problems have engaged students of his writings. Did he translate all or only the greater part of the *Organon?* And what knowledge did the Middle Ages have of his work?

For the benefit of those to whom the name of Aristotle is more familiar than his works, we may note that *Organon,* meaning "instrument" of scientific knowledge and argument, was the title given long after Aristotle's time to the collection of the following writings by him: *Categories; On Interpretation; Topics; Sophistici Elenchi; Prior* and *Posterior Analytics.*

From his own words we learn that Boethius was occupied with the *Categories* of Aristotle in the year of his consulship, 510. For he writes at the beginning of the second book of his Latin rendering of this work: "And if the burdens of consular office hinder me from devoting all my leisure and all my labour to these studies, yet to instruct citizens in this

---

[24] Bubnov, pp. 99ff.; Havet, *Lettres de Gerbert,* p. 6. On p. 118 he suggests that there may be a mention in Gerbert's Letter 130—written to the monk Rainardus—of this same work of Boethius.

[25] *De instit. arithm.* I, 1: *Quibus quattuor partibus si careat inquisitor, verum invenire non possit.*

[26] *Var.* I, 45; my page 149.

doctrine does seem to be part of a magistrate's care for the State. Nor should I deserve ill of my fellow-countrymen if, seeing that the vigour of early times transferred to this One City of ours the rule and governing of other states, I should at least do my part in informing the manners and morals of our City by the methods of Greek philosophy." [27] Translation alternated with comment in the four books which Boethius gave to this task.

The *De Interpretatione* of Aristotle was translated and expounded by Boethius in two commentaries: the first, comparatively brief and simple, in two books; the second, intended for those who wished to go more deeply into the subject, in six books. The chief sources on which he drew in this second commentary were the Aristotelian scholars Porphyry, whom he calls elsewhere a "man of the highest authority," and Syrianus.[28] He tells us, moreover, in the midst of the second work that he is making an abridged edition of it. If he ever did, it is now lost to the world.[29] This second commentary is regarded through its learning and intellectual power as the high-water mark of the labours of Boethius on logic.

The influence of Porphyry lies also on another work of Boethius, which, again, took two forms. The first was a commentary on a translation which the rhetorician C. Marius Victorinus had made of Porphyry's *Introduction* (*Isagoge*) to the *Categories* of Aristotle. We are given to suppose in the beginning of this commentary [30] that it is winter-time, and that Boethius and a student friend of his are enjoying a vaca-

---

[27] *PL* LXIV, col. 201. That some of the work of Boethius on Aristotle was accomplished before 510 is indicated by Cassiodorus, *Var.* I, 45, dated in 507.

[28] Commentary I, Preface, p. 31, 6 Meiser; Commentary II, Preface, p. 7, 5 Meis.; bk. IV, 10, p. 321, 20 Meis.; *De syll. cat. PL* LXIV, col. 814 C.

[29] Comm. II, bk IV, 9, p. 251, 9 Meis.

[30] Brandt, *Philologus*, LXII, p. 152 (cf. ed. Schepss-Brandt, *C.S.E.L.* XLVIII, p. xxix), places this earliest of the logical writings of Boethius, after the writings on the "quadrivium."

tion in the "mountains of Aurelia." [31] As the north wind howls outside the house they settle down comfortably before the fire to entertain themselves by trying to unravel the knotty tangles of dialectics. "Now we have made all our Christmas calls and done our duty to our families," young Fabius pleads, "can't we have a real holiday? Won't you please keep your promise and explain to me what that frightfully learned Victorinus meant in his translation of Porphyry's *Introduction?*"

So in those good old days Boethius and his undergraduate gladly whiled away two evenings in philosophical chat. The dialogue is given here in two books, one for each evening.

Not content with this exposition, some time afterward Boethius made a much longer commentary on the same *Introduction* of Porphyry. This time he accomplished five books of interpretation, and in his zeal for clearness and accuracy made for their basis his own translation of Porphyry's Greek. It was a very close and literal rendering and somewhat wounded his literary conscience, though his scientific mind felt that the charm of words must be ruthlessly disregarded in dealings with logic. His decision must have comforted many since his day! Continuous narrative in this work replaces the easier form of dialogue, and the interpretation is intended for students far more advanced than young Fabius. At its beginning Boethius maintains that logic is indeed part of philosophy. [32]

One more labour of annotation remains for our Boethius. This is a commentary made by him on the *Topica* of Cicero, a work on rhetorical questions. The commentary, as we have it, is incomplete. Only five books and the greater part of a

---

[31] Perhaps, as Brandt suggests (ed. p. viii), in some country-house near the *Via Aurelia*.

[32] *Edit. secunda*, I, c. 1, p. 135; c. 7, p. 154, Schepss-Brandt. On Boethius on logic as part of philosophy see L. Baur, *D. Gundissalinus: De divisione philosophiae*, p. 289.

sixth are to be found, though Boethius states clearly elsewhere that he "sweated over his seven books." [33] He aimed
in this work to supplement another commentary on the same
Topica, made by the same Marius Victorinus.

But Boethius was not only translator and commentator.
We have a whole series of independent works of his, mostly
dealing with his beloved logic: *On the Categorical Syllogism;*
An *Introduction to Categorical Syllogisms; On the Hypothetical Syllogism; On Division; On Topical Differences.*
Originality, again, was not the chief characteristic of these
books. So far as was possible, they harked back to Aristotle,
to Porphyry, to Theophrastus, Eudemus, Themistius and
Cicero. [34] At the beginning of the *On the Hypothetical Syllogism* there are some pleasant words on the joy of sharing the
fruits of one's research with a friend, though the friend
addressed here is unknown to us. Nothing lay to hand in
Latin on this difficult subject, and a clear-minded sympathy
must have been gladness untold.

So much, then, for the Boethian logical *corpus* as we have
it, duly certified. References in some of his extant works
point to other writings of his, now lost to us, and still others
have been wrongly listed under his name. [35]

Before we discuss the appearing of the other parts of Aris-

---

[33] *De diff. top. PL* LXIV, col. 1173 C. The text is found *ibid.* coll.
1039ff.

[34] For texts see *PL* LXIV. For a detailed account of these logical
treatises of Boethius see Carl Prantl, *Geschichte der Logik im Abendlande,*
I, 1855, pp. 679ff.

[35] Among his lost works are: *On Physics (Comm.* II on *De interpr.* p.
190, 13 Meiser); *On Mechanics* (Cass. *Var.* I, 45, 13 Momm.); *Cate-
gorica Institutio (De syll. hyp. PL* LXIV, 834 B, 835 A); *De ordine
Peripateticae disciplinae (De divis. ibid.* 882 D). The following, assigned
to Boethius in Migne, are not by him: *De definitione (PL* LXIV, 891ff.),
by C. Marius Victorinus (cf. John of Salisbury, Webb, ed. *Meta.* p. 147);
De unitate (PL LXIII, 1075ff.), by Dominic Gundisalvi of the 12th century (ed. P. Correns, *Beiträge zur Gesch. der Philosophie d. Mittelalters,*
I, 1, 1891). The *De rhetoricae cognatione* and the *Locorum rhetoricorum
distinctio* consist merely of excerpts from the *De differentiis topicis.* See
Schanz and Bardenhewer V, *s.v.* Boethius.

totle's *Organon* in Latin translation, it will be necessary to turn for a moment to the tradition of Aristotle's works. Only two of his treatises on logic, the *Categories* and the *On Interpretation,* were in general use in the eleventh century, and these not in their original Greek, but in the translations of Boethius.[36] These, and the original works of Boethius on logic, with the work done by him on Porphyry's *Isagoge,* and the books of Marius Victorinus, with, also, the legacies left to scholars by Augustine, by the Pseudo-Augustine, by Martianus Capella in his *Nuptials of Mercury and Philology,* by Cassiodorus and by Isidore of Seville, in writings which held most valuable matter from works of Aristotle, lost since the time of these borrowers, made up for this time the sum in practice of its library on logic. Two-fifths alone, then, of the *Organon* were known fully or generally to students during the lapse of centuries, as Abelard in his *Dialectica,* written about 1121, bears mournful witness.[37] Subsequent scholarship described this two-fifths as the *Logica Vetus,* the "Old Logic." The remaining three parts of Aristotle's *Organon*— the *Topics,* the *Sophistici Elenchi,* and the *Analytics, Prior* and *Posterior,* were still in any complete form, either in Greek or Latin, generally unknown in the first two decades of the twelfth century.[38]

We may trace to two sources the introduction, a little later on in this same century, of these remaining parts, called in distinction the *Logica Nova,* the "New Logic." One source centred in Toledo of Spain, whither Arabs had carried the writings of Aristotle in Arabic version. There, from about

---

[36] There were doubtless some Greek texts, as of the *Categories,* in the monastery of Bobbio in the 10th century (Hauréau, *Hist. de la phil. scolastique,* I, p. 217, note), but a knowledge of Greek was generally wanting.

[37] Abelard knew most, if not all, of the *Organon* before he died: Rashdall (ed. Powicke and Emden) I, p. 350.

[38] Abelard: *Dialectica, Ouvrages inédits,* Victor Cousin, 1836, p. LI, p. 228; Prantl II [2], pp. 100f.; J. G. Sikes, *Peter Abailard,* 1932, pp. 272ff.

1135 onward, scholars, attracted by this rich treasure, were busily engaged in translating many of Aristotle's works on logical and on physical science.[39]

Yet before this time the "New Logic" had come into the hands of scholars in the West. Under the year 1128 we find inserted in the chronicle of Robert de Torigny, Abbot of Mont Saint Michel, a statement that "James the Clerk of Venice translated from Greek into Latin and annotated some books of Aristotle: namely, the *Topica,* the *Analytica (Priora* and *Posteriora),* and the *Elenchi,* although there was available an older translation of these books." [40]

Is this older version that of Boethius, and, if so, what had become of it since it was made in the sixth century? And was the version of these three works which was used by the later Middle Ages the genuine work of Boethius himself?

Some critics are of the opinion that the version which was circulated in later mediaeval days as the work of Boethius was not really by him. James of Venice, they believe, was its author.[41] On the other hand, the theory that the translation of these three books used by scholars of the twelfth century onward was, indeed, the genuine work of Boethius finds support from Charles Homer Haskins.[42] He has brought forward a piece of evidence from a thirteenth century manuscript in the library of the chapter of Toledo. This manuscript contains three different renderings into Latin of the *Analytica Posteriora:* one from the Arabic, and the one current under the name of Boethius, and another not found elsewhere, so far as we know. A preface accompanies this last version, in which we are told that the writer, whose name is not given,

[39] Sandys, *Hist. Class. Schol.* I [3], pp. 527, 561f.; Haskins, *Studies in the History of Mediaeval Science,*[2] 1927, pp. 1ff.

[40] Pertz, VI, p. 489. On this evidence see Haskins, c. XI.

[41] M. Grabman, *Die Gesch. d. scholastischen Methode,* I, 1909, p. 150, following J. Schmidlin; cf. Bardenhewer, V, p. 254.

[42] For the following see Haskins, *ibid.* pp. 228ff.

has been invited to make a translation of the *Posteriora*. "For the translation of Boethius which we have is incomplete and its text is bad. Moreover, professors in France say that although they do possess a translation and commentary by James, yet this translation is little used and they do not dare to employ it in their lectures." This was due, no doubt, to the difficulties of the poor text.

This Preface bears witness to the version of James of Venice, to a lack of its use, and to the existence of an older text, here definitely assigned to Boethius.' From evidence given us by Boethius himself we may believe that he did translate the *Analytica*, as he twice refers to such a rendering, mentioning expressly both the *Priora* and the *Posteriora*.[43] He also speaks repeatedly of his *"Analytics,"* in such terms as *in Analyticis nostris* and *in Analyticis diximus*, which seems to point to a commentary by him on this work,[44] and he mentions a translation and a commentary made by himself for the *Topica*.[45] Not one of these commentaries has come down to us, and there is no reference to either translation or commentary for the *Sophistici Elenchi* in any work assigned to Boethius. Since, however, as soon as the treatises of the *New Logic* gained currency in Latin form early in the twelfth century, they were regularly known under the name of Boethius, and since later writers, such as John of Salisbury, in quoting a Latin translation as "of Boethius" used a version similar in the parts quoted to that printed by Migne, we may think, not without reason, that we still have in the *Patrologia* the rendering, much corrupted in places, which Boethius

[43] *PL* LXIV, *Commentary* on Cicero's *Topica*, 1051 B; *De diff. top. ibid.* 1184 D.

[44] *PL* LXIV, *De syll. categ.* 812 A, 822 B, 830 D, and under the title *Resolutoria* (see LXIV, 539 D), 816 B, 816 C. See Brandt, *Philologus*, LXII, p. 250, for all references.

[45] *PL* LXIV, *Comm. on Cic. Top.* 1051 D, 1052 B; *De diff. top.* 1173 C, 1191 A, 1193 D, 1216 D.

made of the three works in question, in spite of the necessity
of assuming that it was not used from the sixth till the twelfth
century. Possibly it was discarded for this long period through
discouragement on account of its bad text and through lack
of interest in the higher branches of dialectic.[46]

So much for the purely philosophical works of Boethius.
As an original authority on logic he has little claim for renown. He founded no new school. He has even been blamed,
with Martianus Capella and Cassiodorus, for much of the
blundering of the logic of the Middle Ages.[47] Yet his worth
is inestimable for his tradition of Aristotle, both by direct
translation and by quotation and interpretation in those
"original" works in which he depended so greatly upon
Porphyry and other Greek exponents of Aristotle. Without
Boethius Aristotle would have been lost to the West in the
Dark Ages before the revival of learning in the twelfth century. As we have seen, their knowledge of the "Old Logic"
was derived in pre-eminent degree from his work; the introduction of the "New Logic" into the West was due at first,
we may think, to his labours, re-appearing after long lapse
of time.[48] As has often been remarked, he was the last of the

---

[46] Other details regarding the treatises of the "New Logic" may be
repeated here for the sake of clearness. Otto of Freising (died 1158) first
introduced, we are told, the *Topics, Analytics* and *Sophistici Elenchi* to
Germany (Pertz XX, p. 451); Gilbert de la Porrée (died 1154) refers to
the *Analytica* as available for students (*PL* CLXXXVIII, 1268); Thierry
of Chartres in his *Heptateuchon* (circ. 1141) treats of the whole *Organum*
except the *Anal. Post.*; John of Salisbury in his *Metalogicon* (1159) deals
with the whole *Organum*, including all the works of the "New Logic."
C. Webb, editor of John of Salisbury, cites the Latin version of Aristotle
commonly used by John as the work of Boethius "without qualm," and
notes that the *Thesaurus* does the same (ed. *Policraticus*, p. XXVII). John
mentions a "nova translatio" (*Meta.* II, 20, ed. Webb, p. 111), we do
not know by whom, and at times quotes from a version different from
that in Migne (see Webb, ed. *Pol.*, pp. XXIIIf. and also in *John of Salisbury, Great Mediaeval Churchmen Series*, pp. 159f.). For details given
above see Prantl, II², pp. 105f.; Haskins, *Mediaeval Science²*, p. 226.
[47] Prantl, I, pp. 680f.
[48] P. Mandonnet, *Siger de Brabant*, 1911, c. 1, pp. 7ff.

Romans to hand on from his own familiar knowledge of their original the great wealth of the Greeks in science logical and mathematical; in a way worthy of his great predecessor Cicero he brings to an end the direct transmission by the Romans of their magnificent inheritance of culture. The barbarian races who occupied Italy knew no Greek and depended, when they know of things Greek at all, upon a Latin intermediary.

But, in his pre-occupation with Aristotle and logic, Boethius meant far more to Churchmen of the earlier Middle Ages than did Cicero. For logic, or dialectic, as it was commonly called, was a safe and valuable instrument for the Christian pilgrim in this naughty world. Study of pagan writings on other branches of philosophy, arguing of God and His dealings with men, of men and their dealings with one another, was regarded as waste of time, or worse, in this Christian era. Far better to elevate the soul, if not the mind, by studying and digesting the countless miracles laid to the credit of saintly prayers, or heroic deeds of austere life. The devil surely lurked in pages written on ethics and moralities by heathen philosophers, waiting to ensnare the unwary by his bait of delicate words. Logic was impersonal and far removed from charm of style. Moreover, it sharpened the intellect for battle against the adversaries of the Lord. A weapon was a weapon, whether used for good or for evil, and a Christian must fight well-armed. Further, this armour did not turn its edge inwards against him who used it; for was not Christianity based on ultimate truth?

In a far different way the same result obtained for the barbarian. Logic was far better suited for the young energy of the barbarian mind than the ancient refinements of matter and style of pagan classics. Here was something on which the "new man" could exercise his own mind in argument, easier than the effort of bringing his cruder thought into harmony with an ancient civilization already dead and gone. The subtle ponderings of Aeschylus on Divine justice, of Sophocles on human fate, the rebellious mind of Euripides, the intellectual searchings of Plato and the Neo-Platonists after God, did not specially concern the young students of Gothic and Frankish and Lombard blood, descended from men of practice and achievement rather than of meditation on mysteries. It warmed their blood to argue, as long as the argument was the chief thing rather than abstruse metaphysics.

In either case logic was a tool, whether of apologetics or of education. And Boethius fully deserved the gratitude of all future students, readers of the Latin tongue, for the care with which he shaped this Latin weapon of logic. Roger Bacon remarks in his *Opus Majus* that "alone of translators did Boethius thoroughly understand both the language into which and the language from which he was translating." To the philosophers of the Middle Ages it was one of his great services, and this time an original one, that he made most valuable additions in his translations from Aristotle to their Latin philosophical vocabulary and fixed the meaning in Latin equivalents of Greek philosophical terms.

The influence of the secular science of Boethius on mediaeval times is, indeed, a subject more meet for volumes than for paragraphs.[49] The "Quadrivium" owed far more than its name to him. Its curriculum of education depended on his treatises, as did that of the preliminary "Trivium," the course of the three arts. Of these, whether in England, France or Germany, dialectic or rhetoric required Aristotle, translated or summarized by Boethius, or Isidore of Seville, borrowing from Boethius. In the fourfold courses, arithmetic,

[49] See the excellent discussion by H. R. Patch, *The Tradition of Boethius,* 1935.

music and geometry required Boethius, together with Martianus Capella.[50] In the early years of the thirteenth century the course for the Master's degree in Arts at Paris prescribed in Rhetoric the third book of the *Ars Major* of Donatus and the *Topics* of Boethius; later on we find the *Divisions* of Boethius prescribed together with the *Topics*.[51] At Oxford late in the same century candidates for the degree of Bachelor of Arts were required to have heard once the logical works of Boethius with the exception of the *Topics,* Book IV.[52]

Again, Boethius was both food and stimulant to those who sat in the professorial seats of the mediaeval schools. He gave them both the words they used and the dialectical form of argument in which they expounded their matter by way of mouth or pen. Already in his works the *dubitationes,* the *quaestio,* the *solutio,* so beloved of Saint Thomas Aquinas and the Schoolmen, play their logical part.[53] Already in the eighth century Alcuin was busy with him. He included Boethius among the writers he proudly listed as stacked on the shelves of the Library of his Cathedral School at York. He drew on Boethius in his dialogue, *On Dialectic,* a conversation with Charles the Great, who had called him to preside over his Palace School at Aachen. He taught his pupils there from this same source, and in the early years of the ninth century he instructed in Boethius his monks in the Abbey of St. Martin at Tours.[54]

[50] Clerval, *Les Écoles de Chartres au Moyen-Age,* 1895, pp. 117ff.; 220ff.

[51] Rashdall, I, pp. 400ff. Cf. Haskins, *H.S.C.P.* X, 1909, pp. 75ff. for evidence of Boethius as prescribed in Europe in the last quarter of the 12th century.

[52] Rashdall, III, p. 153.

[53] Grabmann, I, pp. 157ff. He gives here an interesting list of logical terms in the Latin of Boethius with their Greek equivalents; cf. p. 172. See also L. Baur, *D. Gundissalinus: De div. phil.,* p. 351, on the six characteristics laid down by Boethius (*Comm. I on Porphyry's Introd. init.*) as necessary for every reasoned exposition.

[54] *PL* CI, 843; A. F. West, *Alcuin,* 1892, pp. 37, 105.

Among these was Raban, who carried his vast erudition to the School of Fulda in Germany, including his study of Boethius *On Arithmetic*.[55] In Reims late in the tenth century Richer, of fame as chronicler, was listening to the mighty Gerbert disentangling dialectical knots of the *Introduction* and the *Topics* as explained by Boethius.[56] We can imagine Gerbert ever and anon taking up his Boethius on Aristotle and on Porphyry as he passed from his teacher's chair at Reims to his abbey at Bobbio and finally to his Papal See in Rome. In St. Gall early in the eleventh century Notker Labeo was drawing crowds of enthusiastic listeners as he expounded Boethius on the mysteries of dialectic.

Perhaps most famous of all homes of training in dialectic in the eleventh century was the Cathedral School at Chartres, brought into renown by the labours of Fulbert, Bishop of Chartres, who had himself been Gerbert's disciple in liberal studies. Under him and under the three great Chancellors of Chartres who in the twelfth century in turn continued his work, Bernard of Chartres, Gilbert de la Porrée, and Thierry of Chartres, the courses of the *trivium* and the *quadrivium* as expounded by Boethius were carried on from day to day and hour to hour. Fulbert speaks of Boethius as one "read in the secular schools" and quotes his poetry in company with that of Vergil himself.[57] Gilbert de la Porrée imbibed so well the principles of Aristotelian dialectic in the current Latin mediaeval rendering, that of Boethius, as we may think, that he proceeded further to rival his master in his *Book of the Six Principles,* held afterward in the schools of logic a worthy successor to the Boethian treatises. Thierry of Chartres dis-

---

[55] Cf. the *De Computo: PL* CVII, 671D.

[56] Pertz, *Scriptores,* III, p. 617. Peiper, ed. *Consol. Philos.* 1871, pp. xxxixf. gives two little poems in honour of Boethius, ascribed to Raban and to Gerbert.

[57] *On the Acts of the Apostles,* XII, 1; *PL* CXLI, col. 284.

cussed through its Latin version all of the *Organon* of Aristotle in his *Library of the Seven Arts,* the two great tomes he bequeathed at his death for the guidance of future students in his Cathedral School.[58]

The same fountain of Aristotelian dialectic, bubbling through the channel of Boethius, sparkled in the twelfth century in the Cathedral School of Notre Dame at Paris, established at the beginning of this period by William of Champeaux. Here and later on near Paris at Saint Victor were sown the seeds of the University of Paris as students flocked to hear William discussing thorny dilemmas; here the foundation was laid of that passion for logical precision which has always been characteristic of French studies in liberal arts. Here Abelard, already impatient to argue the points debated by his master, sat under William of Champeaux; here Abelard in his turn made Paris far more renowned as the centre *par excellence* of logical training. Hither John of Salisbury was drawn by Abelard's renown to study in his lecture-room. We can picture to ourselves the hungry desire of Abelard to learn more of Greek philosophy than the prevailing ignorance of Greek and the scanty volume of Latin translations available for himself and his students would allow.

But John of Salisbury could not be held permanently by logic alone, however sparkling. Chartres soon called him away from Paris to sit at the feet of Richard "l'Évêque" and of William of Conches, "second only to Bernard of Chartres in his rich store of literary learning." William himself wrote a commentary on Boethius' last work.[59] The method of teaching at Chartres, John tells us, had been developed by Bernard, and he praises with enthusiasm its day's work with

[58] Clerval, *op. cit.,* p. 244; R. L. Poole, *Illustrations of the History of Medieval Thought and Learning,*[2] 1920, c. iv.

[59] C. Jourdain, *Notices et Extraits,* xx, pt. 2, pp. 40ff.

its alternation of literary exercise and religious devotion as
laid down by the master.[60] It was literature which John
loved above all, and in his *Metalogicon* he rebelled against the
passion for logic for its own sake which ran like fire in the
schools of Europe of the earlier twelfth century. "Just as
the sword of Hercules is of no use in the hand of a pigmy
or a dwarf, but lays low all it meets like lightning in the hand
of Achilles or Hector, so dialectic, if stripped of the might of
other disciplines, is so to speak, maimed and useless. But if
it be vigorous with their power, it avails to destroy all falsehood." [61] Dialectic, then, or logic, which came to the same
thing, must be firmly supported by a thorough training in
her sister art of grammar, which, of course, involved long
study of literature.

John knew his Boethius from end to end and his Aristotle
both through Boethius and through other source,[62] as the
pages of the *Metalogicon* prove. As we have seen, he knew
the whole *Organon* when he published the *Metalogicon* in
1159. He wonders why the *Topica*, the *Analytica*, and the
Sophistici Elenchi of Aristotle have been so long lost to the
world, and rejoices that the *Topica* has at length "been as
it were raised from death or, at least, from sleep by some diligent and zealous student of our age to recall the érring and
to open to its seekers the way of truth." [63] Among the logical
treatises of Boethius he especially admires the *On Division*
for its "singular grace of vocabulary and nicety of expression." [64] As Fulbert did, he quotes the verses of Boethius in
company with those of Vergil, and calls Boethius "more
excellent in faith and in knowledge of the truth." [65] Yet the
way of truth to John did not mean the disquisitions of
Boethius on Aristotle as a substitute for straight translations

[60] *Metalogicon*, I, 24.
[61] *ibid*, II, 9.
[62] See my note 46.

[63] *Meta.* III, 5.
[64] III, 9.
[65] II, 1.

of the text of Aristotle itself, and he blames bitterly those who rest on the inferior authority without striving to get as near as may be to the fountain head: "Against those who set aside the judgment of the ancients and dismiss the books of Aristotle, content for the most part with Boethius alone, many things could be said. But no matter, for it is pathetic to all men to see the imperfection of those who scarcely know anything, because they have spent their time and substance on Boethius alone." [66]

But among the professors of these times Boethius had a yet deeper effect. It was he who fanned the flame of conflict that was to occupy philosophical minds through all the Middle Ages—the struggle between Nominalism and Realism in their various forms. The distinction between Aristotle and Plato had already been made by Cassiodorus in writing to Boethius: *Plato theologus, Aristoteles logicus.*[67] The question turned for Boethius, as for later philosophers, on the reality of the existence of *genera* and *species*. Aristotle held that as universals and incorporeal they existed only in bodies apprehended by the senses; Plato believed that as universals they had a real existence apart from sensible bodies. Porphyry had refused to give judgment on this problem: "For it is a very deep matter and needs further enquiry." [68] At first Boethius decided in favour of Plato and Realism, when he was writing his first commentary on Porphyry's *Introduction*.[69] But later on he changed his mind. In the second and more learned commentary on the same work of Porphyry, after carefully pondering the doctrines of both Plato and Aristotle in this matter, he declared: "I have not thought it fitting to decide

[66] IV, 27.
[67] *Var.* I, 45. See on this question H. F. Stewart, *Boethius: An Essay,* 1891, c. vii; Sandys, *H.C.S.* I³, pp. 253ff.; p. 526.
[68] *PL* LXIV, col. 82A, quoted by Boethius.
[69] I, 10, ed. Schepps-Brandt, pp. 25f.

between their positions; it would need too deep probings into philosophy." [70]

From this observation springs the picture given of Boethius in the twelfth century by Godefroi of Saint Victor. He is describing in rhymed verse the crystal streams of the seven liberal arts as distinct from the foul waters of mechanical sciences, and the progress of philosophical enquiry in the great figures of its history: Plato, Aristotle, Porphyry, Donatus, Boethius, Priscian. Here, then, Boethius sits hesitating between the claims of Aristotle and Plato:

> Assidet Boethius, stupens de hac lite,
> Audiens quid hic et hic asserat perite,
> Et quid cui faveat non discernit rite,
> Nec praesumit solvere litem definite. [71]

The fire of conflict burned on merrily, fed by his doubt. Fuel was added in the eighth and ninth centuries, on the side of Aristotle by Raban, on the side of Plato by Johannes Scottus. Thence it flared up into the fierce conflagration which from the twelfth till the fourteenth century blazed in every great European school and set the disciples of Saint Francis and Saint Dominic to battle for intellectual truth.

Here, then, we have a tiny view of the work of "Boethius, last of the Roman philosophers," for the professors, for the secular thought of the Middle Ages. But only half of this famous description has yet been quoted. It concludes with "Boethius, first of the scholastics." The term implies the union in harmony of secular and spiritual learning and dates its rise from 787 when Charles the Great, in a letter to the Bishops of France, sounded the call for a revival of secular learning among her clergy. Clerical training in the seven

[70] I, 11, ed. S-B, p. 167. But see Rand, *F.M.A.*, p. 146.
[71] Quoted by Hauréau, I, p. 120. On the "poem" of Godefroi, entitled *Fons Philosophiae,* see Raby, *Secular Latin Poetry,* II, p. 13.

liberal arts was diligently pursued in the Palace School of Aachen. From thence it slowly spread, till many Cathedrals possessed their own Schools, in which the courses of the "Trivium" and the "Quadrivium" were taught in subordination to the principles of the Christian creed. This called forth a new technique on the part of Catholic scholars, the using of secular learning for the confirming and the elucidating of Christian doctrine in the minds of thinking men at large. In this, once more, Boethius had already led the way.

The statement rests on his *Sacred Treatises:* four, or, we may think with reason, five in number. Furthermore, on them hangs the belief that Boethius was a Christian, and, withal, an earnest adherent of his faith.

In the nineteenth century there was much scepticism as to the genuineness of all these writings. It was held that, as Boethius undoubtedly wrote the *Consolation of Philosophy* in uttermost stress and in the last crisis of his life without giving any direct evidence of a Christian belief, he could not have been author of a number of theological treatises dealing with this. Such feeling was strong enough to conquer the clear ascription to Boethius of four such brief works.[72] The publication, however, in 1877 by Usener of that fragment from the *Family History* of Cassiodorus known as the *Anecdoton Holderi* has settled the question with regard to these four in the minds of all except the determinedly sceptical.[73]

This fragment tells us concerning Boethius that "he wrote a book on the Holy Trinity and some chapters on dogma and a book against Nestor." [74] Now Cassiodorus, as a contem-

---

[72] See F. Nitzsch, *Das System des Boethius; Dict. Christ. Biog. s.v. Boethius* (where the suggestion is made that another Severinus, possibly some Saint Severinus, was their author).

[73] As Nitzsch in *Realencyk. f. Theol. u. Kirche*, III, 1897, p. 278.

[74] *Anec. Hold.*, p. 4.

porary and friend, must have known what Boethius wrote. Both internal evidence and the testimony of manuscripts have confirmed this view, and with belief in the authenticity of at least four of the five *Theological Tractates* extant under his name we may confidently look upon Boethius as a Christian philosopher and theologian.[75]

How, then, does the philosopher who longed to harmonize Plato and Aristotle for the world of scholars approach the Queen of sciences? Exactly as we should expect, so far as these four treatises go, Numbers 1, 2, 3 and 5. Here he seeks another and an even higher harmony. At the beginning of the first one, known as *On the Trinity*, he writes to his father-in-law, Symmachus, to whom he dedicates the work: "I have long pondered this problem with such mind as I have and all the light that God has lent me. Now, having set it forth in logical order and cast it into literary form, I venture to submit it to your judgment, for which I care as much as for the results of my own research. You will readily understand what I feel whenever I try to write down what I think if you consider the difficulty of the topic and the fact that I discuss it only with a few—I may say with no one but yourself. It is indeed no desire for fame or empty popular applause that prompts my pen; if there be any external reward, we may not look for more warmth in the verdict than the subject itself arouses. For, apart from yourself, wherever I turn my eyes, they fall on either the apathy of the dullard or the jealousy of the shrewd, and a man who casts his thoughts before the common herd—I will not say to consider but to trample under foot, would seem to bring discredit on

[75] See, from the body of literature on this question, especially E. K. Rand (*Johannes Scottus*, in Traube, *Quellen und Unters.* I, 2, 1906; *H.S.C.P.* XV, 1904, pp. 27f.; *Founders of the Middle Ages*, 1929, pp. 149ff.; *Boethius*, Loeb ed. 1926, pp. xf.): A. Hildebrand, *Boethius und seine Stellung zum Christentum*, 1885: Viktor Schurr, *Die Trinitätslehre des Boethius*, 1935, pp. 1ff.

the study of divinity. So I purposely use brevity and wrap up the ideas I draw from the deep questionings of philosophy in new and unaccustomed words which speak only to you and to myself, that is, if you deign to look at them. The rest of the world I simply disregard: they cannot understand, and therefore do not deserve to read. We should not, of course, press our inquiry further than man's wit and reason are allowed to climb the height of heavenly knowledge." And at the end a similar hope is expressed: "We must not in speaking of God let imagination lead us astray; we must let the Faculty of pure Knowledge lift us up and teach us to know all things as far as they may be known.

"I have now finished the investigation which I proposed. The exactness of my reasoning awaits the standard of your judgment; your authority will pronounce whether I have seen a straight path to the goal. If, God helping me, I have furnished some support in argument to an article which stands by itself on the firm foundation of Faith, I shall render joyous praise for the finished work to Him from whom the invitation comes." [76]

The keen desire to make trial of his long devotion to Aristotelian dialectic in its application to the mysteries of theology was natural, once we admit that Boethius was a Christian, whether he wrote these works in his eager youth [77] or in his riper age. [78] It is here that we see him as the forerunner of Saint Thomas and the Schoolmen of the thirteenth century in their passion to relate after their due order the things

[76] From the translation by H. F. Stewart and E. K. Rand, Loeb edition, 1926, pp. 3f., p. 31. This edition and the sorely needed translation of the *Opuscula Sacra* of Boethius are indispensable for any student of Boethius; to them he is referred here for the philosophical details of these works.

[77] *Anec. Hold.* ed. Usener, p. 54; *P.W. s.v. Boethius,* col. 600; Stewart, *Boethius,* p. 126.

[78] E. K. Rand, *Jahrbb. f. kl. Phil. Supplbd* XXVI, 1901, p. 438, on evidence of style; Manitius, p. 24; Schurr, pp. 224f.

learned by men of natural reason and the things revealed to them from without of supernatural faith.[79]

The scholastic method is already foreshadowed through the treatment in this first pamphlet of the doctrine "That Trinity is One God, not three Gods." After the aim of the work has been set forth, we find, next, a statement of the Catholic Faith regarding this doctrine; then a description of the scientific method of theological enquiry, based on Aristotle; then the application of this method to that particular doctrine.[80]

The treatise *On the Trinity* was well known throughout the Middle Ages. Alcuin praised its author in the eighth century as "learned in tomes both philosophic and divine;[81] in the ninth Hincmar, Bishop of Reims, referred to it and to Tractates II and V in his *De una et non trina Deitate;*[82] Johannes Scottus, the great Irishman who presided over the Palace School at Aachen in the time of Charles the Bald, and his pupil, Remigius of Auxerre, toward the end of the same century wrote commentaries on it and on others of these *Sacred Treatises*.[83] In the twelfth century Abelard studied it,[84] in the thirteenth it was in the hands of Albertus Magnus,[85] and was made the subject of a special commentary by his great pupil, St. Thomas Aquinas.[86] Especially interesting is another commentary written by Gilbert de la Porrée, Bishop of Poitiers from 1142, "the one saint whom Bernard of Clairvaux unsuccessfully charged with heresy." [87] Certain statements in this exposition of Boethius, *On the Trinity,* brought upon Gilbert the displeasure

---

[79] Stewart-Rand, Loeb. ed. pp. xiff.; de Wulf, *Hist. Med. Phil.* I⁶, Eng. ed.³ pp. 110–114.

[80] See Grabmann, I, pp. 169ff. on B. in his theological treatises as pioneer for the Scholastics in vocabulary and scientific form. For explanation of the matter of these treatises see Stewart, *Boethius,* c. V.; Schurr, *op. cit.*

[81] *PL* CI, 76 B. Hildebrand, pp. 165ff.

[82] *PL* CXXV, 522 B, 525 A, 537 A, 582 A, 584 B.

[83] ed. E. K. Rand, *Johannes Scottus;* see my note 75.

[84] *Introd. ad Theolog.* I, 25.

[85] Albertus Magnus wrote a Commentary on Boethius, *De Divisione.*

[86] *Opusculum* LXIII.   [87] R. L. Poole, *op. cit.,* p. 113.

of the Church. He was tried before Pope Eugenius III at the Council of Reims in 1148 and discharged without punishment on his promise to satisfy his accusers with regard to the text of his book.[88] John of Salisbury, who cites these theological works of Boethius in his *Metalogicon*,[89] was present, he tells us, at the Council of Reims. We can picture him watching the fiery zeal of Saint Bernard there, declaring against Gilbert that in his Commentary on Boethius were found "certain things worthy of condemnation by the wise because they accorded not with the precepts of the Church or were unseemly by reason of their strange novelty of language." Gilbert was also roundly accused in Commentaries on the same work of Boethius written in this twelfth century by the "Pseudo-Bede," possibly Gottfried of Auxerre, and by Clarembaud, Archdeacon of Arras, himself a pupil of Thierry of Chartres.[90]

In the sculptures which make beautiful the West Front of the Cathedral of Chartres the Seven Liberal Arts are represented, together with their greatest exponents: Priscian, Aristotle, Cicero, Pythagoras, Nicomachus, Euclid and Ptolemy. At least, so experts have been content to believe. Boethius has not been discovered,[91] perhaps, it has been thought, because of a shadow cast on his work by this Commentary of Gilbert de la Porrée.[92] But Martianus Capella has not been identified there, either, and Saint Bernard himself defended Boethius.

The second of these *Theological Treatises* is also concerned with the Holy Trinity. It is dedicated to "John the Deacon" and was frequently known by that title.[93] Attempts have been made without any definite result to identify this John with Pope John I (523–526) or Pope John II (533–535). He, whoever he was, exchanged letters with Ennodius and with Avitus,

---

[88] *Historia Pontificalis*, Pertz, XX, pp. 524ff.; *Gaufridi Epistula ad Albinum*, PL CLXXXV, col. 587.

[89] II, 20; III, 2; IV, 35: ed. Webb, pp. 107, 127, 205.

[90] Peiper, ed. p. L; Grabmann, I, pp. 166f.

[91] But see H. R. Patch, *op. cit.* p. 37.

[92] Sandys, 1³, p. 673.   [93] *e.g.* in Hincmar of Reims.

Bishop of Vienne in the fifth century. We have an interesting letter by him on the Baptismal Office, written at the request of Senarius, the friend of Ennodius, for his instruction.[94] Boethius addresses this John with great respect at the end of this little work as one expert in the doctrine of the Church: "If my words are true and in keeping with the Faith I beg you tell me so. But if peradventure you disagree in any point, look carefully at what I have written and try to bring into harmony both faith and reason." Here again Boethius strikes the key-note of his purpose. The authenticity of this second treatise is attested, not only by superscription but by reference in later writers, as in Hincmar of Reims and St. Thomas Aquinas.[95] The pamphlet is essentially logical in spirit, and its beginning tersely states its aim: "The question before us is whether Father, Son, and Holy Spirit may be predicated of the Divinity substantially or otherwise. And I think that the method of our inquiry must be borrowed from what is admittedly the surest source of all truth, namely, the fundamental doctrines of the catholic faith." [96]

The third treatise, addressed to "the same," is equally logical in treatment. It is often referred to briefly as "The Hebdomads" of Boethius, since he writes to John at its beginning: "You ask me to state and explain somewhat more clearly that obscure question in my *Hebdomads,* concerning the manner in which substances can be good in virtue of existence without being absolute goods. . . . . I confess I like to expound my *Hebdomads* to myself, and would rather bury my speculations in my own memory than share them with any of those pert and frivolous persons who will not tolerate an argument unless it is made amusing." [97]

[94] Bardenhewer, V, p. 259; *PL* LIX, coll. 399ff.; Rand, *Jahrbb.,* p. 444.
[95] *PL* CXXV, 522 B, 582 A; Hildebrand, pp. 205ff.
[96] From the translation by Stewart and Rand, Loeb ed. p. 33.
[97] *ibid.,* p. 39.

The meaning of the word "Hebdomads" has been variously explained: as the name of a society in which Boethius and his friends, such as John and Symmachus, and probably Cassiodorus, met periodically for philosophical discussion,[98] or as a work in seven parts, after the manner of the *Hebdomads* of Varro.[99] The scientific method is next introduced: "As is the custom in treatises on mathematics and other sciences I have set forth terms and rules throughout in developing my argument." Thus we have in orderly sequence the introduction, the statement of general principles, the *quaestio* or question in point, and, lastly, the *solutio* or conclusion, arrived at by means of the general principles laid down before.[100] Saint Thomas Aquinas made also a detailed commentary on this work, which attracted him through this very scientific method.[101]

More famous in antiquity was the fifth of these treatises, much longer than any of the others, a reasoned argument against the heresies of Eutyches and Nestorius. It, also, is dedicated to "John the Deacon, his revered Father, by his son Boethius." Boethius states at the beginning that he has lately been present at a meeting to hear a letter, no doubt the one sent in 512 by Eastern Bishops to Pope Symmachus asking for direction regarding these errors,[102] and that the reading of the letter has stirred up a theological turmoil in his mind. No one else, however, of all who were present seemed to be worried, and he concluded with much disgust that they must all be very stupid! After thinking things over for a long time he has de-

[98] Hildebrand, p. 289; Stewart, *Boethius,* p. 132.

[99] Rand, *Jahrbb.* p. 443; Loeb ed. p. 38. Father Schurr (*op. cit.* pp. 97ff.) dates No. II before No. I, as an elaboration of its argument. He also finds the motive for these philosophical treatises on the Mystery of the Trinity in the recent writings of certain Scythian theologians on this subject. For review of Fr. Schurr's work see E. K. Rand, *Speculum,* XI, 1936, pp. 153ff.

[100] Grabmann, I, p. 173.

[101] *Opusculum* LXII. See also *Opusc.* LXIII, prologue.

[102] Mansi, VIII, p. 224; Stewart-Rand, p. 73. Tractate V would thus seem to antedate I, II, and III. Schurr, pp. 127ff., 224f., 227.

cided to write down his own conclusions and to submit them
for judgment to this director of his mind in matters of faith.
Once again he argues in logical course: First, the terms to be
used, Person and Nature, must be defined; then the two opposing heresies, of Nestorius and of Eutyches, must be overthrown;
lastly, what is of Catholic belief on this matter must be clearly
set forth.

It is in this treatise that Boethius laid down his well-known
definition of "Person," a definition finally accepted, after full
discussion, by St. Thomas Aquinas and still regarded as valid:
"Person is the individual substance of a rational nature." [103]
After the unfolding of the various points of attack against the
heresy of Nestorius, that there were Two Natures and Two
Persons in the Christ, and that of Eutyches, that in Him were
Two Persons but only One Nature, Boethius finds the solution
of the problem in the Aristotelian mean between two extremes:
the belief in the One Person and Two Natures which is the
creed of the Catholic Church.

We come now to the controversy which has so long centred
in the fourth tractate, *On the Catholic Faith*. For many years
this has been held spurious, even after the fragment discovered
by Alfred Holder spoke for the genuine authorship of Boethius
in the case of the other four treatises, either by direct mention
or by their indirect inclusion in "some chapters on dogma."
The difficulties regarding No. 4 are both internal and external. [104] From the point of internal evidence the great prob-

---

[103] *Comm. in quattuor libros sententiarum*, I, *dist.* XXV, *qu.* 1; *Summa,*
I, *qu.* XXIX, 1 and 2. "That definition of the person that inspired the
whole Middle Ages, and weighs so heavily on the development of modern
ethics": E. Gilson, *The Spirit of Mediaeval Philosophy,* 1936, p. 204.
[104] See on this especially E. K. Rand, *Jahrbb.,* pp. 407ff.; Stewart,
Boethius, pp. 138ff.; Hildebrand, pp. 299ff.; Usener, *Anec. Hold.,* pp. 49f.;
Bardenhewer, V, p. 258. All these, as scholars in general, decided here
against Boethius as author. Since these dates both Rand and Stewart have
decided in favour of his authorship of this Tractate IV; see their Loeb
edition, 1926, pp. 52f., and Rand, *Founders of the Middle Ages,* p. 156.

lems have been the simple style and content of the work, entirely
different from the dialectical argument and scientifically logical form of the other four theological papers. We have here
simply a plain statement of the Catholic faith, composed in
easy language and popular manner. For this reason critics
have suggested other authors: John the Deacon might have
written it for one of his spiritual children; or another Severinus,
possibly Saint Severinus of Noricum, who was, indeed, a mis-
sionary and not at all a philosopher. On the other hand, it is
true that part of the fifth tractate is also written in plain style,
that Boethius in his proven work was not always writing in
scientific language. He wrote at times in simple and easy
words; he wrote various kinds of verse in his *Consolation of
Philosophy*. The man, whom the four tractates we have discussed reveal as a firm Catholic, might well have been content
on occasion to write a plain statement of his faith, perhaps for
some unlearned friend. If he could aid the learned of his time
by his dialectic, he might well have been willing to help some
younger or less educated reader. Moreover, the words of Cassiodorus, "some chapters of dogma," suit this fourth treatise
much better than either the second or the third, to which they
are generally applied.[105] So far as the theological content goes,
the work could quite reasonably be dated in the lifetime of
Boethius.

With regard to external evidence the MS. tradition dates
back to the ninth century. If Boethius did not write the tract,
it may have been sent to him by a close friend, such as John
the Deacon, his Father in the Church, or by some other man
with whom he was accustomed to talk of spiritual things. It
would thus have been found among his papers at his death and
published with them. We have such instances of the inclusion
of the work of other men, as that of Marius Victorinus, in the

[105] Stewart-Rand, Loeb ed., p. 53.

corpus of Boethius. Serious ground for hesitation to assign it to Boethius comes from the fact that there is very little MS. evidence dating before the twelfth century for the author's name and the title of the work and that the paper holds no introduction, and no words of personal import at its end. All the other four treatises are expressly assigned to Boethius, either by name (I, II, V), or by the words "Of the Same" (III) ; all have a definite introduction, and all, except the third, some concluding words of a personal nature. Against this, various lines of defence have suggested that Tract IV might have depended, as one of a series, upon mention of the name of its author in the tracts preceding it in the same volume; or that Boethius himself deliberately omitted his name from this short composition. If it be spurious, it is difficult to see why it should have been inserted between Nos. 3 and 5, unless the *Tractates* were published in two parts. Much importance has been attached to the appearance of the words ACTENUS BOETIUS ("Here ends the work of Boethius") between Tractates III and IV in red capitals in the ninth century Codex Augiensis, inserted by the hand of the copyist or one of his assistants. This subscription, however, died with the copy, as this manuscript was not perpetuated. It may well have been due to a writer's error. Lastly, the lack of scholia and commentaries from which this particular tract has suffered may reasonably be explained by the eager interest of scholars in all matters of dialectic throughout the Middle Ages. A simple confession of faith hardly called for interpretation. This might explain its neglect by students like Abelard and Gilbert de la Porrée, though in the ninth century Remigius of Auxerre annotated all five tracts.

At least, MS. tradition does not render the authorship impossible, and it is pleasant to think that Boethius, as other learned men have done since his day, could lay aside his erudition to sum up his creed in the simple language of his own devotion, for the assurance of his own heart or the enlightening of some enquirer after God. His last words may be translated here as an indication of the character of the whole:

"There are, therefore, three truths by which ye shall know the Catholic Church throughout the world. All she holds, she holds either by authority of the Scriptures, or by universal tradition, or of special and particular custom. Of these, the authority of the Scriptures and the universal tradition of the Fathers bind her whole body; particular rules and special governances support and direct her individual parts, according to differing locality and the counsel deemed expedient by each. Herein now lies the one great hope of the faithful: the coming of the end of this world, when all corruptible things shall pass away, and men shall rise again for judgment, each to receive his merits and to remain for ever and eternally where he has deserved to be. This alone is the reward of blessedness, the contemplation of the Creator, so far as the created may be able to contemplate its Creator. Then shall the ranks of Angels be filled again from the number of the blessed in that City on high, whose King is a Virgin's Son. There unto men for their eternal joy and delight, for their meat and for their work, shall be His perpetual praising."

But it is time that we look back again to the life of Boethius the man, whom we last saw prospering magnificently as Master of Offices in 522. He was now a ripe scholar as well as statesman, renowned not only in Rome and Ravenna but in East and West, wherever the Roman learning and the Latin tongue were still esteemed. He was still in his forties and might confidently look forward to many further years of his beloved research and successful administration. His great aim of harmonizing the Aristotelian and the Platonic philosophy was in steady progress, though still far from its goal; Theodoric needed supremely the support of wise and cultured men, and all looked well on the outside for his future career.

Within, however, things were far from well. Theodoric, in spite of his honest strivings after *civilitas*, after harmony, peace, order and beauty in his composite kingdom, was, after all, a Goth and an Arian—in other words, a barbarian and a heretic. He was proud of his race and of the religion of his fathers. Boethius belonged to the aristocratic circles of Rome; he had been trained from his childhood in Greek and Latin culture; he was a steadfast adherent of the Catholic Church. Friction was inevitable, even if sternly repressed and never allowed to escape in disloyal word or act. As Boethius felt, so did his fellow-Senators, and Theodoric must have been nervously aware in his heart of the gulf which separated him from the nobler of his subjects. As time went on, the fair record of the greater part of his reign seems to have been darkened by fear and suspicion. This was natural enough. Yet there is no need for us to press forward the story that this King, so keen on toleration and justice for his citizens, of whatever blood or religious faith, now began to yield to the devil's machinations, ordering a Chapel of Saint Stephen on the outskirts of Verona to be destroyed and forbidding any Roman to carry weapons, even as much as a knife.[106] Undoubtedly the time was a difficult one for Theodoric, and it did not help matters for him that the Pope who succeeded Hormisdas in 523, John the first, was resolutely opposed to tolerance of any deviation from the Catholic belief.

The King's irritation, at first somewhat vague, was sharply

[106] See the *Anonymous Valesianus,* one of our chief authorities for this section, who does not hesitate to speak against Theodoric: 27 (83). The narrative is probably entirely unfair here to the Gothic King: see Cessi (*R.I.S.,* XXIV, 4, pp. CXXIVf.); Pfeilschifter, pp. 156f. Agnellus also reports action by Theodoric against the Christians: ed. Holder-Egger, p. 304.

stimulated by change in the religious attitude of the Imperial government in Constantinople. The Emperor Justin the first, who had followed Anastasius of Monophysite tendency in 518, was himself an orthodox Catholic and was steadily urged on against all forms of heresy by his nephew Justinian, the power behind his throne. At this time Justin was meditating, if not already declaring, strict legislation against the Arians, even an edict that their churches in the East must be surrendered to the Catholic See. When the edict did come, Theodoric was enraged at such an affront to his own creed.[107] But we may think that he had been disturbed in mind long before, suspecting that Catholics in Italy were secretly yearning toward Constantinople. No doubt they were attracted by the orthodoxy of the East and the stability of its Emperor, who held his throne by a right of tenure to which the Goth could not lay claim. No doubt even those who felt it their duty to support Theodoric as one who had deserved well of them and their country did sometimes turn eager eyes eastward toward the traditional Emperor of Rome and the supporter of their faith. The King in the West must have tossed at times by night on his bed, dreaming uneasily of this very thing.

On the other hand, the position of Boethius had its own point of danger. Among the courtiers of the King in Ravenna, ever ready to flatter and acquiesce in the royal will, he stood out, we may imagine, as a rock of uprightness and stern virtue. Public life for such men forms a target of attack, and we find Boethius lamenting afterward to his Lady Philosophy the hard fight he had fought in the cause of honour:

"Following, then, this authority" (of Plato), "I longed to transfer what I had learned at leisure in secret to the conduct of public administration. You and God, who has placed you in

---

[107] We are not sure that the edict enforcing these was issued before the death of Boethius (Bury, *L.R.E.* II, p. 156).

the minds of the wise, are my witnesses that nothing but the common aim of all good patriots brought me to public office. Thence have come to me grievous and implacable quarrels with wicked men, and in the free following of my conscience I have oftentimes right willingly given offence to the powerful by maintaining what is just.

"How often I have checked Conigatus when he was attacking the fortunes of some weak man! How often I have turned aside Trigguilla, Chamberlain of the King's Palace, from some wrong he had plotted, or even set into action! How often I have protected those unhappy men whom the barbarian greed was vexing with endless slanders unrestrained, though thereby I exposed my own authority to peril. Never did anyone drag me from justice to injustice. I sorrowed for the ruin of people in the provinces by private robbery and public taxation as deeply as the victims themselves. I took up the cause of Campania in a season of dire famine when hard and inexplicable terms of purchase seemed likely to bring about a lack of food there. I opposed the Praetorian Prefect, I fought the matter out before the King, I won my case, and such terms were not exacted. When the dogs of the Palace had already eaten up in greedy hope the wealth of Paulinus, a man of consular rank, I dragged him from the very jaws of those seeking to devour him." [108]

At times, too, Boethius could be very outspoken. He writes of a certain Decoratus as a "right worthless rogue and a spy," though Cassiodorus sang the official praises of Decoratus for Theodoric. Ennodius, also, wrote to Decoratus as his friend. [109] But Boethius declared roundly he never would hold office in company with such a man. The man, nevertheless, was Quaestor under Theodoric, and, we may think, in the very

[108] *Cons. Phil.*, I, 4 (prose), 26ff.
[109] *Variae* V, 3 and 4; Ennodius, *Epistles*, IV, 17.

year in which Boethius languished in prison. Apparently his
enemy flourished in his disgrace.[110]

The stage was set, prepared for tragedy if only a sufficient
argument should present itself. It came suddenly. Certain
letters, sent by a Senator named Albinus or by his friends [111]
to the Emperor Justin at Constantinople, were intercepted in
Italy by an official named Severus, a most zealous minion of
the law, as it would seem. In these letters were words which
were interpreted as conveying a treacherous desire for negotia-
tion with Justin, a hinting at the "freeing of Rome" from the
Ostrogothic rule.[112] The discovery was promptly reported by
Severus to the officer whose business it was to collect all information relevant to cases brought before the royal Consistorium, or Court of trial for persons accused of treason. The
officer (referendarius) of the moment was named Cyprian,
and he was serving under Boethius himself, the Master of
Offices. It was a difficult matter for Boethius. He would
naturally be reluctant to press a charge against Albinus, a
friend of his and a fellow-Senator; moreover, ex officio he was
a member of the Court which would try the accused. We
need not think that Boethius had had any hand in sending to
Justin foolish letters of doubtful loyalty; such a course is in
keeping neither with his scrupulous honesty both intellectual
and moral nor with the sagacity which had raised him high
in the King's counsels. But we may well imagine that he had
keenly sympathised with Albinus and other Senators in a
common desire to be ruled in those days from Constantinople
rather than from Ravenna; he may possibly have known of
correspondence with Constantinople.

[110] Mommsen dates *Variae* V, 3 and 4 in 524, before Sept. 1. See, on
Decoratus, Sundwall, *Abh.*, pp. 112f.

[111] Suidas *s.v.* Σεβῆρος. See on all this matter Bury, *L.R.E.* II, pp.
153ff.; Sundwall, pp. 243ff.; Cessi, *R.I.S.* XXIV, 4, pp. CXLVIIIff. For
the Catholic enthusiasm of Albinus, see Sundwall, p. 88.

[112] *Cons. Phil.* I, 4 (prose), 89f.

At any rate, with or without the official consent of his superior, Cyprian referred the matter to Theodoric, who was at the time in Verona, and conscientious loyalty drove Boethius there at once to defend Albinus in his own person. We still have his words to Theodoric: "This accusation by Cyprian is false. But if Albinus did do this deed, then also I myself and all the Senate did it together with him. But the thing is false, Lord King." [113]

His honesty was fatal to himself. For Cyprian after some hesitation, whether caused through his own reluctance or through fear of the consequences, went on to include his superior in the charge of treason, supporting the accusation, it was said, by evidence of false witnesses. It was certainly a shock for Theodoric to hear that two of the leading Romans, one of whom was his own Master of Offices, had been charged with treason against his throne. It was a greater shock to find good ground for fearing that members of the Senate, how many he did not know, were in league against him. In his angry mood he doubtless remembered that Justin had specially favoured Boethius in 522 when he allowed Theodoric to raise his two sons to the consulship. [114] He may also have been told of a work which Boethius had lately published on the Catholic doctrine of the Trinity. Was there on foot a movement of the Catholic Romans to drive his race from the throne of Italy? The fact that the accusers of Boethius, Cyprian and others, were themselves Catholics did not allay this fear. Someone must suffer, and in his rage he seized the victim ready to his hand, this man so calmly confronting his royal power with bold words, and eagerly he lent ear to the proceedings in the Consistorium.

Boethius tells us something about accusation and accusers. On behalf of the whole Senate he withstood the charge of

[113] *Anon. Val.* 28 (85).   [114] Mommsen, *Ostgoth. Stud.* p. 382.

traitorous action, brought, as he says, against that Order by the King. On his own behalf he resisted the statement, very probably pressed by his subordinate officer, Cyprian, that he had tried to obstruct justice by preventing the presentation of evidence against the Senate.[115] He resisted, further, the charge of "sacrilege," in which commentators have seen an accusation of magic practice, possibly drawn from the skill of Boethius in mathematics and astronomy. In passionate words he protested afterward his innocence to his Mistress, the Lady Philosophy, both for her own assurance and for the knowledge of men to come.

The accusers were Cyprian and also three other men brought forward as witnesses; Basilius, Opilio, and Gaudentius by name. Of Cyprian Boethius tells us, continuing the defence of his own public life: "I faced the wrath of Cyprian, the informer, lest unfair accusation should condemn Albinus, once Consul. Do I seem to have piled up sufficiency of grievous enmities against myself?"[116]

Cyprian appears, however, in another light in two letters of Theodoric, in which his merits as *referendarius* are sung and he is admitted to the office of Count of the Sacred Largesses. This was in 524.[117] Like Decoratus, he flourished in his opponent's fall. Special stress is laid on his loyalty to the throne of Italy; it is just possible that we may detect here a covert reference, by contrast, to Boethius and his recent accusation.

The characters of the other three accusers are more directly attacked by their victim. He declares, continuing the argument quoted above: "But I ought to have been safer in the hands of other men, I who through my love of justice reserved for myself no refuge among the King's courtiers. Yet who

---

[115] Sundwall, p. 244. He points out that *Variae* V, 41 shows Cyprian a man both bold and adroit.

[116] *Cons. Phil. ibid.* 51ff.   [117] *Variae* V, 40f.

were the men who by their informing struck me this blow?
One was Basilius, who had been banished from the King's
service and was forced by his debts to lay information against
me. Others were Opilio and Gaudentius, men sentenced by
the King to exile because of innumerable acts of dishonesty.
When the King heard that they would not obey this order and
had fled to sanctuary, he proclaimed that if they had not left
Ravenna by a certain day they should be driven out with
branded foreheads. What could be more severe? And yet on
that very day information against me was accepted from these
same men."

Here also we have contrary evidence in two letters of Cassiodorus written for Athalaric in the year 527.[118] Opilio was a
brother of Cyprian and, according to Cassiodorus, equally
loyal to Theodoric. The two letters tell of his rewarding by
bestowal of the same office of Count of the Sacred Largesses.
In one of them we may very possibly see a reference to the
trial of Boethius, by this time matter of history; Cassiodorus
had had special cause to be concerned about the fate of his
fellow-citizen. His words here seem rather to be the cautious
expression of one who really sympathized with his friend, now
condemned and dead in disgrace, than indication of judgment that Boethius had been guilty. They also appear to con-
tain an implicit warning to Opilio to watch his official steps.
"You are going to enjoy," the royal letter runs, as penned by
Cassiodorus, "all the privileges and emoluments which fell to
your predecessors, and we pray that those who stand firm in
their own deeds may not be shaken by any contrivings of slan-
der. There was a time when even judges were troubled by
informers. But you have no bad conscience. Lay aside fear,
therefore, and enjoy the fruits of your honours." If this does
refer in any way to the fate of Boethius, the word *delator,*

[118] *ibid.* VIII, 16f.

"informer" or "spy," is certainly a daring one. It was the word used, as we have seen, of Cyprian, Opilio's brother, by Boethius himself.[119]

There lies a strange contradiction in the thought that Opilio, whom Boethius could describe in 523 or 524, when he was writing his *Consolation,* as one guilty of innumerable frauds, punished with exile and threatened with branding, should three or four years later be honoured with office in the State. Apparently Athalaric and his Regent Mother chose the officers whose aid they desired among their Gothic subjects without looking too closely into their history under Theodoric. Cassiodorus, we may suppose, wrote his missives of congratulation as an official servant of the Crown without allowing his private conscience to overrule obedience to the sovereign for whom he worked.[120]

The evidence was found sufficient to arrest Boethius and to cast him into prison at Pavia together with Albinus. He was also stripped of his high dignity, and Cassiodorus himself was made Master of Offices in his place. But the King in his anger went further. He stopped the hearing before the Consistorium and cast aside legal procedure by assuming in his own person the conduct of the trial at Pavia, after summoning thither the Prefect of Rome to assist him in judgment. State magistrates and Senators who composed this Court of Treason were relieved of all responsibility concerning the matter; this rested by his own determination with Theodoric. The Senate was so terrified of implication in the charge of high treason after hearing of the words of Boethius that it passed special decrees of compliance, declaring him guilty.[121]

[119] Hodgkin, *Letters of Cassiodorus,* p. 363.
[120] Basilius (*Var.* VIII, 17) seems to have been related by marriage to Opilio. He may be the Roman Senator charged with magical practice in *Var.* IV, 22, 23. Stewart, *Boethius,* p. 49, thinks this charge may possibly explain the feeling of Boethius against him.
[121] *Cons. Phil. ibid.* 8of.

Meanwhile Boethius remained in prison, ignorant of all that was happening, till the royal deliberations ended in sentence of death and confiscation of property.[122] We do not know much about these deliberations or even how long they actually lasted; according to Boethius himself forged letters formed part of the evidence. By the time the sentence was carried out in 524 he had endured nearly a year of captivity. Records differ as to his end. Our chief authority declares that he was transferred from Pavia to another prison in Calvenzano, near Milan, and was there put to death with torture: "A cord was tied round his head and drawn so tightly that at length his eyes burst from their sockets, and he was then despatched by a blow from a club."[123] Fortunately the horrible record is placed in doubt by two other versions, which state: one, that he was beheaded,[124] the other, that he was killed by a sword.[125]

The sequel of Theodoric's quarrel with Constantinople is interesting. According to evidence of chronicle, when the edict against the Arians had been published, he sent for the Pope John himself, and when he arrived at Ravenna, curtly bade him get to Constantinople and obtain from Justin relief for those who did not desire adherence to the Catholic faith. The Pope went reluctantly, but was received at Constantinople with all honour. He obtained the relief, except that Arians already converted to Catholicism were not permitted to return to their former creed. On his return, however, he was received by Theodoric in an angry mood and was actually cast into prison, where he died shortly after.[126] His funeral was carried out with great distinction, and he was subsequently enrolled among the Saints of the Church. An honourable exception among terrified Senators

[122] Both the *Anon. Val.* 28 (87) and Procopius, *Hist. Wars,* V, 1, 34, witness to the illegality of the King's procedure.
[123] *Anon. Val. ibid.*
[124] Agnellus, ed. Holder-Egger, p. 304.
[125] *Liber Pontificalis,* I, ed. Duchesne, p. 276.
[126] *Anon. Val.* 90–93; *Lib. Pontificalis,* I, p. 276.

at this time was Symmachus, who, while Boethius was still alive in prison, "grieved for his injuries." [127] His grief cost him dear. He must have shown it clearly; for he, also, was arrested and put to death in 525.

Remorse, we read, came quickly to Theodoric for these hasty acts of spleen. He is described to us by a contemporary writer as beset by fears of conscience, doubtless aggravated by the sickness which troubled these last days of his life. After recording the aristocratic birth and the high standing in the State of both Symmachus and Boethius, the narrative goes on: "They were earnest disciples of Philosophy and foremost in love of Justice and they ministered of their substance to the need of many, both citizens and strangers. Thus they enjoyed great renown and brought to envy men of evil character, who with their lies persuaded Theodoric that the two were plotting revolution. So he slew them both and made forfeit their goods to the treasury. A few days later as he sat at dinner his servants placed before him the head of a great fish, and it seemed to him just like the head of Symmachus, lately killed. For it looked at him in a dreadful threatening manner with its teeth clenched on the lower lip and its eyes fixed in a grim and cruel stare. Sudden terror seized the King, and shivering with cold he hurried to his bed, where he buried himself in a heap of blankets hastily brought by his servants at his call. The doctor, Elpidius, was summoned, and Theodoric confessed to him with tears the whole story of the crime he had committed; but his grief and pangs of conscience constantly tormented him till he died a little later. This was the first and the last wrong done by the King to his subjects in condemning both of these men without first trying their case as he was wont." [128]

In years to come Boethius was honoured as a Martyr by the Church. Already in Paul the Deacon's *History of Italy* we read

[127] *Cons. Phil.* II, 4 (prose), 18.　　　　[128] Procopius, *ibid.*

that while Pope John and his fellow-ambassadors "were tarry-
ing to return from their mission to Constantinople, Theodoric,
driven by the fury of his wickedness, slew with the sword Symmachus and Boethius, Catholic men," [129] though we know that
Pope John did not start for the East till after the death of
Boethius. If Theodoric's fear of the alliance of Catholics in
Italy with Constantinople and his vexation at the hostility
toward the Arians of both the Pope in the West and the Emperor in the East can raise Boethius to the rank of martyr for
his faith, then surely he merits a martyr's place. But since
his prosecutors, Cyprian and the rest, were also Catholic, his
trial could not actually have been based on religious grounds.[130]

It is also true that a cult of "Saint Severinus Boethius" has
continued down the ages, though here, again, it would be difficult to say how much the fame of another Severinus may be
indirectly responsible for this, through confusion of persons.
The Cathedral of Pavia still holds his relics, and the observance
of his feast-day there on the 23rd of October was formally
sanctioned by the Sacred Congregation of Rites in the year
1883.

To the days when Boethius lay in torment of suspense and
discouragement we owe the best known of his works, the
Consolation of Philosophy. Many have asked why Boethius
seemed to ask aid of philosophy rather than of his religious
faith as he sat in the shadow of death, alone and imprisoned;
many, as we have seen, have denied for this reason that he was
a Catholic Christian at all. But surely a man's book need not
show all his self. Boethius might well have written a treatise
in like circumstances on mathematics or on music for the re-
lieving of his mind while, unknown to the public of future days,
morning and evening and at noontide he offered his prayers

[129] *PL* XCV, 978.
[130] Bury, *L.R.E.* II, p. 156, note. Cf. (on the theology of Boethius as
the innocent cause of his downfall) Rand, *Speculum*, XI, 1936, pp. 155f.

for the comfort of his soul and the keeping of his faith. He may well have wanted for years to write such a book, "In Praise of Philosophy," and have seized this time of enforced leisure, with the difference that she was now to stand forth as his friend in sorrow, as before in joy. There is nothing that is hostile to the Catholic religion in her counsel as given here. On the contrary, a man's faith might well find support from her reasoned argument.

To her, then, Boethius now turned, while the reserve of his inner soul in those last hours forbade the revealing of his colloquies with God. It may be that he desired further to use his knowledge of philosophy for the enlightening of others beset by problems like unto his own, men to whom the truths of religion would not so surely appeal. If this was his thought, he succeeded as he never dreamed. In the Middle Ages his book was read by all men, found everywhere, in places both sacred and secular. It trained the young, it comforted the old, it stayed the doubts of the vigorous and of the weaker brethren alike. Men, learned and simple, theologian and lay, marked and digested its pages for the sake of others as of themselves. Its pithy definitions gave food for argument to Saint Thomas Aquinas and the Schoolmen ; its subtler passages gave thought to countless commentators.[181] Already in the ninth century Asser, teacher of King Alfred, was busy at this work. In the same century Alfred made his famous version in Anglo-Saxon, the forerunner of translations into many other tongues. Among them those by Notker Labeo or his pupils into Old High German in the eleventh century and by the monk Maximus Planudes into Greek in the fourteenth, are perhaps of special interest for their language. Far better known is the prose rendering of Chaucer. He was ever devoted to his dear

[181] Cf. E. T. Silk, ed. *Saeculi noni in Boetii C. P. Commentarius,* 1935. For the influence of Boethius in general here see H. R. Patch, *op. cit.*

"Boëce," whatever he was writing, and especially in his tale of *Troylus and Cryseyde*. A little later came the translation of John Walton, and we may remember, also, a rendering by Queen Elizabeth of the year 1593. Among the innumerable recollections of Boethius in prose and poetry two shall be mentioned here: in English literature the brief summary of John Lydgate, in Italian the picture given by Dante. Lydgate wrote of him as slain for his faith:

> But touching Boys, as bookis specefie,
> Wrotte dyvers bookis off philosophie,
> Off the Trynyte maters that were dyvyne,
> Martyrd for crist and called Severyne.[132]

Dante places him among the flaming spirits that make glorious music around the throne of God: "The sainted soul that from martyrdom and from exile came to this peace." His bones, as Dante told, were laid, long after his death, under the Golden Ceiling in Saint Peter's Church at Pavia.[133]

And now to the book itself.[134] It was written in a medley of prose and verse, such as Varro and Martianus Capella had used before and Bernard Silvestris of Tours and Alan of Lille were to imitate. Verse alternated with prose for the relief of the mind from application to logical argument, written in a variety of metres, with many traces of the influence of Seneca's tragedies. At times we find real poetry, at times mere versification. That Boethius was given to writing poems we know from his own and from other witness.[135] The prose is clear and simple, easy to read, and of a Latin sufficiently pure and classical to cause no difficulty.

[132] *Fall of Princes*, VIII, 2657–2660.
[133] *Parad.* X, 126ff.
[134] Ed. with trans. E. K. Rand and H. F. Stewart, Loeb ed. 1926; G. Weinberger, *C.S.E.L.* LXVII, 1934.
[135] *Cons. Phil.* I, 1 (verse); Cassiodorus, *Anec. Hold.* p. 4: *condidit et carmen bucolicum*. For delightful translations of verse in the *C.P.* see Helen Waddell, *Mediaeval Latin Lyrics*,[4] pp. 48ff.

The relation of Boethius to his sources is, again, a matter of varying judgment. These sources are undoubtedly the teachings of the Stoics, of Plato and the Neo-Platonists, and of Aristotle, and yet these component borrowings have been transfused into a whole which bears a new and original impress from the mind of the author himself. We have here the tree of a philosophy rooted in ancient theory, bearing a fruit all its own. And so, while we see the matter of the *Timaeus* and of the *Gorgias,* the thought of Proclus and of Plotinus, the substance of the lost *Protrepticus* of Aristotle clearly in evidence, we see them through the mind of the Roman philosopher and thinker and man of this sixth century. And more. We see the pagan doctrines through the mind of one who knew in his own religious experience something of that philosophic contemplation of God which Christian men have always held as part of their inheritance. Philosophic reasoning here led Boethius to the contemplation of the Divine, nurtured him in its high thought, till in this same book he passed beyond its ken to the vision of the Personal God whence springs Christian belief.[136]

At the beginning of the work we find him in the full misery of his changed fortune, suffering the torments of reflection in his prison while he ponders on his injuries and dreads worse to come. As he sits in this deep sadness, he is suddenly amazed by the vision of a Lady, familiar and yet strange to him. Her face is vigorous as of one in youth, yet it bears the thought of untold time; her stature seems to vary, now of human height, now rising high beyond man's gaze. She is clad in a robe that carries in its lower part the Greek letter *pi* to mark her skill in practical meditation, in its upper part the letter *theta,* denoting her knowledge of contemplative science in

---

[136] See Rand, *H.S.C.P.* XV, pp. 1ff., and, in *Founders of the Middle Ages,* pp. 177f.; Klingner, *De Boethii Cons. Phil.* 1921, pp. 117f.

ways beyond reason or intellectual imaginings. Steps fashioned in her dress lead from the lower to the higher part; but her clothing is torn by the violence of men in snatching fragments for their use.

It is the Lady Philosophy. She quickly perceives the unhappy mood of her disciple, so different from the earlier promise of his philosophic studies; but she determines rather to aid him by remedies than to waste time in complaints. Gradually the mist of depression clears a little from the mind of Boethius, and he recognizes his Mistress and Healer, long known to his life.

Now Philosophy begins her mission of succour. She reminds Boethius of the heroes of adversity in past time, of Socrates, of Zeno, of Seneca. Such as they care nothing for tyrants or adverse happenings; for a mighty fortress of philosophy stands ever ready to receive them in the hour of their need. Thither they may retire and laugh merrily from within at those who run after vain trifles outside. Philosophic indifference is their sure armour, dreading nothing, desiring nothing that may chain them to earth.

At her bidding Boethius opens his sorrow; he tells her of his upright administration and the wrongs done him by false charges, wails that the good are afflicted and the wicked rejoice. In answer Philosophy grieves that he has wandered in his complaining so far from his native country, the land of soul's content in God, and sets to work to bring him back: "If you truly remember your own native land, you know that it is not ruled by a democracy as the Athenians once were ruled. It owns

Unus Deus et Pater omnium,[137]

Who rejoices in the multitude, not in the banishment of His

[137] The Latin Bible may perhaps replace here Homer's Greek.

citizens, Whose service is justice and perfect liberty. Are you ignorant of that most ancient law of your City, which ordains that none may be an exile who has willed to settle his dwelling within her? For there is no fear that he who is held safely by her rampart and fortifying should deserve to be an exile. But he who ceases to wish to dwell within her ceases also to deserve this.

"And so the sight of this prison of yours does not concern me so much as the look upon your face. Not the walls of your library at home with their adornment of ivory and crystal matter to me so much as the house of your mind. There I have gathered, not books, but my ancient doctrines, for the sake of which books are prized." [138]

The complaints that Boethius has made are true enough, and far more might be said, the Lady continues. But in his present state of distress remedies, mild remedies at first, must be applied for his healing. One or two questions then bring out the real trouble. He remembers, indeed, that God is the source and ruler of all the world, but he has forgotten how and by what means God governs it. "Now I know," replies Philosophy, "another, yes, and the greatest cause of your sickness. You no longer understand your true nature. Now, then, I have fully discovered the reason of your bitterness and so the means to win your rescue. You are confounded through forgetfulness of yourself, and for this reason you have grieved as an exile, robbed of your possessions. You do not know what is the real end of things, and so you think that worthless and wicked men are powerful and happy. You have forgotten by what helm the world is guided, and so you think that Fortune veers now this way, now that, without control. These are grave reasons, not only for sickness, but even for death." [139]

Yet there is still hope. For Boethius, even in this great

[138] I, 5, 9ff. (prose).   [139] I, 6, 39ff. (prose).

unhappiness, still knows that the world is ruled by divine reason. From this tiny spark the fire of life shall again blaze up in him. From this starting-point Philosophy will build up her cure of instruction.

First, then, it is entirely wrong to think that Fortune has shown a new and strange side of herself to him. For she is changeable of her own true nature and has ever been so. Why, then, be surprised when she shows herself in her true self? Everyone who takes Fortune as mistress must accept her as she shall be, bound by her own character to alter at some time, however constant she may be for a long period: "You have given yourself over to the will of Fortune. Then you must submit to the ways of your mistress. Do you want to stop her revolving wheel? But, most stupid of mortals, it is no longer the wheel of chance if it stays unmoved!" [140]

The arguments which Fortune might bring forward in her own defence are now reviewed and found just and reasonable from her standpoint. Of her own she gave, of her own she has taken away. The turning of her wheel is within her own right, to swing up and down as she will. Why should Boethius expect treatment different from that meted out to other men? Further, Philosophy recalls all the blessings which have fallen to him in life, both domestic and political. Not now for the first time has he suddenly come as a stranger upon the stage of this world. To which Boethius answers in that cry which meets us again on the lips of Francesca, tossed in outer darkness upon the wind of torments, the grief of Tennyson for Arthur Hallam:

A sorrow's crown of sorrow is remembering happier things. [141]

Yet, urges Philosophy, your wife still lives and your sons, dearer to you than your own existence. What man, more-

[140] II, 1, 58ff.   [141] II, 4, 4ff.

over, that lives can boast of fortune that shall give to him unmixed joy, be it of wealth or ancient lineage or wife or children? He who is blessed in one respect ever cries for his lack in another, and no earthly happiness remains stable. The only true happiness of man is found within himself, the chief of his own possessions. While he remains ignorant of the ways of Fortune, he cannot rest in peace, fearing her fickle habit. And, come what may, earthly fortune must desert the soul at its passing from this world of time. Have not many men sought and attained happiness in the rejection of temporal fortune, deliberately choosing pain and torment, even death itself?

By this time the healing touch of Philosophy has begun to take effect in the sick soul, and she warms to her work with increased vigour of longing to expose the futility of false fortune. If a man's possessions are bad, she declares, they are but a trouble to him; if they are good, their goodness is inherently their own, not of the man who only possesses them from without. Beauty and riches can only adorn a person; they must always be external to his real self; and how can mere clothes or servants add to a man's inner store of blessedness? "Other creatures, truly, are happy in their own possessions. But you, with mind made in the image of God, do you seek the adornings of your high nature from the lowest things, and do not understand how great wrong you do your Creator? He willed that the human race should excel all earthly creatures; you thrust your dignity down below the very lowest. For if it be granted that what each man holds as his Good is more precious than the man himself, then you rank yourself inferior to the cheapest things by judging them to be your Good. And this is only what you deserve. For human nature is such that it only rises above other things when it knows its own true character, but is cast down below the beasts if it ceases to understands itself. Ignorance of self is natural to other living creatures; for men it is a sin." [142]

The same is true regarding honours and offices of the State, which are the source of great harm when held by bad men and are only of profit in the hands of good citizens by reason of the personal virtue of their recipients: "So it comes about that public offices do not magnify virtuous men, but virtuous men magnify their offices." [143] This desire of fame and glory is the special weakness, however, of great men. Yet how foolish it is! Reflect, observes Philosophy, that only a quarter of the world is inhabited by men, and much of this is taken up by seas and marshes and desert lands where no one may dwell. Why should anyone want to show forth his renown in this "tiniest point of a point"? Reflect, also, that in this little space there are assembled many races of different languages, manners and views of life—how can one man's fame reach very far? And what seems splendid to one race will seem blameworthy to another.

This is true enough of life. It is even more true when we think of death, which brings oblivion to most men's work in course of time. And what of a man's fame when brought face to face with eternity? Do men expect or desire earthly renown after death? Truly, we believe that the soul lives on. But will she crave to be still entangled in the things of this unstable world?

Yet, sometimes, Philosophy allows, Fortune does deserve well of men, and this, strangely enough, when she frowns upon them. For here, in changing, she not only shows her true self, but she reveals to those whom she deserts what store of happiness is really theirs in the friends that remain steadfast, the most precious of riches.

By now, through this method of reasoning, interspersed with the relaxation of song, Philosophy has cleared away the

[142] II, 5, 75ff.   [143] II, 6, 11ff.

outer débris that had choked entrance to the happiness still latent in her patient's soul. And so, after a brief moment of recollection for the gathering of her resources, she now approaches more nearly to his higher self. Now she will teach him what is that happiness which is the end and aim of all men: "And that is the Good which utterly satisfies its possessor. It is truly the Highest Good, containing within itself all good things. If any good were absent from it, it could not be the Highest Good, for something to be desired would still be left outside it." [144]

Yet men in their blindness do not recognize their true joy, and seek lower blessings, vainly supposing these to be the perfect good which they are all trying to attain by false paths. So "like drunken men they cannot find their way home." Such lesser goods are worldly wealth, honours, power, glory and pleasures, all of which men seek by natural inclination. Not one of these in itself can satisfy. They are prone rather to create their own craving for further possession and to bring with them their own sorrows, as being each and in their total union incomplete and lacking the sum of all goodness. They are but parts divided off from that undivided good which is the real desire of mankind. And this undivided perfect good is perfect happiness, a joy which in itself contains all gifts which a man can desire, and will render him in lack of nothing: neither wealth nor power nor reverence nor fame nor any manner of content.

Where, then, are we to seek this ideal happiness? Before trying to solve this problem Philosophy stays to ask help from the Father of all. Her petition is put in form of a hymn, from which students in the Middle Ages were gladly to regain much of the teaching of the *Timaeus* of Plato, still lost to them. [145]

The final search is now entered upon, with the premise that

---

[144] III, 2, 5ff.   [145] III, 9 (verse).

the existence of every imperfect postulates a perfect. If there were no standard of perfection, nothing could be imagined as imperfect, spoiled of previous perfection and corrupted by this corrupt world.

We start in the certainty that God is good. Moreover, as such, He must be the Perfect Good, since He is chief of all things. That He could not be if there were anything more excellent or older than He; for the perfect must have existed before the imperfect. He must be the Perfect Good in Himself; for otherwise He must have received the Perfect Good from a source greater than Himself, in which case He would not be Him whom reason acknowledges as God. God, also, as God, is the beginning of all things, and as such the Author of all good. But the perfect good is in itself perfect happiness; therefore, God is both perfect happiness and perfect goodness alike.

If, then, continues Philosophy, we learn to know perfect goodness, we shall learn to know God. Perfect goodness is found in the union of all blessings and gifts which severally would be incomplete in virtue. Perfect goodness, moreover, possesses the quality of wholeness; for anything that is maimed or incomplete is so far lacking in good. Perfect goodness, we may therefore say, is identical with wholeness, with one-ness, with unity. But everything craves that wholeness for itself, that soundness and completeness of its parts, which is unity. Therefore everything strives after perfect goodness, and this goodness is the goal and end of all things.

Boethius is then allowed to catch his breath while Philosophy sings a song, of interest for its Platonic doctrine that human learning is but a remembrance of light given to the soul before her descent to this earth.

Now at last the disciple recalls his former knowledge, forgotten for the time under the burden both of the flesh in general and of his own sorrow in particular: that God rules the world and all within it by means of Himself, Who is Perfect Goodness. "He is, we may say, the rudder and the helm by which this world's body and its workings are kept stable and unspoiled." [146]

From this there follows immediately another conclusion. Since all things of their own nature are striving after perfect wholeness, which is one-ness, which, as we have seen, is perfect goodness, or, under another name, perfect happiness, all things in following their natural desire must be really striving to find God.

Another thought also arises. Since God is all-powerful and can do all things, but is unable to do evil, we must conclude that evil is nothing and does not exist. This kindles a new spark of grief in Boethius, as he hears that evil is to be believed non-existent! So Philosophy leaves her logical instruction for a while to calm him in a song of Orpheus and Eurydice. [147]

The listener, however, can hardly wait for the end, before he bursts out with the question: "Why, under God's rule, are wicked men powerful and good men lacking in power?" Philosophy answers that this is not true. Here he has touched upon a great matter, and its unfolding will lift him swiftly as it were on wings, to bear him once more to the native country of his soul.

We have seen, she begins again, that all men strive eagerly for happiness. As happiness is their chief good, both the virtuous man and the evil man strive equally after goodness, the one rightly, the other in mistaken fashion. Since, therefore, the virtuous man attains his object of goodness and the bad man fails, of necessity the virtuous possesses power and the bad lacks it. In proportion as a man's character is worse, so does he fall further short of his goal by his error of judgment, and so the

[146] III, 12, 40ff.   [147] III, 12 (verse).

more does he lack of power. He must either fall short through blind ignorance, weakest of qualities, or through frailty itself, in that he sees but is not able to compass that end of good which he really desires. No man, however, is wholly evil or he could do nothing at all. For evil is nothing, as we have said.

Further, we may argue thus: That all real power is to be desired, and that all desirable things are desired because of their goodness. But the possibility of committing crime is not desired because of its goodness, and accordingly the possibility of committing crime is not real power at all.

By these stages, therefore, we are brought to the conclusion of Plato in the *Gorgias:* "Only the wise are able to do what they want to do. The wicked are able to carry out their immediate pleasure, but they cannot fulfil their real desire. They do their pleasure and think to obtain the Good they desire by the things which please them. But they gain it in no sort at all, for the wicked cannot attain to happiness." [148]

Now good and evil have opposite destinies, led thereto by their opposite qualities. Since goodness is the reward of the good, wickedness must be the reward of the bad. But, as goodness is happiness, so wickedness is misery. Therefore the bad man is miserable. And more. Since all that is exists in so far as it is whole, or, in other words, in virtue of its one-ness, and since the Perfect One-ness or Unity is the Perfect Good, therefore, all that exists is good. On the contrary, whatever has ceased to be good has ceased to exist; therefore, as evil has no existence, so bad men, in so far as they are bad, are not real men at all.

Presently Boethius, who is now feeling much better, sympathetically utters the pious wish that bad men had not this power of doing their imagined pleasure. Philosophy replies that this very power is in itself their punishment, since evil

[148] IV, 2, 140ff.

is misery. The bad man, indeed, who is punished is really happier than the bad man who escapes penalty. For penalty, in so far as it is just, is good, and, therefore, the bad man's badness is mixed with some proportion of good when he is bearing the penalty for his sin. On the contrary, the bad man unpunished is in a parlous state, for injustice is thereby added to his burden of badness. For this reason criminals should be brought to tribunals of justice, as sick men, even if unwilling, are brought to a doctor. Indeed, on reflection they ought to be glad to be punished that they may thus obtain something of goodness in their evil plight. Moreover, none should hate the wicked, but should rather regard them as sick souls in need of a physician. Hatred of the criminal is a sin against reason, seeing that crime is a disease of the mind.

Here the Lady Philosophy and her patient begin to find themselves in deep waters. For Boethius naturally wants to know why the good are punished and the bad are rewarded. Why do men sin here, in a world governed, not by chance, but by the Divine Will? Does God force men on to the destiny His foreknowledge sees awaiting them? The answer to this most difficult problem involves discussion of such weighty matters as the simplicity of Providence; the consequence of Fate; sudden accidents; the knowledge of God; predestination and free-will. Little time is now left to the two after so long talk. Yet Philosophy will try to treat of the question of Boethius in some brief sort.

From this point the colloquy takes a new turn, as its writer attempts some new step toward the harmonizing of the old, old connection in human thought between God's foreknowledge of man's destiny and the doctrine of man's predestination.

He begins with his famous definings of Providence and of Fate. They may best be given in a translation of his own words: "Providence is that very Divine Reason which is seated in the Most High Lord and disposes all things. Fate, on the other hand, is inherent in the things that are moved, and is the means whereby Providence intertwines all things in their own due order. Providence embraces all things alike, however different, to infinity; Fate moves things one by one, according to different places, forms and seasons. Therefore, the exposition of this temporal order of ours in one single view foreseen by the Divine Mind is Providence; the same view, when its various parts are arranged and displayed in their different times, is called Fate."

Whatever, then, the immediate agency by which things are done, "it is clear that Providence is the immovable and simple form of events that are to be; Fate is the movable intertwining and the order in time of the events which the Divine Simplicity has bidden come into being. Therefore, all things which are under Fate are also subject to Providence, to which even Fate itself is subject. Some things, indeed, under the will of Providence rise above the ordered sequence of Fate." [149]

What, then, is chance? Here we find another definition of note in later times. "Chance is the unforeseen result of a combination of causes in acts done for some purpose." [150] It is brought about by Fate emanating from Providence in accordance with the will of God.

This brings us to the final enquiry: whether men have free will or are constrained by necessity? The answer is unhesitating: human nature, in so far and in such degree as it is endowed with reason and guided by it, is, indeed, possessed of free will. [151] But not, therefore, in equal measure. Supernatural and divine beings have clear judgment and pure will and efficient power for the carrying out of their wishes. Human souls are less free when they descend from the heav-

---

[149] IV, 6, 32ff.; 56ff. [150] V, 1, 53ff.
[151] Cf. Boethius, *De Interpret.* ed. Meiser, II, p. 196, and E. Gilson, *Spirit of Med. Phil.,* p. 311.

enly vision into bodies, still less when they forsake the light of reason through weakness or vice.

But God in his Providence foresees all things, embraced in one simple view. Then must not all that God foresees as going to happen, happen of necessity? And how can man be free to act as he would, caught in this chain of inevitable sequence? For we cannot believe that God sees uncertainty in His gaze, lest we bring down His foreknowledge to the level of human opinion.

The cause of this dilemma of man, Boethius asserts, rests on an initial error, "the belief that knowledge of things is only derived from the character and nature of the things themselves. The truth is just the opposite. Knowledge of each thing known depends, not upon its own character, but upon the varying faculties of those who know it." [152] The different faculties, ranging from lower to higher—sense, imagination, reason, intelligence—know and understand things in a corresponding degree of gradually ascending power. The higher faculty includes in its knowledge of any object all the knowledge of the faculty or faculties below it in power; so that, finally, intelligence must be said to possess all the powers of apprehension owned by sense, imagination and reason together.

It would, therefore, be foolish of the lower faculties of knowledge, which can but grasp the sensible or the imaginable, to deny that reason has a higher power, seeing that it can grasp the universal. And in like manner it would be foolish of human reason to refuse to yield in comprehension to the Divine intelligence. For reason cannot by her own light see the things of the future which lie open to the mind of God.

If, then, we would understand somewhat of the knowledge of God, we must also understand somewhat of His nature.

[152] V, 4, 72ff.

God is Eternal. And if we can understand in some degree the meaning of eternity, we shall know of the nature and thus of the knowledge of God. Eternity, we may say, is the whole and perfect possession at one and the same moment of everlasting life, whereas whatsoever lives in time is constantly passing from past to present, and so on to the future. There is nothing in time which can embrace at one and the same moment the whole space of its life: yesterday, today, and tomorrow. But that which at one and the same moment embraces and holds the whole plenitude of everlasting life, to which nothing of the future is wanting nor anything of the past is lost or gone, that rightly is called eternal. Of necessity the Eternal is always present and in possession of itself; of necessity it has present with it and before its mind the infinity of moving time.

It is true that the perpetual movement of temporal things by its constantly passing periods tries to imitate the infinite presentness of the unmoving eternity of the Divine Mind. But time, the perpetual, can never be eternity embracing all knowledge, past, present and future, in each moment of its consciousness. For we have observed that every judgment comprehends the things subjected to its knowledge by means of its own nature and comparative power. So the knowledge of God, being both Eternal and One, embraces in its one-ness, in its perfection, all things, that have been, that are, and that shall be, ever and always, at one and the same time. These things are in perpetual motion, while God, seeing all from beginning to end, is Himself unmoved, is unaffected by the passage of time. We may regard, then, His power not so much as foreknowledge, but rather as never-failing perfect all-knowledge, surveying the plain of human experience in its totality as from some lofty height.

Why, therefore, should we think that those future things

which the Divine Mind includes in its comprehensive grasp of
all time are necessarily bound upon man's will, any more
than we think that the things which men see every day must
necessarily happen merely because men see them happening?
We see the sun rise, and call it necessary; we observe other
men walking, and call it voluntary. Neither event is constrained to happen just because we see it happen. So with
God, Who sees, without compelling them, both the necessary
and the voluntary things that shall be. For with Him present, past and future are all one.[153]

This is the end of this meditation in captivity, and Boethius
now places on the lips of his Mistress the thoughts that were
staying his soul as he awaited, he knew not what, in those
months before his death: "There remains, therefore, freedom
of will unspoiled for men, and the laws are not unjust which
hold out prizes and penalties for wills freed from all necessity.
God ever abides in His foreknowledge, spectator on high of
all things; and eternity, ever present to His vision, concurs
with the judgment our actions shall gain for us, awarding
prizes to the good and punishments to the wicked. Hopes and
prayers laid up in God are not in vain; if they be rightful
they cannot fail of fruit. Fight, then, against sins, cultivate
virtues, lift up your mind to rightful hopes, stretch out to the
highest your humble prayers. A great constraint toward good
life is declared unto you, if you will not to deceive, in that
you live before the eyes of a Judge Who beholds all things."

Cassiodorus, Ennodius, Boethius: these are the three last
sounds from the train of Italy's culture before it plunges into
the long tunnel of the Dark Ages. Flashes of light may occasionally illuminate its buried course, but they do little save

[153] Cf. F. H. Brabant, *Time and Eternity in Christian Thought*, 1937,
pp. 62ff. for the influence of Boethius here upon the mediaeval schools.

reveal the darkness. Italy recked little of ancient culture in the time of Gregory the Great, and it was in Spain and in Celtic lands, in Ireland and in Britain, in Gaul nurtured by Ireland, that classical learning still found its lovers when these three were dead and gone. Even already, if the metaphor be not too strained, the rising cliffs that mark the tunnel's approach have cut off from these three much of the freshness and the radiance of the open horizon. Yet all three worked on in the twilight of Roman letters, fearing the coming night, hoping for a new dawn, if from the barbarians themselves. All refused to despair. There is something courageous even in the rhetoric of Ennodius; something higher, perhaps, than the careless blindness of Sidonius Apollinaris. Cassiodorus only retired when he felt he had nothing more to offer his country in political service; from his retirement and his old age he was to offer her a legacy far greater than any of his workings in active life. The scientific translations and commentaries of Boethius were to influence mightily the coming Schoolmen. But the work that influenced the world and is always connected with his name came from his prison, written without books, without scholars, in loneliness and weariness of life. These are strange things; yet not strange, to those who know the world's history.

SELECT BIBLIOGRAPHY

PROCOPIUS: *History of the Wars,* Loeb ed. vols. III–V, 1919–1928.

—— *Anecdota (Secret History),* Loeb ed. 1935.

J. B. BURY: *History of the Later Roman Empire,* vols. I and II, 1923.

—— *The Invasion of Europe by the Barbarians,* 1928.

EDWARD GIBBON: *Decline and Fall of the Roman Empire,* ed. Bury, vols. IV–V, 1909–1911.

T. HODGKIN: *Italy and her Invaders*[2], vols. III–VI, 1896–1916.

—— *The Letters of Cassiodorus,* a condensed translation, 1886.

F. GREGOROVIUS: *History of the City of Rome in the Middle Ages*[4], trans. Hamilton, I, 1900.

LOT-PFISTER-GANSHOF: *Histoire du Moyen Age,* I, 1928.

H. GRISAR: *History of Rome and the Popes in the Middle Ages,* Eng. trans. ed. Cappadelta, vols. II–III, 1912.

F. LOT: *The End of the Ancient World,* trans. Leon, 1931.

W. P. KER: *The Dark Ages,* 1911.

H. ST. L. B. MOSS: *The Birth of the Middle Ages,* 1935.

SIR CHARLES OMAN: *The Dark Ages*[6], 1923.

—— *England before the Norman Conquest*[6], 1924.

W. G. HOLMES: *The Age of Justinian and Theodora,* vols. I and II, 1905–1907.

E. K. RAND: *Founders of the Middle Ages*[2], 1929.

C. FOLIGNO: *Latin Thought during the Middle Ages,* 1929.

THE GATEWAY TO THE MIDDLE AGES

C. C. Mierow: *The Gothic History of Jordanes,* 1915.

Boethius: *Consolation of Philosophy,* ed. E. K. Rand, with trans. of "I. T." revised by H. F. Stewart, 1926.

—— *The Theological Tractates,* ed. E. K. Rand, trans. Stewart and Rand, 1926.

H. F. Stewart: Boethius: an Essay, 1891.

H. R. Patch: *The Tradition of Boethius,* 1935.

C. H. Haskins: *Studies in the History of Mediaeval Science,* 1927.

E. Gilson: *The Spirit of Mediaeval Philosophy,* trans. Downes, 1936.

M. de Wulf: *History of Mediaeval Philosophy,* I^e, Eng. ed.^{a}, 1935.

H. Rashdall: *The Universities of Europe in the Middle Ages,* ed. Powicke and Emden, vols. I–III, 1936.

O. M. Dalton: Gregory of Tours: *The History of the Franks,* trans. and commentary, vols. I and II, 1927.

Sir Samuel Dill: *Roman Society in Gaul in the Merovingian Age,* 1926.

T. Scott Holmes: *The Origin and Development of the Christian Church in Gaul,* 1911.

D. Tardi: *Fortunat,* 1927.

E. Briand: *Histoire de Sainte Radegonde,* 1898.

L. Eckenstein: *Women under Monasticism,* 1896.

F. J. E. Raby: *A History of Christian-Latin Poetry,* 1927.

—— *A History of Secular Latin Poetry in the Middle Ages,* vols. I and II, 1934.

Alban Butler: *Lives of the Saints,* revised Thurston and Attwater, 1926–1934.

W. J. Rees: *Lives of the Cambro-British Saints,* 1853.

H. Williams: ed. and trans. *Works* of Gildas, 1899.

—— *Christianity in Early Britain,* 1912.

SELECT BIBLIOGRAPHY

J. E. LLOYD: *A History of Wales,* I, 1911.

EUGIPPIUS: *Life of Saint Severinus,* trans. G. W. Robinson, 1914.

C. F. ARNOLD: *Caesarius von Arelate,* 1894.

A. MALNORY: *Saint Césaire,* 1894.

BARING-GOULD and FISHER: *Lives of the British Saints,* vols. I–IV, 1907.

COUNT DE MONTALEMBERT: *The Monks of the West,* vols. I–III, 1896.

ADAMNAN: *Life of St. Columba,* ed. W. Reeves², 1874.

JONAS: *Life of St. Columban,* Univ. Pennsylvania, *Translations and Reprints,* II, 1902, No. 7.

J. A. DUKE: *The Columban Church,* 1932.

—— *History of the Church in Scotland,* 1937.

LOUIS GOUGAUD: *Christianity in Celtic Lands,* trans. Joynt, 1932.

J. F. KENNEY: *Sources for the Early History of Ireland,* I, 1929.

W. A. PHILLIPS: ed. *History of the Church of Ireland,* I, 1933.

JOHN RYAN: *Irish Monasticism,* 1931.

W. K. LOWTHER CLARKE: *The Rule of St. Benedict,* 1931.

PAUL DELATTE: *Commentary on the Rule of St. Benedict,* 1921.

F. CABROL: *Saint Benedict,* trans. Antony, 1934.

CUTHBERT BUTLER: *Benedictine Monachism²,* 1924.

E. G. GARDNER: ed. *The Dialogues of Saint Gregory,* translation of ann. 1608.

GREGORY THE GREAT: *The Pastoral Rule,* trans. Bramley, 1874. *Pastoral Rule; Selected Letters,* trans. Barmby, *Nicene and Post-Nicene Fathers,* XII, *Morals on the*

Book of Job, trans. *Library of the Fathers,* vols. I–III, 1844-1847.

G. F. BROWNE: *King Alfred's Books,* 1920.

F. HOMES DUDDEN: *Gregory the Great,* vols. I and II, 1905.

P. BATIFFOL: *Saint Gregory the Great,* trans. Stoddard, 1929.

INDEX

ANN ARBOR PAPERBACKS

reissues of works of enduring merit

The University of Michigan Press   *Ann Arbor*